TO A SUCCESSFUL PHD IN BUSINESS & MANAGE

ROADMAP

TO A SUCCESSFUL PHD IN BUSINESS & MANAGEMENT AND THE SOCIAL SCIENCES

THE DEFINITIVE GUIDE FOR POSTGRADUATE RESEARCHERS

Glauco De Vita, Jason Begley and David Bowen

Peter Lang
Oxford · Bern · Berlin · Bruxelles · New York · Wien

Bibliographic information published by Die Deutsche Nationalbibliothek
Die Deutsche Nationalbibliothek lists this publication in the Deutsche
Nationalbibliografie; detailed bibliographic data is available on the Internet at http://dnb.d-nb.de.

A catalogue record for this book is available from the British Library.

Library of Congress Cataloging-in-Publication Data
Names: De Vita, G. (Glauco) author. | Begley, Jason, author. | Bowen, David, 1956- author.
Title: Roadmap to a successful PhD in business and management and the social sciences : the definitive guide for postgraduate researchers / Glauco De Vita, Jason Begley, David Bowen.
Description: 1 Edition. | Oxford : Peter Lang, 2021. | Includes bibliographical references and index.
Identifiers: LCCN 2021027918 (print) | LCCN 2021027919 (ebook) | ISBN 9781800795686 (paperback) | ISBN 9781800795693 (ebook) | ISBN 9781800795709 (epub)
Subjects: LCSH: Industrial management--Study and teaching (Graduate) | Industrial management--Research. | Social sciences--Study and teaching (Graduate) | Social sciences--Research. | Doctor of philosophy degree.
Classification: LCC HD30.4 .D483 2021 (print) | LCC HD30.4 (ebook) | DDC 658.0076--dc23
LC record available at https://lccn.loc.gov/2021027918
LC ebook record available at https://lccn.loc.gov/2021027919

Cover design by Brian Melville for Peter Lang.

ISBN   978-1-80079-568-6 (print)
ISBN   978-1-80079-569-3 (ePDF)
ISBN   978-1-80079-570-9 (ePub)

© Peter Lang Group AG 2021

Published by Peter Lang Ltd, International Academic Publishers,
52 St Giles, Oxford, OX1 3LU, United Kingdom
oxford@peterlang.com, www.peterlang.com

Glauco De Vita, Jason Begley and David Bowen have asserted their right under the Copyright, Designs and Patents Act, 1988, to be identified as Authors of this Work.

All rights reserved.

All parts of this publication are protected by copyright.
Any utilisation outside the strict limits of the copyright law, without the permission of the publisher, is forbidden and liable to prosecution.
This applies in particular to reproductions, translations, microfilming, and storage and processing in electronic retrieval systems.

This publication has been peer reviewed.

Contents

List of figures, tables and appendices   vii

Preface   ix

List of abbreviations   xvii

GLAUCO DE VITA
1 The nature of doctoral research and becoming a postgraduate researcher   1

JASON BEGLEY
2 How to write a PhD application and academic proposal   17

DAVID BOWEN
3 Completing a literature review   49

JASON BEGLEY AND GLAUCO DE VITA
4 The key attributes of an excellent PhD thesis   75

GLAUCO DE VITA
5 Managing up, managing your time and managing your wellbeing   113

JASON BEGLEY
6 Making the most of training and development opportunities   139

JASON BEGLEY
7 Strategies to deal with difficulties and major crises   159

DAVID BOWEN
8 Annual progress reviews — 191

DAVID BOWEN
9 Talking about, presenting and publicising your research — 211

GLAUCO DE VITA
10 Final checks of the thesis, preparing the *viva* and dealing with amendments — 237

GLAUCO DE VITA
11 All you wanted to know about publishing from your PhD but never dared ask! — 267

GLAUCO DE VITA
12 Preparing for life after the PhD and career options — 301

About the authors — 325

Index — 327

Figures, tables and appendices

Figure

Figure 2.1.	Thesis template	28

Tables

Table 5.1.	Typical misalignment of expectations between PGRs and supervisors	116
Table 7.1.	UK domiciled qualifiers by disability and sex, postgraduate research	167

Appendices

Appendix 5.1.	PGR's GANTT chart of PhD schedule for second year	135
Appendix 10.1.	An authentic example of an examiner's pre-*viva* report	263
Appendix 10.2.	An example of the menu of PhD award recommendations available to examiners	265

Preface

The motivation for this book came from Postgraduate Researchers (PGRs) themselves. Time and time again in my daily interactions with them, they ask for advice ranging from how to structure the thesis and publish from their research to last-minute tips on how to prepare for their annual progress review or *viva voce*. In my conversations with the Postgraduate Research Lead in the Faculty of Business and Law at Coventry University (UK) – Dr Jason Begley, second-named author of this book – we often discuss recurrent issues that prospective and existing PGRs also raise with him. These issues usually revolve around how to go about preparing the best possible PhD proposal and better cope with the stresses of academic life, including how PGRs could better manage their time, their relationship with supervisors and, more generally, their wellbeing. Of course, we regularly run many workshops and training sessions to cater for PGRs' thirst for knowledge. In such seminars we unpack many such issues to help them develop the right mindset and expectations of what it means to become a PGR, understand the inherent challenges and fulfil the tasks necessary to successfully complete the PhD. However, as one cohort of PGRs runs its course, new candidates embark on their doctoral journey. This raises, once again, the need for us to explain and clarify to them the skills and processes necessary to facilitate the successful completion of their doctorate.

Having worked closely in my capacity as Associate Dean for Research and Knowledge Exchange at a previous university with another PhD programme director – Dr David Bowen, third-named author of this book – I was already well aware that such issues, needs and demands for doctoral training are widespread across universities. Hence the idea for this book, to provide a useful and comprehensive contemporary guide to current and future PGRs on how to start and complete a PhD successfully and, for supervisors, how to fulfil their responsibility to guide their PGRs in this endeavour.

There are obviously already several books that offer guides to the secrets of a successful PhD completion. However, their quality varies, and some are rather dated. To better appreciate the distinctiveness of our contribution, it is perhaps worth looking first at the existing provision in this area.

Some of the existing texts take a supervisor-focused rather than a PGR-centred approach to the subject of completing a doctorate (see, e.g., Green, 2005, *Supervising Postgraduate Research: Contexts and Processes, Theories and Practices*, or Lee, 2020, *Successful Research Supervision: Advising Students Doing Research*). Although these books contain helpful advice, they are explicitly aimed at early career academic supervisors rather than PGRs as their target audience. As a result, they build on a teacher- or instructor-led paradigm (rather than a 'learner-led' educational model) that appears to run antithetical to the view that a PhD is, ultimately, an endeavour that starts and ends with the doctoral researcher. Placing emphasis on the supervisor's role in the PGR-supervisor relationship also brings with it a set of assumptions and expectations about educational and motivational responsibilities that are not naturally conducive to offering useful guidance to PGRs operating in academic environments where less than ideal supervision is carried out (a point I elaborate on in this book when discussing how PGRs should go about 'managing up'). On this note, it is worth highlighting that we refrain in this volume from referring to PGRs as 'students'. We do so to draw an important distinction between their status and that of undergraduate- or postgraduate-taught students, and to raise attention to how they are to be viewed by staff and Higher Education (HE) institutions (HEIs). Some PGRs are mature learners, and some work part-time or even full-time alongside their study. Many of them are fully involved in the academic life of the school, department or research centre in which they do research. Alongside working on their PhD, they teach, mark assignments and exams, help organise conferences, contribute to their university's research output and, most importantly, to the vibrancy and richness of the scholarly culture characterising the learning environment. The 'student' nomenclature, with its supposed connotations of dependence and immaturity, also downplays the level and quality of thought and analysis that is required to achieve the PhD award. After all, doctoral research is not judged as 'student' work, and it is often of publishable standard. Apart from mandatory methods training and supervisory guidance, the award is the fruit of a long journey where the PGR has been required to self-regulate and work autonomously to produce original independent research that makes a significant contribution to knowledge as judged by senior peers.

With respect to content and style, at one end of the spectrum of existing texts on completing a PhD are those that employ a purely pragmatic, marketing-like approach. These books tend to offer interminable lists of easy solutions and quick fixes often without providing any reasons, underlying justifications or theory-based evidence as to why suggested behaviours should be expected to be beneficial. Some of these texts are illustrated pocket guides aimed at demystifying the PhD process, which often adopt a vignette-like, light-hearted stance to the subject (see, e.g., Williams et al., 2010, *Planning Your PhD – Pocket Study Skills*). The problem with this approach is that in attempting to provide a highly digestible and very basic understanding to ensure comprehension by all, it can end up trivialising, obscuring even, the inherent complexities and challenges of the doctoral journey. The value of a sense of humour notwithstanding (an essential life skill), I remain sceptical of the actual worth of the sort of 'Complete Idiot's Guide' to completing a doctorate. Hyperbole aside, doing a PhD is probably an ambition still best reserved for those who do not fall into the clinical classification of 'idiot' or who share traits with the layperson's interpretation of the term.

At the other end of the spectrum are those books that, in spite of their valuable insights, tend to offer a narrative skewed towards the bureaucratic infrastructure of doctoral level institutional offerings. These texts are often replete with information about formal procedures and associated rules and responsibilities that universities and departments have for providing an adequate level of service, content of limited usefulness and marginal relevance to the immediate needs of PGRs. *How to Get a PhD – A Handbook for Students and Their Supervisors* by Phillips and Pugh (2015) is a case in point.

This is not to say that along with the rich doctoral education literature from academic journals, we do not take note of, draw on even, some of the useful advice that is offered in many previously published PhD handbooks. On the contrary, we cite and pay homage to many of them throughout our book. One such text stands above all others: Umberto Eco's (2015) wise and witty guide *How to Write a Thesis*, a real gem! Who better to help with thesis writing than a venerable public intellectual and novelist, a distinguished academic and a widely celebrated author of influential works on semiotics, right? That said, although its first English (translated) edition only became available in 2015, the book was written (in Italian) in the mid-1970s, almost half a century ago. Moreover, Eco's '*Come si fa una tesi di laurea - le materie umanistiche*' (a literal translation would be 'How to write a dissertation in the humanities') was intended for the original research that was required of students pursuing the Italian equivalent of a bachelor's degree (the first, post-secondary, degree called '*Laurea*') – not quite the same as the contemporary requirements of a PhD thesis. In addition, Eco wrote his 'dissertation-writing' manual, which was never revised or updated, before the advent of widespread word processing, the World Wide Web, digital libraries, online portals of archival and cataloguing systems, and electronic databases of peer-reviewed literature. It should come as no surprise, therefore, that alongside the inspiring and timeless wisdom imparted by Eco, his book also devotes entire chapters to archaic 'technologies' such as handwritten note and index cards. The book also contains long sections on matters such as formatting requirements (which are nowadays highly standardised, just like the codified citation styles in common use) and how to overcome the limitations of local libraries, with tips that, as a result of the passage of time, are rather anachronistic and of little use to contemporary PGRs. Finally, as per Eco's acknowledgement in his own 'Introduction' to the original 1977 edition, his book deals mainly with 'dissertations' in the humanities. Since his experience relates to studies in literature and philosophy, his examples are naturally confined to such topics – examples that may not always be illuminating for PGRs in business and management–related disciplines.

I have similar yet inverse-related subject qualms about other admirable and well-written 'how-to' PhD guides, which, despite recognising that disciplines vary, try to speak to PGRs across all academic fields, nonetheless. *The Unwritten Rules of PhD Research* by Rugg and Petre, 2010; and *Authoring a PhD: How to Plan, Draft, Write and Finish a Doctoral Thesis or Dissertation* by Dunleavy, 2015, are eminent examples. The problem is that across disciplinary fields there are significant differences in PhD practices as well as assumptions and expectations of what a PhD thesis should look like and how to go about research.

As indicated by its title, the aim of our book is to provide the most comprehensive if not 'definitive' roadmap to a successful PhD completion in business and management and the social sciences. Our ambitious attempt adds to what has gone before by dealing explicitly with the deficiencies and lacunae of existing provision as highlighted above. First, although much of the content will be of considerable benefit to any PGR in any discipline, this book is written for and specifically aimed at PGRs studying in business schools and social sciences departments in disciplines such as, *inter alia*, international business, marketing, management, organisation studies, tourism and hospitality, accounting, finance, law and economics. Moreover, while the book makes frequent reference to the British system, most of the advice applies across countries and the book, therefore, can be used and widely implemented globally.

Second, unlike any other PhD handbook, we provide detailed advice to both *aspiring* and *current PGRs* on aspects pertaining to the *entire* doctoral journey. Following our introductory chapter on the nature of doctoral study, our thorough coverage takes the reader through a storyline that starts from how to write a first-class academic proposal as part of the PhD application process, a topic hardly ever dealt with in similar books, through to how to prepare for life after the PhD, another aspect far too often ignored by comparable PhD manuals. In so doing, we fill other important gaps in currently available texts.

Third, our writing style unapologetically alternates a formal, literature-based, academic writing narrative (where PGRs are referred to in the third person), with a more intimate, more direct and conversational personal style, where we refer to our audience of aspiring and existing PGRs as 'you'. The former text provides a scholarly account of the education landscape and doctoral study context–dependent knowledge, with frequent reference to relevant literature, theory and educational psychology. The latter passages centre around specific practical guidance that is informed, at strategic points throughout the text, by stories of the lived experience of past PGRs (duly anonymised, of course) as well as our personal professional anecdotes and real life examples of 'how to' and 'how not to'. These many suggestions include how to and how not to write a PhD application, how to deal with crises such as that posed by the Covid-19 pandemic (particularly in terms of alternative strategies for data collection), how to make the most of Annual Progress Reviews (APRs), how best to prepare for the *viva* and adjustments to be made for an online (remotely hosted) PhD oral examination, how to maximise the probability of publishing from the PhD material, how to choose the best academic journal to target, how to address PhD examiners and journal reviewers' requests for amendments, how to engage with and publicise the research through social media, and considerations related to career opportunities outside as well as within academia. In-depth discussion of such aspects, which have received hardly if any coverage by other volumes in this area, also make our book up to date in dealing with the contemporary challenges PGRs face.

Finally, our compendium of useful information and tools draws from decades of experience in teaching at all levels of educational provision (from undergraduate programmes through to the Doctorate of Business Administration), publishing in academic journals of high repute, successful PhD supervision and examining, and in our role as strategic and academic directors of doctoral programmes in different universities. Supervisors too should benefit greatly from reading this book, even simply as recipients of much of the implicit or tacit knowledge which surrounds the realm of 'best practice' supervision, rarely shared by academics. We have made every effort to articulate such tacit knowledge explicitly in order to make visible our expertise with many examples drawn from our own lived experiences of PGR selection and PhD supervision and examining, and associated lessons learned.

....

I am happy to acknowledge the superb environment for teaching, learning and research within the Centre for Business in Society (CBiS) at Coventry University (UK), and the support of Professor Lyndon Simkin, Executive Director of CBiS, Professor Nigel Berkley, Institute Director (Responsible Business, Economies and Society), and many colleagues.

My heartfelt gratitude goes to Jason Begley and David Bowen, for embracing my vision for this book and for their excellent contributions

Preface

to it. They have been ideal co-authors. Additionally, I thank Tony Mason, Senior Commissioning Editor, and the team at Peter Lang, for allowing us the editorial freedom to shape this work in the way we envisaged.

Our collective appreciation extends to the friends, colleagues and former PGRs who gave their time to read early drafts of the chapters in this book and helped improve it in innumerable ways. Peter Case, Adrian Parker, Tom Donnelly, Laura Spira, David Cushman, Donato Vozza, Emmanouil Trachanas, Sailesh Tanna, Paul Noon, Daniel Ganly, Fabio Carbone, Yun Luo, Eliana Lauretta, Oluwatosin Lagoke and Runda Gao in particular provided us with insightful points for reflection and critical feedback, and we can only hope that the final version is worthy of their wisdom.

This book is dedicated to our families, friends and all our past, current and future PGRs.

– *Professor Glauco De Vita*

Abbreviations

ABS	Association of Business Schools
AD	Anno Domini
AJG	Academic Journal Guide
APR	Annual Progress Review
AR	Augmented Reality
BBC	British Broadcasting Corporation
BRIC	Brazil, Russia, India and China
CAUTHE	Council for Australasian Tourism and Hospitality Education
CEO	Chief Executive Officer
Covid-19	Coronavirus Disease SARS-CoV-2
CSQ	Customer Survey Questionnaire
CV	Curriculum Vitae
DBA	Doctorate of Business Administration
DMP	Data Management Plan
DoS	Director of Studies
DTA	Doctoral Training Alliance
DTP	Doctoral Training Partnership
ECR	Early Career Researcher
EDP	Eisenhower Decision Principle
EL	Entrepreneurial Learning
ESRC	Economic and Social Research Council

EU	European Union
FT	Full Time
HASS	Humanities, Arts and Social Sciences
HE	Higher Education
HEI	Higher Education Institution
HESA	Higher Education Statistics Agency
IBV	Institutional Based View
IELTS	International English Language Testing System
IMF	International Monetary Fund
IT	Information Technology
NGO	Non-Governmental Organisation
OA	Open Access
OECD	Organisation for Economic Co-operation and Development
OIA	Office of the Independent Adjudicator
ONS	Office for National Statistics
PGR	Postgraduate Researcher
PRES	Postgraduate Research Experience Survey
PT	Part Time
QAA	Quality Assurance Agency
Q&A	Question and Answer
QE	Quantitative Easing
RDF	Researcher Development Framework
REF	Research Evaluation Framework
RSA	Republic of South Africa

SALSA	Search, Appraisal, Synthesis, Analysis
SCT	Social Capital Theory
SMART	Specific, Measurable, Achievable, Realistic, Tangible
SME	Small and Medium Sized Enterprise
STEM	Science, Technology, Engineering and Mathematics
THE	Times Higher Education
THES	Times Higher Education Supplement
TOEFL	Test of English as a Foreign Language
UKCGC	UK Corporate Governance Code
UKRI	United Kingdom Research and Innovation
VR	Virtual Reality

GLAUCO DE VITA

1 The nature of doctoral research and becoming a postgraduate researcher

Preamble

What's a PhD worth? Why is it worthwhile to pursue such a qualification? What is the nature of doctoral research and what is required to become a successful postgraduate researcher? The **aim of this chapter** is to answer these questions in order to highlight the value of doctoral research, the arduous but highly rewarding task of becoming a competent professional researcher, and the significant personal and professional development associated with the achievement of a PhD. The chapter concludes by outlining what the book is about, for whom it is intended and how to use it.

Why doing a PhD is not 'a waste of time'

In the 2010 Christmas double issue of *The Economist*, a deeply disconcerting article entitled 'Why doing a PhD is often a waste of time' appeared. Few articles I have read in my lifetime contain more banalities and inaccuracies surrounding the experience and usefulness of embarking on a Doctorate of Philosophy (PhD). Given the nature of this book, it appears opportune, therefore, to begin by dissecting the article's claims to unveil their sheer vapidity and in doing so to highlight why doing a PhD is not a waste of time.

The first outrageous claim made in the article in question relates to the alleged widespread dissatisfaction among PhD students said to be fuelled by perceptions of doctoral work as "*slave labour*" characterised by "*seven-day weeks, ten-hour days, low pay and uncertain prospects*". The article goes on to denounce inherent problems with "*the system*" that produces research doctorates – reductively described as mere training for a job in academia – and an oversupply of PhDs that far outstrips the number of job openings in universities. Such claims contain several misconceptions. Whilst there will always be a thin tail of whining postgraduate researchers (PGRs), some of whom may well have genuine reasons to be dissatisfied, the most recent official UK Postgraduate Research Experience Survey (PRES) of 2019,[1] the largest survey of its kind in the UK (one of the largest markets of PhD enrolments in the world), tells a very different story of the big picture. PRES (2019) draws together the key learnings from a dataset which represents the views of over 50,000 PGRs across 107 UK Higher Education (HE) institutions (HEIs). According to the PRES report, the PGR experience across the UK university sector is a positive one, with an overall satisfaction rating of 81%. Of those doctoral students who 'disagreed' with the statement "*I agree that I was satisfied with my experience*", which was 10%, only 4% 'definitely disagreed', and 9% of respondents 'neither agreed nor disagreed'.

The claim that universities work their PhD students to death is also preposterous. A Tier 4 visa issued for full-time degree level studies in the UK, caps the number of hours that PhD students from overseas can work to a maximum of twenty hours in any one week. Home PhD students have no such limit, but in my entire career I have never come across a full-time PGR who taught more than eighteen hours per week. In fact, extra teaching hours – mostly relating to leading seminars rather than delivering lectures – are generally in high demand and relatively short supply across UK universities. Such hours are mostly offered by HEIs and undertaken by PGRs (alongside their attendance in teaching qualifying courses) as part of PGRs' wider academic development.

The accusation of an "*overproduction*" of PhDs, suggestive of the need for universities to practice academic birth control, must also be

---

[1] See <https://www.advance-he.ac.uk/reports-publications-and-resources/postgraduate-research-experience-survey-pres>.

called into question.[2] To start with, the huge expansion of doctoral education, especially over the past two decades, is actually a good thing. Right up to the 1960s, even a first (undergraduate) degree at university was the privilege of the few, one mostly reserved to aspiring academics in the developed world. The article in question itself acknowledges that *"by 1970 America was producing just under a third of the world's university students and half of its science and technology PhDs"*. This is despite America having, at the time, only 6% of the world's population. Since the year 2000 doctorates awarded in all OECD countries have grown by nearly 50%, effectively ending the hegemony of the United States as the main producer of PhDs.[3] Second, although within the social sciences the majority of newly qualified doctors do indeed take employment within academia, many increasingly find work in other sectors since a PhD gives PGRs the skills to work in a range of jobs across different industries. This is why although it is true that, in certain years and countries, more PhD students obtain a doctorate than there are job openings for university lecturers,[4] this does not mean that having a PhD does not provide a competitive job market advantage for plenty of other available occupations. As reported by the UKRI, Economic and Social Research Council,[5] data from the Longitudinal Survey of the Destinations of Leavers of Higher Education show that six months after graduating, 66% of leavers were in employment in the UK and 17% were working overseas. Over three years from PhD graduation, such percentages increase to 71% and 18%,

---

2   This is not to say that PhD entry requirements should be relaxed. Anything but, especially at a time when many weaker universities have begun to treat PhD fees as an important source of income, and to put pressure on academic staff to take on more and more self-funded PGRs.
3   By 2018, thanks to the expansion and wider geographical distribution of the development of doctoral education, countries like Slovenia (3.8%), Switzerland (3.1%) and Luxemburg (2.1%) had a higher share of the population with a doctoral degree than the United States (2%), though the United States still has the highest number of doctoral graduates in absolute terms, 71,000 in 2017 (Hutt, 2019).
4   But note that several fast-developing economies, particularly from the BRIC countries, still denounce a significant shortage of PhDs.
5   See <https://esrc.ukri.org/skills-and-careers/postgraduate-careers/careers-in-social-science/>.

respectively. As many as fifty-eight different career paths were described by the 255 social sciences respondents. Although teaching and lecturing in HE was by far the most common employment for social sciences respondents (40%, increasing to 42% over three years), other common pathways from the survey data included working as researchers in industry and the third sector, as commercial, industrial and public sector managers; in marketing, sales, media and advertising positions; and as business and financial professionals. These data corroborate the views from relevant literature emphasising both that a PhD offers great advantages over other job candidates and the increasing attractiveness of doctoral graduates to non-HE employers (see, e.g., McGagh et al., 2016). As noted by Diamond et al. (2014) and Bryan and Guccione (2018, p. 1125), the recruitment of PhD holders *"yields collective knowledge, skills, networking, and prestige benefits to organisations making doctoral graduates assets of significant value to organisations"*.

The Economist's article also claims that having a PhD may offer no real financial benefit, may not lead to permanent academic employment even years after graduation and may even reduce earnings. Nonsense! Having a doctorate is a significant advantage in the labour market. If the multi-decennial experience of the employability of our past doctoral graduates is anything to go by, the stereotype of PhD candidates being 'overqualified' for jobs in industry, is nothing more than a myth. Having a PhD qualifies you for many positions in industry, and PhD-qualified professionals are in high demand (more on this point in Chapter 12 of this book). Applicants holding a PhD have the lowest average unemployment rate of any level of educational attainment. According to the OECD 'Education at a Glance 2019' report,[6] the average employment rate for PhD holders is a whopping 97%. Moreover, gaining more years of higher education impacts always positively on earnings potential, and individuals who hold a doctorate also earn the most over their lifetime when compared to other degree types. A study in the *Journal of Higher Education Policy and Management*

---

6   See <https://esrc.ukri.org/skills-and-careers/postgraduate-careers/careers-in-social-science/>.

by Bernard Casey (2009) shows that British men with a bachelor's degree earn 14% more than those who could have gone to university but chose not to. The 'earnings premium' for a PhD (defined in the study as the difference over the working lifetime of the earnings of an individual obtaining a doctorate relative to a person who could have gone to university but who chose not to) is 26%. For women, obtaining a doctorate warrants an even higher earnings premium, of 38%. In some subjects, women's earnings premium associated with a PhD qualification is higher still, 42% in social sciences, 47% in mathematics and computing, and 55% in medicine and related studies.

In addition to doctoral graduates' deep specialist subject knowledge, non-HE employers value a range of PhD-related skills that include, but are not limited to, the ability to collect, interpret and evaluate data, wider research and analytical skills and a proven capacity for critical thinking. These skills and cognitive abilities allow doctoral graduates to distinguish themselves by knowing how to bring a fresh perspective to problems, create knowledge rather than just repackage it and innovate. Doctoral graduates also offer a proven ability to work as part of a team as well as independently, within a relevant ethos, formulate evidence-based arguments, question assumptions, communicate concisely, clearly and accurately (orally and in writing), present information, positively respond to critical feedback, manage their own time and wellbeing, and take responsibility for their own development. These are the very skills that, in a world increasingly driven by knowledge-based economies that favour innovation, make universities the 'motors' of a nation's economy and doctoral graduates the newest form of renewable energy. As Neumann and Tan (2011, p. 611) eloquently elaborate:

> … the tacit assumption within doctoral programs that the doctorate is a preparation for an academic career may be challenged. Some argue that although universities are a key institution in the knowledge economy they are under pressure to redefine their place and role within this new division of labour […] The knowledge economy is more than simply higher knowledge intensity, and the doctorate represents more than greater technical skill and ability to conduct research. There are also social and moral aspects to advanced research, and to how the doctorate can promote effective participation in communities of knowledge.

In a global climate increasingly characterised by 'anti-intellectualism', faltering levels of trust in science and experts and a political agenda pushing for a merely utilitarian and reductionist notion of 'useful' knowledge as knowledge usable solely in the pursuit of profit, interest and money, it is paramount to advocate the wider economic, moral and societal value of knowledge, research and the producers of knowledge. Doing a doctorate is much more than just obtaining an educational qualification that increases one's job prospects and earnings potential. Indeed, the careerism narrative obfuscates the value of knowledge, ideas and the ability to think as critical assets not only in most professions but in everyday life. In addition to the benefits of having a PhD for the holder of the doctorate and for organisations, there are social gains associated with knowledge spill-overs to the economy at large and to wider society. The power of education to change lives and communities should not be underestimated. This view resonates with the notion of research, education and the production of highly qualified and educated individuals as a 'common good' (Casey, 2009), a path to knowledge, truth, free thinking and emancipation that might raise the abilities and wellbeing of all people and society at large; a point conveniently ignored by *The Economist*'s article discussed above.

Becoming a postgraduate researcher

Becoming a PGR is a process. It involves a long and at times lonely journey of transformation best described as 'a rite of passage', a transitional process of moving from one social status to another (van Gannep, 1960; Turner, 1969). Such a process entails a liminal phase of discovery and self-discovery fraught with ambiguity and uncertainty, challenges and steep learning curves. I could unpack the profound significance of the academic blurb contained in the previous sentences by citing ten times as many journal articles from the higher education literature that have concerned themselves with the process of self-discovery many doctoral students go through. Yet, I find the reflection by one of my past PGRs on her lived experience, to be more touching and authentically authoritative than any academic narrative could ever be to exemplify the notion of the PhD as a 'rite of passage'. She wrote:

> As a black woman, a mother, and a wife, returning to doctoral study after many years in work was a transformative experience, a rebirth even. The initial fears of tackling demanding academic and intellectual challenges soon gave way to a sense of rediscovery of my skills and abilities that had become dormant but were still in me, somewhere, and were dying for being put into use again. The PhD allowed me to do just that, find my inner voice and express myself; to do something for me. Not just rediscover myself, but grow, and develop yet another identity to become the best I could be. The process was fraught with tough challenges, setbacks, and at times mixed emotions, including feelings of guilt and selfishness, which were painful to process. When asked about what my PhD was about, my answer is, 'I got a PhD in … me'. But I am happier of being the 'new me', despite the arduous road I journeyed, and the tough obstacles I faced on the way. I now feel a better version of myself and I can give more to anyone around me because of it and be a great example to my children. This is what life, after all, is about: dreams, ambitions, challenges, learning, discovery, and change.

But, of course, as we have seen, along with new understandings and a new way of looking at things, slowly forming a new identity of the self, the task of becoming a doctoral researcher can be framed and is typically assessed in terms of describing the skills doctoral graduates develop. Bryan and Guccione (2018) refer to the myriad of skills highlighted in the UK-sector document 'The Researcher Development Framework' (Vitae, 2011), delivered following Sir Gareth Roberts' (2002) report on UK STEM PhD graduate skills. The report lists as many as sixty-three descriptors across four domains and twelve sub-domains, encompassing *"the knowledge, intellectual abilities, techniques and professional standards to do research, as well as the personal qualities, knowledge and skills to work with others and ensure the wider impact of research"* (Vitae, 2011, p. 2). Bryan and Guccione (2018) draw specific attention to the 'value-added factors' such as cultural awareness, self-efficacy, leadership and working relationships. But it is worth highlighting other skills that can also be said to be critical for becoming a successful postgraduate researcher.

To start with, to complete a major research project over a three-year period, it is useful to feature good project management as a critical success factor. High-quality planning, from setting achievable aims and objectives and feasible milestones through to identifying necessary resources, including access to data and/or information gatekeepers, will be a crucial competency to carry out the project to successful completion. Equally important will be the ability to handle an inevitably tight project budget, which for many PGRs will have to be managed in parallel to keeping a grip on personal and domestic finances.

Learning how to keep the data safe and re-usable will also be key. Whether the results you obtain from the study involve statistical results, interview material or archival evidence, data management skills will become essential also to ensure you comply with the legislative, contractual, ethical and university policy requirements that you must adhere to in the management of your research data. This process will entail compiling a comprehensive Data Management Plan (DMP) that is generally part of the requirements to obtain ethical clearance for your PhD project. Your DMP should specify, among other things, methods for data collection and quality assurance processes, plans for data storage during the project to keep your data safe and secure, processes for documenting your data during the project, details of how you will share and preserve your data after the end of the project, and the length of time that the data must be preserved.

Closely linked with data management is the necessity of developing IT skills. Although you might consider yourself already a confident user of IT, you will most likely need to learn new software packages such as Stata or, for qualitative research, NVivo, online platforms and programmes or new analytical tools for working with large amounts of data.

But acquiring new skills aside, which will be given ample coverage throughout the rest of this book, the transformative process of becoming a PGR is mostly about developing a new mindset, way of thinking and attitudes, that align to the very nature of what doing research is about. Below I expand on the nature and essential features of doctoral research whilst also highlighting the fundamental mind shifts that such features require of those intending to embark on a PhD and that I deem as necessary for success.

The nature and distinguishing features of doctoral research

How many times have I heard PGRs say things such as *"tell me what to do"*, *"but I wasn't told I should learn about this"* or even *"but I wasn't specifically asked to read all the published work in the field"*? Too many. The nature and most distinguishing feature of doctoral research compared to Masters or other forms of postgraduate education, lies precisely within this fundamental misunderstanding. Doctoral education places you in the driving seat, it is a process that needs to be led by you; it is *your responsibility*, *your thesis*, *your PhD*. You are no longer part of a structured undergraduate or postgraduate course. There is no pre-defined syllabus, no set assessments, coursework assignments, teachers or module leaders. You need to manage your own learning, your time, your budget, your development, your wellbeing and all the working relationships within and outside academia you are likely to establish to reach your goal. Obviously, you will not be alone, there will be people around to help you, *"but the responsibility for determining what is required, as well as for carrying it out, remains firmly with you"* (Phillips and Pugh, 1994, p. 2).

Indeed, becoming accustomed to working with a large degree of autonomy whilst learning to recognise at which crucial times you or the progress of your research project will require the support of others, is key. Relevant others include supervisors, librarians, administrative staff, fellow doctoral candidates, career advisors, family and friends, and at times individuals in the private sector who may provide access to data. However, even such support cannot be unqualified. In the case of supervisors, it is 'autonomy support' that should be cultivated. As observed by van Rooij et al. (2021), 'autonomy support' can be understood as giving the 'PhD student' space and opportunity to make his or her own choices, encouraging autonomous behaviour and treating the PGR's point of view and ideas with respect.

Critical in this context is the concept of self-regulated learning. Defined as *"an active, constructive process whereby learners set goals for their learning and then attempt to monitor, regulate, and control their cognition, motivation, and behavior, guided and constrained by their goals and the contextual features in the environment*" (Pintrich, 2000, p. 453), self-regulated learning relates to the cognitive, metacognitive, behavioural, motivational and emotional/affective dimensions for effective learning and academic achievement (Zimmerman, 2008; 2013). During a PhD, it is through this self-directed process that learner PGRs will transform their mental abilities into task-related skills and the writing of the thesis into a magical process of self-realisation.

Indeed, evidence from doctoral education literature suggests that self-regulated learning is a good predictor of the time needed for the completion of the thesis and is also strongly correlated with intrinsic task value (Kelley and Salisbury-Glennon, 2016). Motivation, a key component of self-regulated learning, is, of course, paramount to accomplish the task. Motivation, in turn, depends on self-efficacy, which refers to the extent to which an individual is confident that he or she can perform the task and accomplish the goal (Bandura, 1997). Self-efficacy is of great importance for self-regulated learning because it affects how learners engage and persist at challenging tasks. Research has shown that, in academic settings, learners with higher self-efficacy are better able to engage with a difficult task and are more likely to persist at it even in the face of initial failures compared to low-efficacy learners (Pajares, 1996). On the other hand, PGRs with lower levels of self-efficacy tend to engage in self-handicapping behaviours in order to avoid being perceived (or perceiving themselves) as incompetent (Schwinger and Stiensmeier-Pelster, 2011).

Alongside autonomy, taking responsibility for your own learning and development, and being able to self-regulate, two additional defining features of doctoral research that distinguish it from other types of postgraduate education and which require analogous mindset shifts many PGRs tend to struggle with, are worth highlighting.

The first such shift is about gaining a genuine appreciation that doctoral research is not just about learning all there is to know about a topic, that is, mastering a field, which is what Master degrees are about. It is about creating new knowledge and bringing new ideas, theory and reliable evidence into existence in a way that adds to the scientific field and advances knowledge. This is where the attributes 'originality' and 'contribution' come into play as core criteria in the assessment and, ultimately, the award of a PhD.

The second defining feature of doctoral research and associated mindset shift relates to embracing the inherent uncertainty that inevitably accompanies the search for that original idea or new solution to the problem you are tackling. There will be uncertainty also in finding your own voice and, as rightly noted by Dunleavy (2003, p. 28) *"Framing your own view while still grounding your work in an established academic tradition and some part of the contemporary discourse of your discipline, is a knack that takes time to develop."* In fact, you may not even know for quite a while during your doctorate whether the main research question of your project has an answer at all, let alone what that answer may be. Research is undertaken precisely because we don't know everything.

This notion of uncertainty is an integral part of the process and experience of doing research. The most accurate and inspiring description of the symbiosis between research and uncertainty I have ever come across, is the 'dark mansion' analogy offered by Sir Andrew Wiles, the British mathematician who was awarded the 2016 Abel Prize (widely regarded as the Nobel for mathematics) for solving Fermat's last theorem, a conjecture that had remained too difficult to prove for many centuries. His experience of doing research, Wiles said, *is like entering a dark mansion …*

> One goes into the first room, and it's dark, deeply dark. One stumbles around, bumping into the furniture, and gradually you learn where each piece of furniture is. And finally, after six months or so, you find the light switch. You turn it on, and suddenly it's all illuminated, and you can see exactly where you were. (Extract taken from BBC – Horizon, 1996, 'Fermat's Last Theorem')

In essence, without uncertainty and research, discovery would be impossible. And even what constitutes a discovery is a moving target, as other researchers all over the world are part of that 'race against time' to make that novel contribution you too are eagerly working towards before others 'get there'. Whilst you may feel uncomfortable with this notion of scientific uncertainty, you must learn to thrive on it, through great curiosity, perseverance, passion, enthusiasm and the desire to make a real difference through your work. The extract below, from the reflective statement of one of my past PGRs, captures the 'uncertainty' challenge well as follows:

Becoming a PhD researcher took some getting used to. Perhaps the greatest challenge was learning to cope with the unpredictability and state of suspense that surrounds some tricky research phases characterised by great uncertainty, where things weren't working out and I felt I had little or no control. I remember, for example, getting stuck for a long time on a methodological problem that appeared unsolvable with the techniques in my toolbox. I recall feeling defeated and even thinking of throwing in the towel on my research career. Yet, my love for research, and sticking to it long enough brought rewards. When those methodological problems were resolved (also with the help and support of my supervisor), the joy of succeeding more than made up for the weeks if not months of frustration I had experienced. I have learnt that it is impossible to be defeated if you never give up.

About this book and how it will help

The aim of this book is to provide the most comprehensive roadmap to a successful PhD completion, thus offering a very useful guide for *aspiring* and *existing* doctoral researchers in business and management disciplines and the social sciences (including, *inter alia*, international business, marketing, management, management education, organisation studies, tourism and hospitality, accounting, finance, law and economics). Although we often refer to the British postgraduate research system/framework, the book is written for a global audience of prospective and existing doctoral researchers. As such, it can be used, and implemented as a core text in PhD induction programmes, across countries. Academic supervisors, too, should find this book a valuable resource on how they can fulfil their responsibility to guide PGRs toward a successful completion of their doctorate.

We aim to share the craftsmanship of doing research in the way artisans or chefs would, to pass down their artistry, knowledge and skills. Hence, it is a book intended for those who really are passionate about learning the craft, who are willing to let themselves be inspired and who are prepared to work hard. If you think these stipulations can be innocuously compromised, think again. To those approaching this book looking for ways to cut corners or, even worse, trickery to get a PhD, we say firmly, *this book is not for you*. Similarly, don't expect us to advise you on the content to put in your thesis. That is *your* task. Building on Eco's (2015) 'prepared meal' analogy, the purpose of our writing is not to serve a ready-meal but rather help you understand the value of quality ingredients, the importance of taking the time to plan, of the processes to follow and of the hard labour that must go into preparing a meal of gourmet quality.

There is no set expectation of how prospective PGRs, current doctoral researchers and supervisors should read this book. We don't necessarily anticipate that you will read it sequentially from Chapter 1 through to Chapter 12 in one go (though doing so may be the best way to maximise your enjoyment from it). Although our compendium can be said to be a hybrid between a research monograph and a 'how to' manual that takes the reader more or less chronologically from the initial challenge of applying for a PhD place through to seeking employment after completion, each chapter stands alone in offering relevant advice at every given stage of the doctoral journey. We recommend reading it thoroughly, of course, from cover to cover, and keeping it as an essential companion for going back to relevant chapters as needed, even after taking employment in academia as a lecturer, early career researcher (ECR) and/or supervisor.

The book doesn't include action summaries, questions with model answers or exercises to apply concepts and practise new skills, sections typically skipped even by the keenest of readers of such texts. It is not a self-study skills text as such, therefore. Yet, it does provide innumerable points for reflection, food for thought and many suggested strategies throughout. To those who find our narrative and normative register excessively prescriptive, we say resolutely, this is the price we are happy to pay in order to offer firm, practice-based and ethically grounded advice in areas where others are not prepared to take a robust stance. That said, we advise PGRs as well as supervisors reading this book to take time to consider each suggestion carefully. We recommend evaluating the significance and relevance of such strategies and how they can be tried out, adopted or discarded as seems useful to each individual's way of working and studying, and through dialogue and negotiation, a multitude of PGR-supervisor relationships.

Each chapter begins with a 'Preamble', a brief introduction that outlines the problem statement, context and indicative content. This preliminary section also states the aim of the chapter, clarifying its main purpose and relevance. Every chapter ends with 'Some final words of encouragement'. This is a kind of epilogue that serves as a concluding comment to what has been covered; a finale aimed at directing thoughts and emotions into a positive headspace and at instilling motivation in readers keen on tackling challenges, overcoming obstacles and accomplishing goals.

References

Bandura, A. (1997). *Self-Efficacy: The Exercise of Control*. New York: Freeman.
BBC - Horizon (1996). Fermat's Last Theorem. Documentary available at: <https://www.dailymotion.com/video/x223gx8>
Bryan, B. and Guccione, K. (2018). Was it worth it? A qualitative exploration into graduate perceptions of doctoral value. *Higher Education Research & Development*, 37(6), 1124–1140.
Casey, B. H. (2009). The economic contribution of PhDs. *Journal of Higher Education Policy and Management*, 31(3), 219–227.
Diamond, A., Ball, C., Vorley, T., Hughes, T., Moreton, R., Howe, P., and Nathwani, T. (2014). *The Impact of Doctoral Careers*. Leicester, UK: CFE Research.
Dunleavy, P. (2003) *Authoring a PhD – How to Plan, Draft, Write and Finish a Doctoral Thesis or Dissertation*. London, UK: Macmillan International Higher Education.
Eco, U. (2015). *How to Write a Thesis*. London, UK: MIT Press.
Hutt, R. (2019). Which countries have the most doctoral graduates? World Economic Forum, available at: <https://www.weforum.org/agenda/2019/10/doctoral-graduates-phd-tertiary-education/.>
Kelley, M. J. and Salisbury-Glennon, J. D. (2016). The role of self-regulation in doctoral students' status of All but Dissertation (ABD). *Innovative Higher Education*, 41(1), 87–100.
McGagh, J., Marsh, H., Western, M., Thomas, P., Hastings, A., Mihailova, M., and Wenham, M. (2016). *Review of Australia's Research Training System*. Melbourne: Australian Council of Learned Academies.
Neumann, R. and Tan, K. K. (2011). From PhD to initial employment: The doctorate in a knowledge economy. *Studies in Higher Education*, 36(5), 601–614.

Overall, N. C., Deane, K. L., and Peterson, E. R. (2011). Promoting doctoral students' research self-efficacy: Combining academic guidance with autonomy support. *Higher Education Research & Development*, 30(6), 791–805.

Pajares, F. (1996). Self-efficacy beliefs in academic settings. *Review of Educational Research*, 66, 543–578.

Phillips, E. M. and Pugh, D. (1994). *How to Get a PhD*. 2nd Edition. Maidenhead, UK: Open University Press.

Pintrich, P. R. (2000). The role of goal orientation in self-regulated learning. In: Boekaerts, M., Zeidner, M., and Pintrich, P. R. (Eds.). *Handbook of Self-Regulation* (pp. 451–502). New York: Academic Press.

Roberts, G. (2002). SET for Success – The Supply of People with Science, Technology, Engineering and Mathematical Skills. The Report of Sir Gareth Roberts' Review. See <https://webarchive.nationalarchives.gov.uk/+/http://www.hm-treasury.gov.uk/ent_res_roberts.htm>

Schwinger, M. and Stiensmeier-Pelster, J. (2011). Prevention of self-handicapping: The protective function of mastery goals. *Learning and Individual Differences*, 21(6), 699–709.

The Economist (2010). Why doing a PhD is often a waste of time. Available at: <https://medium.economist.com/why-doing-a-phd-is-often-a-waste-of-time-349206f9addb.>

Turner, V. (1969). *The Ritual Process: Structure and Anti-structure*. Chicago: Aldine.

Van Gennep, A. (1960). *The Rites of Passage*. London, UK: Routledge and Kegan Paul.

Van Rooij, E., Fokkens-Bruinsma, M., and Jansen, E. (2021). Factors that influence PhD candidates' success: The importance of PhD project characteristics. *Studies in Continuing Education*, 43(1), 48–67.

Vitae (2011). The Researcher Development Framework. Retrieved from <https://www.vitae.ac.uk/vitae-publications/rdf-related/researcher-development-framework-rdf-vitae.pdf>

Zimmerman, B. J. (2008). Investigating self-regulation and motivation: Historical background, methodological developments, and future prospects. *American Educational Research Journal*, 45(1), 166–183.

Zimmerman B. J. (2013). From cognitive modeling to self-regulation: A social cognitive career path. *Educational Psychology*, 48(3), 135–147.

JASON BEGLEY

2 How to write a PhD application and academic proposal

Preamble

The **aim of this chapter** is to consider the question of how to write a better-quality doctoral application. The chapter starts by outlining the types of PhDs available to applicants to UK business schools and the relative merits of each, to help candidates identify their optimal pathway. It then focuses on various preparations necessary before even starting to draft an application; where to apply, entry requirements, which institutions, schools or research centres to consider, what supervisors may be most suitable, and the thorny issue of the financing of a PhD. Next, the chapter discusses the key features of a PhD research proposal and how the best proposals demonstrate knowledge and understanding of relevant literature, thus increasing confidence in the ability of the applicant to deliver an original study that makes a contribution to knowledge. This section also offers some observations about the application system at higher education institutions themselves, especially online applications. Some discussion will also be directed at how to respond to requests for editorial changes, or worse, outright rejection. The chapter then examines the international dimension to PhD applications, the role of government agencies and the ensuing complexity of applications that need to navigate regulatory barriers. Finally, I return to the question of how to garner support for an application from potential supervisors and institutions.

The first steps in your PhD journey

Why do you want to do a PhD? This is probably the most frequently asked question of PhD applicants and with good reason. It is usually prompted by a rushed application from individuals without a clear sense of what is required of them. A surprising number of doctoral candidates have not fully considered this important matter. Considering they are about to commit a considerable period of their lives to a singular task of great complexity and not a little difficulty, it may seem unexpected. However, potential postgraduate researchers (PGRs) often choose to apply for a doctorate in a speculative manner while still being irresolute and/or uncertain. On many occasions these aspiring researchers fail to appreciate what is actually required of a doctoral student and what skills will be acquired from completing their PhD, namely an ability to undertake high-quality, independent research (if so, please read Chapter 1 if you skipped it).

A PhD is primarily research training leading to a professional research qualification (Rugg and Petre, 2010). While many of the skills are transferable to other areas of life and work, losing sight or being unaware of this central truth undermines decisions to undertake doctoral study. By extension, the uncertain and weakly thought out decision to pursue a PhD will manifest in a poorly conceived and hastily written application that only serves to demonstrate the vacillating thought processes of the candidate. The very best applications have absolute clarity of purpose. They are well-researched, quickly identify the knowledge gap in both theory and literature, offer a clear indication of the academic contributions and societal applications the study is likely to generate at completion and, additionally, demonstrate that considerable thought has gone into pinpointing a suitable supervisor. An excellent PhD application requires months of preparation. Time spent this way on an application is enormously valuable, allowing candidates the opportunity to build the foundations of their work, reading through scholarly works and talking to knowledgeable academics. When these individuals start their PhD, they hit the ground running and don't waste time trying to get to grips with their research topic, expending three of their most valuable resources doing so, time, patience and money in the form of fees.

The initial stage of putting together a PhD application is obvious; you will need to decide on a research topic. The advice to offer is also clear-cut. It needs to be a topic you are invested in, one that will sustain your interest when the early enthusiasm wanes and the research journey becomes difficult. However, not just any topic will suffice. The most frequent reason for rejection of a PhD application is a failure to identify an appropriate research topic that makes both an academic contribution and research outcomes with social value. In business schools, the expectation of doctoral candidates is that, from an academic perspective, they will make a contribution to theory that will add to existing understanding, adapt a theory in new and informative ways, extend theory into complementary disciplines, or provide evidence that reinforces knowledge around an existing debate in a new or novel manner. Sometimes keener applicants wish to overturn existing theory, a lofty ambition that would be beyond even the most seasoned researcher and not expected for a PhD. The second feature of a good research topic is the possible learning that can be derived from the research findings and how they can inform our understanding of the world around us. In particular, the expectation for many business and management or social science theses is that policy recommendations will arise from the doctoral research. Being able to identify how the research topic will benefit society (i.e. the wider societal impact of the PhD study) will vastly improve the quality of the application.

Too frequently PhD applications undervalue either one or both of these two features. However, in my experience, it is the first, the academic contribution, that is more often overlooked. This typically arises because the applicant does not invest enough time going through the literature, erroneously believing that such part of the research will take care of itself at a later date. This usually occurs due to time constraints or because the applicant fears they will be beaten to researching the topic by another candidate. However, without a well-developed question that meets both requirements, the most likely outcome is that the institution will either send the application back for further editing, so wasting valuable time or, worse, reject outright. It is important, therefore, in developing an application that significant time is spent reading through an appropriate amount of literature relevant to the research topic, a point I will return to later in this chapter. You should also seek help from peers, staff from undergraduate courses you attended and from other researchers already involved in doctoral study, including PGRs who have recently completed (as an old Chinese proverb goes, '*To know the road ahead, ask those coming back*'). Feedback from researchers can be particularly useful to help you reflect on the achievability of the PhD study you propose. Not just in terms of the scope of what you plan to investigate and the associated academic territory you will need to cover and add to, but also with respect to your ability to access the required data and complete the intended research within the time and financial constraints of doctoral research. In short, as sternly put by Eco (2015, p. 8), "*you must write a thesis that you are able to write*". This piece of advice may seem banal or trivial, but the fact is that while it is great to have your eyes on the stars, you must also keep your feet on the ground. Many PhD proposals have been rejected precisely because what was being suggested was overly ambitious, infeasible and unachievable.

Having given some consideration to the research topic, the next area of concern for the applicant must be the institution of choice. Not all UK universities are equal and useful rankings are provided through sources such as the Times Higher Education Rankings, the Guardian University Guide, or the QS World University Rankings. However, such broad, prestige-based grading only touches the surface of the information required. Important too is finding out about the research culture of the institution, its track record in terms of completions, its financial commitment to postgraduate research, and the resources and expertise made available for the specific type of research the applicant wants to undertake. It is not always the case that storied institutions with a long tradition of research provide the most supportive environment for PGRs. Frequently, newer institutions, that are investing in research and are eager to establish a vibrant and successful PhD programme, will offer strong incentives and support to PGRs in the form of generous scholarships and funding, as well as bountiful support from administrative and welfare services. Hence, spending adequate time scouting the best opportunities, through contacting staff responsible for doctoral programmes, can prove beneficial.

Researching an appropriate supervisor is a critical step at this juncture. The supervisor you select should be knowledgeable of your discipline and research topic. The temptation is to seek out the most senior researchers to supervise your thesis. However, these senior figures, such as full professors, may be already very busy and may not offer as much time and input as less visible supervisors who are keen to establish their reputation. Conversely, the latter may not be as experienced in supervision, sometimes adding a frisson of unnecessary tension to proceedings. The best way to understand the type of supervisor you might want to become involved with, therefore, is to contact them directly. This will help you form a first impression and possibly a view as to how the relationship might pan out. In some cases, depending on the type of individual you contact, the first exchange can lead to valuable feedback on your research and useful pointers as to what reading material you might start with.

Having considered what institutions and supervisors to approach, the next step is to focus on the options available to you as a potential doctoral candidate. The traditional model of the PhD that emerged over many centuries in Europe and the UK bears similarity with the relationship between a craftsperson and his or her apprentice. As Dunleavy notes, in this approach to PhD studies *"the supervisor will inculcate the right spirit in the doctoral candidate in a hand-crafted way, passing on the accumulated wisdom of the discipline"* (2015, p. 6). The emphasis is on the quality of the relationship between the supervisor and the supervised. Over time this approach has partially given way to models with a greater emphasis on methods training and coursework, as well as teams of supervisors replacing the single reference point for the doctoral candidate, offering greater flexibility. Nonetheless, the importance of the lead supervisor on a team, frequently referred to as the Director of Studies (DoS), remains central to the PhD process.

The route through to a PhD award has also changed over time, branching significantly to offer a range of options to doctoral candidates seeking the most appropriate avenue for their own needs and circumstances. In UK Business Schools, the available options can be captured under four main headings, as examined below.

Full-time doctoral study

Still the most prevalent form of study in UK Business Schools, the full-time doctorate route aligns most closely to the classical style of PhD study. Typically taking a minimum of three years (though this may well vary in some institutions), the PGR will be expected to produce a major piece of work somewhere between 40,000 (STEM) and 80 to 90,000 (Business, Arts, Humanities) words in length, depending on their discipline or data collection method. The PGR will be expected to self-manage and self-regulate his or her own workload, pegged against a series of benchmarks identified by the supervisory team or institution. All deliveries of research output will be the responsibility of the PGR, as will be most administrative tasks. The first year is typically spent in training sessions relevant to research skills, with written outputs providing early indicators of approach to the research topic. The second year will usually involve data collection, with later years spent on the analysis of results and writing up. Typically, doctoral researchers are encouraged to aim for completion at the three-year mark, but the chances of doing so still remain remote with most theses taking much longer than the minimum time recommended, a factor that should be considered in terms of financing a PhD. Additionally, mental stress can be very high during this intense period of study and research. Vitae, the leading UK independent organisation for professional and career development of doctoral researchers and research staff in HE, released a critical report on researcher wellbeing in 2017. Derived from findings based on two major national surveys, the report indicated that 26% of doctoral researchers had considered leaving or suspending their degree programme. These figures rose to 48% and 60% respectively, for those with a disability or an underlying mental health condition (see Chapter 5 for detailed advice on how to manage your wellbeing).

Part-time doctoral study

The part-time option is aimed at those who want a better balance between work and study, with the study period usually set at five years. On the surface at least, this may seem like a tempting pathway to pursue. However, this can prove a more difficult route, as implied by UK completion rates. According to the Higher Education Statistics Agency (HESA, 2020) the average number of full-time doctorates undertaken yearly between 2014/2015 and 2018/2019 was 75,720, with average completion rates being 19,831. The respective figures for part-time doctorates were 24,145 and 3,879. Though a very crude measure, it suggests the percentage completion rates for part-timers are significantly lower.[7] Potential part-time candidates should appreciate that many UK universities regulate for half the number of hours as the full-time route, meaning the targets for progress review panels are still substantial. The possibility of doing a part-time PhD on evenings and at weekends is challenging and most part-time PGRs need to set a significant share of their work week aside to produce a thesis in the time allotted. Moreover, it can be extremely disheartening to candidates to realise that so many years of their life will be spent balancing their time between work and study, with concomitant demands on their free time the further into their research they go. A highly capable and intelligent colleague explained that the reason she dropped out of part-time studies was precisely because she could no longer justify to her young family the time she was spending on her job and her thesis. There was no doubting her capabilities, it was all the other parts of life that got in her way.

The above two programmes of study are the most common type of PhD in UK universities. However, in the last few years several alternative routes to a doctoral award have emerged, with growing popularity.

---

7   Approximately 26% full-time compared to 16% part-time. These figures need to be treated with caution. They are averaged, rounded and do not reflect changes over the lifetime of a research project. Having contacted the agency, I was informed a deeper dive would require significantly more time and investment. *In lieu* I was pointed to the broad figures above and deemed them to be sufficient to make the point.

Professional doctorate

These are 'practical' work-based programmes (typically in fields such as, *inter alia*, law, business and medicine) of study with a research component and are also studied part-time. They can take up to five years, with the first two usually focusing on taught modules relating to research methods, literature reviews and critical analysis. In the latter part of the programme the candidate is expected to produce several written outputs, but not one large piece of work such as a PhD thesis. The purpose of the professional doctorate is to offer those already research active in their careers the opportunity to enhance their research skills to doctoral level while continuing to advance along their career trajectory. As such, this option is usually pursued by those with significant research skills already acquired as part of their job.

PhD by publication

Quite frequently misunderstood, even within HEIs, the PhD by publication route allows researchers with a rich body of existing published work (most typically over half a dozen, mostly single-authored publications) the opportunity to acquire doctoral recognition for the work undertaken so far. The candidate must demonstrate in a document of about 20,000 words in length how the totality of their research specialisation, as demonstrated by the published work to date, is worthy of a doctoral award. It can be a difficult task to put together such a piece of work and one usually reserved for those well-advanced in their specialised field. What has occurred in recent years is an attempt by some institutions to develop a similar approach for early career researchers. What is proposed in this alternative approach is for the candidate to produce a series of research articles in recognised academic journals, articles that are linked around a common theme so that when combined into one body of work they will form the basis of a doctoral thesis. This can be quite challenging, not least because the academic journals the candidate submits work to have to be of an approved standard, usually identified through Business

School ranking lists, for example, the Chartered Association of Business Schools (ABS) list, or through indicators such as journal citations and impact factor, that can be found though sources such as Scopus.[8] If you see a PhD by publication offered at a HEI you will need to determine in advance which type is available and what and how many research outputs will be required.

Writing the PhD proposal

Referring to 'writing up' a proposal, is archaic in many ways, since most doctoral application systems in the UK are now online. It is, therefore, worth pausing a moment before discussing the content and structure of the proposal, to say a few words about the online portal systems and processes used by most UK universities to assess PhD applications.

Most of these portal systems adopt a two-part process to gauge the value of an application. The first stage involves administrative staff, well versed in the regulations and requirements of the university, who examine each application to ensure it meets all the entry criteria for the candidate, including past academic records and achievements, funding capability and, in the case of foreign students, their ability to adequately converse and write in English. For international/overseas candidates applying from outside the UK/EU it becomes even more complicated as there are certain immigration requirements overseen by the national government that they need to be aware of, as will be discussed later.

The second hurdle to overcome is academic. The decision-makers who determine the scholastic quality of an application will be drawn from the research staff and not administration. This can serve to occasionally confuse an applicant. Sometimes aspiring PGRs will have contacted a potential supervisor who enthusiastically champions their application, only to fail due to not meeting the necessary entry requirements (e.g. due to lack of a recognised Master degree). In other cases, the applicant will have been

8   For more information on Scopus see later in this chapter.

steadily progressing through the system only to have their research proposal meet a brick wall when it is deemed of too low a quality by a potential supervisor screening the application. Since falling at the academic stage ends the process, often assessors will give the applicant another chance by sending the application back to the aspiring PGR for editing. It is important then, if your application is not accepted, that you understand why. If you have failed on the entry criteria, there is very little recourse left open other than trying at another institution, since the entry standards are clear and written into regulations. However, if the application comes back requesting further edits to the proposal, this means the academic quality is not up to standard and needs further work. An opportunity then may exist to go away and redraft the proposal according to the feedback received, if any.

Quite frequently in my role as PhD Academic Director I have sent applications back for editing only to receive them again a few days later with minimal or, at best, superficial changes. Probably impatience, or a feeling of being so close to being accepted that this trifling barrier can be quickly bypassed, is what encourages this mindset. However, what applicants fail to appreciate is that this will have been the first time I will have seen this application. Any changes I suggest are serious and require proper revision and effort. For example, if I point to a weak methodology, it will not suffice to add some generic commentary on epistemology. What will be required is a complete rethinking of the way in which the aspiring doctoral researcher intends to pursue the study. If I state that the theoretical contribution is insufficiently clear, or not evident, tacking on extra theory unconnected to the research question and objectives is also not good. That brings us to what a proper PhD proposal looks like in terms of content and structure. Typically, there are three key components to an application, your *Curriculum Vitae* (CV), a personal statement and the proposal of the research question to be addressed.

This is not the appropriate place to discuss at length what is required of a good CV (but see Chapter 12). Suffice to say that it should demonstrate your academic credentials and research skills and achievements; any awards for academic work, institutional support or postgraduate activities (including a research component or dissertation) should be prioritised. In terms of the personal statement, this is an opportunity to offer some insight into who you are, what interests you and, importantly, what motivates you to pursue a PhD. The personal statement is an opportunity to showcase your drive and determination to complete a worthwhile piece of original research, while also establishing your credibility as an able, independent researcher. Take the opportunity to highlight any relevant skills that will help execute your research, and how your chosen topic reflects your previous studies and experience. If at this stage you profess to not understanding what is expected and required, or that you have chosen this path as the one of 'least resistance', then you can expect the reader to harbour doubts about your capacity to deliver a self-directed research project.

Arguably the most crucial component of the application will be the academic proposal containing your research question, approach and justification for examining it. Although there will be differences in application procedures depending on which PhD route you intend to pursue, the process for putting together a research proposal is consistent, reflecting the same logical steps that can be seen in small 10,000 word projects right up to a large 80,000 word thesis. You'll need to start by organising your material and articulating your arguments in order to guide your reader to the main research question and show them the purpose of your research. Structure and clarity of content are crucial in this endeavour. Figure 2.1 below gives a broad overview of what the overall process looks like in a typical research project. The logic of the approach is clear. Each step is informed by the previous one, building on evidence and information gathered, finally culminating in an informed series of findings and recommendations supported by a clear and transparent process, well evidenced and signposted. Similarly, a PhD proposal should be cognisant of the way in which a research question or project is created and pursued, reflecting that knowledge in the development of the proposal.

Any research project, large or small, will broadly follow the steps outlined in Figure 2.1. When crafting a proposal what is required is to show how you intend to develop a research question into a project and, in doing so, address how you will engage with each stage of this process in the next three to five years. Since the academic proposal is such a crucial component

Context	This section focuses on outlining the background to the research for the reader and points to the research question they hope to answer
Research Question	Here the topic being examined by the thesis will be outlined in 3-4 lines, a single statement capturing the overarching aim of the thesis
Research objectives	A subset of the research question, the objectives will state the steps required to answer the research question posed
Literature review	A thorough and expert analysis of relevant existing research and theory to demonstrate understanding of the question and identify where the contribution is to be made
Conceptual framework	A detailed explanation of how theory can be applied to the research question to answer the stated aim
Methodology	A clear statement of the steps to be taken to meet research objectives and fulfil the ideas outlined in the conceptual framework
Data collection and analysis	A series of chapters examining the information gathered, frequently guided by the research objectives and corresponding to the ideas laid out in the conceptual framework
Findings and discussion	A shorter chapter, usually focusing on the broad themes emerging from the research and how they match against the themes discussed in the literature review, i.e. How the thesis contributes to the discipline
Recommendations and conclusion	Recommendations arising from the research, analysis and discussion of the previous chapters, in other words what had been learned from the thesis and how can it be applied to improving knowledge and understanding.

Figure 2.1. Thesis template

of the application process, it is worth going into some detail on the points raised above, with some examples to help explain important concepts.

Context

The first step in writing a proposal is developing the context to your research. It goes without saying that this research topic should reflect your own interests, something that draws you in and enthuses you, something that you are already knowledgeable about but want to investigate in much greater depth. This will require the researcher to create an overview of the problem posed, an explanation of the challenges and why the research question identified is important. Demonstrating the significance of the research question should be a central concern for the candidate. However, some effort should be made to consider how the work will be of value to practitioners and scholars, if only in a few lines. Even though this section of the proposal is not usually lengthy, sometimes no more than a page or two, to develop the context to the thesis will require a broad sweep of critical literature, a task that can take considerable time.

Research question

Having contextualised the problem, the next step is to clearly state the main aim of the proposed thesis. This is commonly referred to as the research aim or main research question and though the wording may be subject to change, with various tweaks over the course of the PhD, the broad thrust will always remain the same, offering a clear direction to the PGR for the entire project. As such, the import of the research question belies its brevity. Academics tasked with the onus of judging the quality of the proposal will inevitably be drawn to this component to see if the candidate's understanding of the phenomenon matches their own expert knowledge of the area. It is important not to rush this stage of the application as a poor foundation will undermine the totality of the proposal. Too often the eager applicant supplies a very far-ranging and complex research question, an overly ambitious aim that would challenge a team of researchers over many years. This is frequently a reflection of an undergraduate mindset, when students are asked to do short essays on broad topics. What many PhD applicants fail to realise is that doctoral research is far more focused and detail-oriented, not conducive to wide-ranging discussions on big, wide-spectrum questions. These are best left to large, well-resourced teams over many years and even decades. Doctoral research is as much about demonstrating your ability to understand the challenges involved as it is answering the hard-to-research questions of the day. The flipside, as Dunleavy (2015, p. 20) notes, is to avoid choosing a less than worthwhile topic:

> Defensively minded theses focus on tiny chunks of the discipline. They may cover a very short historical period, a single not very important author or source, a small discrete mechanism or process, one narrow locality explored in-depth, or a particular method taken just a little further.

The importance of the research question cannot be overstated and getting it right may take many attempts. Contacting a potential supervisor for guidance can greatly facilitate the fine-tuning process. This can help avoid a research question that is insufficiently theoretical, unfocussed or, most importantly, already researched. Saunders and Lewis (2012) offer useful suggestions to help generate ideas, including looking at past theses' titles, past research projects from universities, relevant literature, coursework, media gazing, brainstorming, the Delphi Technique[9] and concept mapping.

An example of a recent research topic I was asked to assess is reported below:

> The primary aim of this study is to explore one way of closing the gap between the value realised by coffee farming communities and that generated by consumer facing operators in the developed markets. The motivation is to explore the adoption of an equity-based model of the trade in coffee which enables small-scale farmers to benefit from the entire coffee value chain as a means to close the value gap. The model, which focuses on collaborative value creation across the value chain, can be an improvement on, or alternative to, the Fair-Trade model. Using Zimbabwe's small-scale coffee farming community as a subject, this project adds to existing literature on co-value creation in the coffee supply chain.

Although the final project's aims and objectives differed to those stated above, the text is notable for its clarity of purpose, the singular aim stated early on, the unambiguous motivation for the work and, crucially, the contribution to both scholarship and practice. This allows supervisors the opportunity to develop, sharpen and improve the original statement over the course of the PhD, while also setting a clear direction and goal for the research itself.

Research objectives

Arising from the research questions are a series of objectives that will need to be developed by the applicant to guide the reader through the planned activities; a step-by-step explanation of how the aspiring PGR intends to address the research question posed. Frequently applicants struggle to differentiate between the research aim and research objectives. While the former can be said to capture the 'What' of the overall purpose of the

---

9   The Delphi Technique involves using a group of people with interest and knowledge in the area to help refine a broader topic into a more specific approach.

work, the research objectives relate to the more specific outcomes connected to the 'How(s)' required to realise the overarching aim. Ideally, objectives will be SMART, that is, Specific, Measurable, Achievable, Realistic and Tangible.

These first steps in a proposal can be quite confusing for candidates since most will have been accustomed to receiving a topic from their lecturers/examiners to demonstrate their understanding and knowledge. Having to now set their own parameters and determine the scope of their activities can prove daunting, confusing and not a little off-putting to those new to this task. However, as noted earlier, the structure and content of a thesis proposal will correspond closely to that of a full thesis. It is, therefore, worth spending time examining existing theses from the discipline that the candidate intends to pursue. You should reflect on how other doctoral students have crafted their research questions and objectives, gaining useful insights into how they are created.

In the example above, the proposed research topic was clearly set out and the expected contribution made explicit. The same application, having stated its purpose, followed with these objectives:

> One of the objectives of this research is to explore if customer facing global coffee businesses chains and operators can secure more sustainable long-term supply chains by creating an equity-based partnership with coffee farmers that lead to more responsible and environmentally friendly coffee farming.
>
> The second objective is to explore the involvement of small-scale coffee farmers up the value chain in an equity shareholding structure as a way to bring higher returns to farming communities.
>
> The third objective is to establish, through analysis, if such an equity-based, value co-creation model can form the basis for an accelerated redevelopment of Zimbabwe's coffee industry using small-scale coffee farmers as drivers of that development.
>
> The fourth objective is to establish if, applied to other agricultural products exported and consumed in developed markets, whether the equity model can drive economic development in the developing supplier markets.

Each objective, states with intent an achievable goal. The work does not aim to explore all aspects of small-scale coffee farming in one country, rather a series of closely related and complementary aspects expected to generate important findings which, in turn, will inform equity models of development. Each objective reflects on the research aim and shows how it will answer the overall question by careful analysis of each of the stated facets. As such, the above represents a good example of what an assessor might hope to see in a proposal, before the process of narrowing and tightening the thesis' aims and objectives begins.

Literature review

A fully crafted literature review in a completed thesis will, typically, be 10 to 20,000 words in length, far more than what will be required just for a proposal. However, understanding how a doctoral candidate analyses and critiques existing research in the field can give valuable insights into how to fashion a briefer document. Worth examining, therefore, is the literature review of a completed thesis, which will be the next step in your proposal.

A literature review offers an overview of significant research material that has been pursued in your area of interest. It draws on a range of sources, including peer-reviewed academic articles and textbooks, professional and trade journal articles, newspaper articles, conference proceedings and reports, for example, government reports and privately financed business reports. The main crux of the work will be drawn from refereed articles, as this represents the most peer-reviewed and widely critiqued material available to researchers. Textbooks, while initially useful for early engagement with a topic, take longer to produce and tend to have a wider focus. While the candidate is not expected to produce a detailed and in-depth piece of work for a proposal, a good knowledge of key literature should be demonstrated along with a critical ability to marshal ideas and highlight what we know from past work and, most importantly, new unanswered questions arising.

It is also important to identify potential theoretical approaches to your research topic to help frame your research question and objectives. Theory should be understood as an approach that helps to explain how concepts or variables are related to each other. It is not having lists of data, variables, references to academic papers or a suggested hypothesis that offer an insight. Theory offers a conceptual lens through which to examine a phenomenon, and it is firmly grounded in well-developed, rigorously scrutinised and well-evidenced approaches to studying specific connections that allow for hypothesis testing. To offer an example, I once supervised a doctoral thesis that used stakeholder theory[10] to explore the relationship between Non-Governmental Organisations (NGOs) and corporate actors. The question the PGR wished to answer was how this relationship was impacted by crisis, the early indications being that it broke down under duress. The approach used to answer this question involved a conceptual framework of the interaction between key stakeholders, developed through intensive investigation of the literature on stakeholder theory. In other words, theory was used as a lens to better understand the organisational relationship between NGOs and specific corporations and how said relationship was altered by crisis. This had been the direction of research travel from the beginning and informed the development of conceptualisation, methodology and evidence collection.

A doctoral applicant, of course, is not expected at the proposal stage to demonstrate a complete and thorough understanding of the theory and concepts they have chosen to research. That said, they are expected to demonstrate knowledge of leading researchers in the field, relevant theories that might be used to examine their research question, as well as an ability to justify choices and critique ideas or approaches. In contrast to the contextualisation at the opening of the proposal, the literature review will focus on critical aspects of the research question and outline dominant and/or conflicting thinking amongst leading researchers, as well as any relevant schools of thought that have shaped the debate under scrutiny. This process can be facilitated by examining the material used in the

---

10   Freeman (1984) is credited with originating the term and underlying principles of stakeholder theory. In brief, the theory states that firms need to prioritise the needs of stakeholders, and not just the shareholders. The theory stresses the interconnections between business and stakeholders (e.g. customers, employees, suppliers, investors and the community). Subsequent research (see, e.g., Freeman et al., 2010) has built layers of understanding and frameworks of interpretation to allow the relationship between firms and stakeholders to be explored.

contextualisation section and deriving key words and key ideas from the material, to be used in seeking out, in particular, high-quality articles in the highest ranked journals. Other approaches that can be considered include using a systematic research review to filter out relevant articles from education portals. Denyer and Tranfield (2009) offer a useful guide to undertaking such a review in their chapter 'Producing a systematic review'.

There are several online portals used by researchers that allow keyword searches of leading journals. Examples of these repositories are listed below:

- *Business Source Complete (EBSCO)*. Dedicated to Business and Management research, it offers access to full-text articles, though there are embargoes on the most recent articles in some journals. It also has industry reports and data lists.
- *Scopus*. An abstract and citation database of peer-reviewed literature offered by the information analytics business, Elsevier. It has access to full-text articles, books and conference proceedings in the fields of science, technology, medicine, social sciences, and arts and humanities.
- *JSTOR*. A digital library containing academic journals, books and primary sources. It also has full-text articles for science, social science, arts and humanities.
- *ProQuest*. A global information-content and technology company, this database offers access to journals, newspapers, reports, working papers, datasets, digitised historical primary sources and approximately 450,000 digital books.
- *Emerald Insight*. Has access to over 300 journals and approximately 255,000 articles in the fields of business, management, engineering, computing, technology and social sciences. It also offers a separate search engine for open access articles.
- *Google Scholar*. A Web search engine tool that ranks and categorises literature across a wide array of publishing formats and disciplines. It can be a powerful tool for a broad sweep of material.
- *Science Direct*. Provides access to scientific research for peer-reviewed journal articles, book chapters and open access content.

All those listed are currently leading providers of research databases, e-journals, e-books and other services that support academic research. They are widely used by business schools in the UK. It is important to note that some journals will require institutional access to paid content, the alternative being costly fees for articles. Some of these portals do make explicit where content is Open Access (OA), *Emerald Insight* being one example. More and more research outputs are being designated as OA (i.e. freely available to the public) but new articles and older archived research can prove very difficult to source without support from libraries and online repositories such as those mentioned.

In conjunction with lists of ranked journals, doctoral candidates will be able to build a picture of research journals and articles relevant to their topic. They will be further guided by impact factors of journals, the number of citations an article receives and the *h*-index[11] of the author(s). Additionally, all work undertaken here can be used in the first year of doctoral study (when most PGRs would be expected to produce a draft of their final literature review). Moreover, should you as a candidate be invited to an interview (in person or online) by potential supervisors, as they attempt to determine for themselves how invested you are in doing a PhD, having a good knowledge of relevant material will increase your confidence and make this process significantly smoother. While not all institutions will insist on an interview, many do. Interviews may be also conducted to get a feel for the personalities involved and whether they are a suitable match. The interview will typically only come after the initial regulatory barriers have been overcome and will involve the likely supervisory team and possibly another senior academic.

A key aspect of the literature review component of the proposal, arguably the most sought-after aspect of this section, is a good analytical ability. Analytical ability is not displayed through a list of ideas or articles nor via a vague sense of discomfort with a key piece of research. It is shown through well-evidenced, well-researched analysis that draws on a range of commentators, and critical reflections on leading research in the chosen discipline. One way to get to grips with this difficult task is to read recent survey articles and follow up on articles that cite key literature. This process has been made substantially easier in modern research as all of the online portals mentioned above will give the researcher the option to follow the

---

[11] The *h*-index refers to the number of citations an author has received as well as the number of references to their work in other journals and articles.

citation path of a document, to see who has supported its findings, who has built on it and those who have identified potential gaps in knowledge that require addressing. Most articles themselves will helpfully caveat their own shortcomings and point to future research pathways. In fact, the aspiring doctoral candidate may consider following these pathways back to the key researchers themselves to explore opportunities for not just doctoral research but a research career pathway.

It is difficult to offer brief examples of good literature reviews since it is often only in the totality or 'gestalt' you learn to appreciate the true quality of a piece of work. Nonetheless, below can be seen two examples of analysis I have recently considered. The first example[12] supplied here was unclear in its research aim but broadly wanted to focus on the impact of climate change strategy on consumer behaviour in the oil and gas industry:

> Saini and Matinise (2013) made an extensive research in consumer behaviour of fuel consumers from retailers, however the study lacked the understanding of the applicability and the factors that influence consumer decision making in the choice of service station, other consumer behaviour models could have been adapted. The sample sizes used are narrow, a wider sample could have been used to attain generalisation. Saini and Matinise (2013) suggested a further testing and validation of Customer Styles Inventory (CSI) model. There was an over depenance on the CSI model other, other models could be explored for the understanding of consumer behaviour. The results from Yvonne and Siyabulela (2013) research call for the revision of the CSI inventory, it might not be applicable in all sectors (Sinkovics et al. 2010).

The review of Saini and Matinise (2013)[13] was banal and vapid. It offered little real detail on content. It referred vaguely to problems of sample size, mentioned but did not expand on other behaviour models, critiqued the Customer Styles Inventory model without explaining what that model was or why it needed further testing, before referencing another piece of work from the same year calling for revision of *"CSI inventory"* (which

---

12 While the references listed in the example text(s) were not used in researching this chapter, I felt it would be appropriate to list them in the footnotes where relevant.
13 Saini, Y. K. and Matinise, S. V. (2013). *An Exploratory Study on Factors Influencing Customer Decision Making: A Case of Fuel Retailing Industry*. Johannesburg, South Africa: University of Witwatersrand.

reads as '*Customer Styles Inventory inventory*'!), but not offering any insights as to what those revisions were or why they needed to be made. Finally, in addition to the numerous grammatical errors and spelling mistakes, the final reference, the one from which the apparent review of "*Yvonne and Siyabulela (2013)*"[14] is drawn from, is actually from 2010.[15] Many of these errors – spelling, punctuation, grammar, referencing – are amongst the easiest mistakes to avoid but also the most likely to draw the ire of an academic asked to review proposals such as this. Vague analysis is also enormously detrimental to a piece of work.

A better example of what is required can be found in the most recent proposal I reviewed and assessed. Here the candidate wished to examine the impact of involuntary employee reductions or 'downsizing' on those workers, 'survivors', who were left after job cuts. The focus of the proposal was the HE sector. It read:

> Noer (1993)[16] recognises the 'survivor syndrome', which survivors experience following a workforce reduction process and is characterised by sadness, guilt and affective changes in feelings about the organisation. The 'syndrome' has been shown to have a negative effect on the productivity of organisations following downsizing (Gandolfi, 2010).[17] Similarly, De Meuse et al. (2004),[18] in a longitudinal analysis on the financial performance of companies that downsized between 1987 and 1998, found that all the companies underperformed for the two years following the downsizing. Campbell and Pepper (2006)[19] also report a loss of interest by survivors in

---

14   This cited source was not in the list of references at the end of the proposal. It most likely refers to Saini and Matinise (2013).
15   Sinkovics R. R., Leelapanyalert K. M., and Yamin M. (2010). A comparative examination of consumer decision styles in Austria. *Journal of Marketing Management*, 26(11–12), 1021–1036.
16   Noer, D. (1993). *Healing the Wounds: Overcoming the Trauma of Layoffs and Revitalizing Downsized Organizations*. San Francisco, US: Jossey Bass.
17   Gandolfi, F. (2013). Employee downsizing of the banking sector in Portugal: A case study. *Journal of Modern Accounting and Auditing*, 9(8), 1105–1118.
18   De Meuse, K. and Tornow, W. (1990). *The Employer-Employee Attachment Continues to Erode as Companies Try to Make Ends Meet*. Washington, DC: Human Resource Planning Society.
19   Campbell, R. and Pepper, L. (2006). Downsizing and Social Cohesion: The case of downsizing survivors. *New Solutions*, 16(4), 373–393.

their jobs after a downsizing process and consequent job dissatisfaction. Conversely, a study by Appelbaum and Donia (2001)[20] suggested that survivors may perceive themselves as valued and become more committed to the organisation. Overall, the effects of downsizing on survivors are summed up by Marques et al. (2011)[21] in three constructs: job insecurity, organisational commitment and innovative behaviour which also represent the themes that usually emerge in the extant literature on the effects of downsizing (ibid.).

This short extract from what was a longer and much more detailed proposal captures the approach required of candidates. It discusses key terms and concepts related to the proposed work, references and summarises key literature in the field while also laying the groundwork for their later explanations of why and how the candidate will address the question of 'survivor syndrome' amongst workers in the UK HE sector after recent job losses and cuts.

Conceptualisation

It would not be expected at this stage of research to have a fully developed conceptual framework, a model for interpreting collected data informed by theory and a detailed methodology. However, it is useful to explain how you envisage theory will be used to interrogate the research question, as this will aid a justification for the methodological approach you choose. Returning to the earlier example of using stakeholder theory to explore relations between NGOs and corporations, the doctoral candidate in question had indicated at an early stage the intent to identify, hierarchically rank and categorise the critical stakeholder groups, using stakeholder theory and analysis to facilitate this process. In turn, this justified the decision to pursue a qualitative methodological approach involving

20 Appelbaum, S. H. and Donia, M. (2001). The realistic downsizing preview: A multiple case study, Part 1: The methodology and results of data collection. *Journal of Career Development International*, 6(3), 128–150.
21 Marques, T., Gonzales, I., Cruz, P., and Ferreira, M. P. (2011). Downsizing and profitability: An empirical study of Portuguese firms in 1993–2005. *International Journal of Business and Economics*, 10(1), 13–26.

questionnaires and interviews to better understand the relationship between these groups.

Methodology

The next step of an application is the one most frequently done poorly, the methodology. I have, in the past, seen methodological sections of academic proposals with as few as three lines, offering up information on the number of interviews they intend to conduct and little else. I suspect this may partly be a case of fatigue. After spending a long time getting the first parts right, a tiring applicant may rush through this stage. My advice here is to take a break after the literature review section and leave the next part to the following days or weeks. Don't try to complete the application all in one go. Confusion may also be a factor, with applicants not sure of what is required here. For example, many will just know they will be using a qualitative approach and try to pad the section with generic information on methodology before explaining that what they really want to do is to complete thirty interviews. At the other extreme are those applicants who over-promise, perhaps choosing a mixed methods approach that belies their own expertise and would require a huge amount of work in a very short period. Concerned about potential gaps in their approach and eager to impress potential supervisors, these applications develop a methodology that tries to cover all bases. But doing so can introduce many hostages to fortune and raise questions about the candidate's ability to deliver. The best research is tightly focused, with a specific research aim or question and associated objectives. The best methodologies reflect that understanding, and in answering the question, 'What is the best method for my data?' provide at least a 'horses for courses' justification as to why the proposed method appears more tailored to obtain reliable evidence than others.

A crucial feature of the methodology discussion is making explicit what you aim to do, how you aim to do it and, most importantly, the availability of the data that will be used to obtain evidence in the thesis. There is little point planning a three-year project if, in the second year, you realise that the data you thought would be available is inaccessible. This means that you will need to undertake exploratory actions to identify whether (or not) you can put into action your research plan. It must be feasible. For example, if your aim is to complete thirty interviews with senior management figures in a specific industrial sector, then you will need to contact these organisations to ascertain their readiness to support a doctoral researcher in this way, as well as the extent of the information they are willing to reveal. Similarly, if you are engaged in more quantitative research that will require specialised datasets, doing an archival dive, either digitally or physically, to determine availability and accessibility, is essential. If these data can only be examined through library services with special permissions, this will need to be mentioned in the application also. Contact the archivist, inquire as to the availability of the material in question, clarify what is achievable in your application, as well as the resources necessary to support these activities. Most universities will have available support, sometimes financial, to pay for data deemed central to a research project, but you cannot expect to make this information known after you start researching. Experts assessing your proposal will be well aware of the challenges around data collection and will want, at the very least to be reassured you have given sufficient thought to what you are proposing and how you intend to deliver. For example, the following is a part of a methodological section on empowering female entrepreneurship in India. The candidate focuses on explaining where the data will come from and its availability:

> Data shall be collected for the increase in the number of women employed in the 14 districts of Kerala over the period of 1997–2018 and empirical analysis employed to determine its impact on gender inequality, nutrition of children, female participation in politics, poverty, corruption, number of female entrepreneurs, child mortality and education attainment. This information is available from the Government website of Kudumbashree, Ministry of Statistics and Program Implementation, India, the National Statistical Organisation of India and from reports available in the Indian National Archives. Other available relevant data for female participation in civic areas such as the legislature, enrolment in schools etc. will also be collected from the same sources to learn their scope for influencing economic development. Apart from the secondary data collected above, field surveys are necessary to measure the household impact of gender policy on overall gender empowerment. The field survey will require the preparation of a binary response questionnaire to the participants.

The data collected will be used to quantify women empowerment on parameters suggested by Biswas (1999)[22] and Israel et al. (1994).[23] A cross-sectional analysis of the collected data will provide insights into the impact of the policy.

Later in the methodology discussion the applicant went into additional detail on further aspects of the approach she intended to take as outlined in the literature, but what can be seen in this extract is the clear explanation of data availability and type. The candidate had researched the appropriate material and sourced it from government organisations, lending credibility to its veracity. The actual data used and how such data would inform the research would be refined during the years of doctoral study, but from the outset the candidate had demonstrated an understanding of what was required in terms of data collection as well as outlining what was available for the study.

References and referees

At the end of your proposal you should include a list of all the material you have cited in the proposal such as academic texts, journal articles, online resources and databases. The reference style should reflect the standard used in the institution where the application is being made, with Harvard and Chicago being the most common styles. Whatever style you use, be consistent throughout.

Some thought should be given to who you choose as a referee for your application. The obvious source for many applicants is former academic staff members or academic supervisors. Other options include employers who know of your wish to become a researcher and who are aware of what it is you wish to investigate as a doctoral candidate. References should offer

---

22 Kumar Biswas, T. (1999). Measuring women's empowerment: Some methodological issues. *Asia-Pacific Journal of Rural Development*, 9(2), 63–71.
23 Israel, B., Checkoway, B., Schulz, A., and Zimmerman, M. (1994). Health education and community empowerment: conceptualizing and measuring perceptions of individual, organizational, and community control. *Health Education Quarterly*, 21(2), 149–170.

an insight into you as a potential researcher and, ideally, strengthen the message you have put forward in your personal statement.

Final steps

Once an application has been crafted and proofread it may be tempting to submit and see what response is generated. However, if you have already approached a potential supervisor and they have responded positively, then it makes sense to ask for some informal feedback on your proposal. Obviously, they cannot offer more than support and useful comments, but if there is any obvious flaw in the work, they may take the opportunity to make you aware of the problem before it is too late. It is important to note at this point that just because a potential supervisor appears happy with an application, it does not mean it will be accepted. Competition can be fierce for the best universities and applications may be returned simply because a more fitting candidate was selected, or supervisory capacity had already been reached. In this instance there is little you can do other than try again with another institution. Yet, it is important to take note of any feedback offered and act on it.

The challenge for the international candidate

This section reflects on the unique challenges faced by PhD applications to the UK HE sector from overseas. The UK has no centralised system for doctoral applications and entry criteria differ from institution to institution. This makes applying to do a PhD a prolonged and time-consuming process, with would-be doctoral candidates having to research many different opportunities. For international (EU or overseas) candidates the challenge is even greater, in terms of knowledge and understanding of the education landscape, cost, requirements to study, as well as all the travails of cultural and, often, linguistic differences. The chapter makes specific reference to the problems that international applicants will encounter when seeking to do a PhD in the UK.

The first obvious additional obstacle for international students relates to a lack of local knowledge of the institutions to which they will apply. While ranking, completions and awards will guide them to better appreciate which institution is suitable for their area of research interest, most foreign applicants will likely be unable to visit the campus. This means they will have to trust accounts that may not always accurately reflect the situation on the ground, particularly in terms of institutional support for foreign candidates. PhDs are big business and institutions are not apt to advertise their weaknesses. Hence, the candidate should be guided by information from previous international researchers who have spent time in third level study in the UK and may have had a quite different experience to the domestic doctoral candidate. Furthermore, some of the nuances of the third level sector may be lost to applicants from abroad. For example, in the UK there are other distinctions between the universities; traditional, storied universities like Oxford and Cambridge are distinct from 'red brick' universities, civic universities established in major industrial cities in the nineteenth century. However, the bulk of both these groups of universities make up the Russell Group, an association of twenty-four UK research-oriented universities which account for approximately two thirds of UK research income. Outside of these leading universities are the 'new universities' (or 'modern universities'), universities that were only designated as such after 1992. While these distinctions may not be immediately apparent from ranking lists, there is significant demand amongst domestic doctoral candidates to attend Russell Group institutions (a self-selected association of currently twenty-four leading universities in the UK), even if the institutions do not always offer the best support for their specific research interest. As a result, international aspirants will, at times, be encouraged to apply to these institutions by well-meaning peers, even when it is not necessarily optimal to do so.

The next major issue for international candidates to consider is cost. Frequently doctoral candidates have already spent considerable time in undergraduate or masters-level research programmes before starting to pursue doctoral studies. This means they will have had considerable financial tribulations even before they undertake many more years of self-directed study. For internationals applicants this bar is even higher. In the first instance, fees for domestic doctoral researchers are subsidised by the UK government. This is not the case for many of their overseas peers (coming from outside the EU), with fees for overseas candidates sometimes three times as high.[24] Even more problematic is that many UK universities will require proof of funds. This can require an applicant keeping a large sum of money in their account for a protracted period. In one case I was made aware of, a candidate had accumulated the appropriate amount of money to satisfy this stipulation. However, in the normal course of a month's spending activities, he had allowed the amount to slip below the financial threshold, albeit marginally, causing the entire process to reset. Since the university only recruited three times a year, he missed the deadline and was forced to delay enrolment by four months.

Probably the greatest barrier to entry for international applicants is language. Most likely, candidates will have to take a language test, with the two most common variants being TOEFL (Test of English as a Foreign Language) and the IELTS (International English Language Testing System). Taking the latter as an example, there are two tests that can be taken, one academic, one general. The tests examine listening, reading, writing and speaking, all scored on a range between 0 and 9. Most UK universities will insist on an average score between 6 and 7 as a minimum across all components, with an emphasis on high scores in writing skills. Furthermore, testing is usually limited to certain times of the year and results can take some time to arrive, furthering delaying entry onto PhD programmes. There are alternative pathways that can be followed, such as first doing a masters and later either doing a PhD or upgrading to one, depending on the institutional offer, but that pathway too will come with

---

[24] The decision by the UK to end its membership of the European Union (EU) has also created further uncertainty for European candidates who benefit from comparable subsidies to UK doctoral researchers. At this time no decision has been reached on how applicants originating from the EU will be treated, but the mere spectre of much higher fees should give these candidates pause for thought.

its own entry criteria and there is no guarantee of progression to a PhD. Some universities offer the opportunity to do English classes to provide refresher courses, but few will allow them *in lieu* of certification from an internationally recognised language test. In other words, there are opportunities to supplement language skills before doing tests, but limited chances of circumventing their necessity. In truth, it would be remiss of HEIs to encourage potential doctoral candidates to apply without the requisite written and spoken skills to complete a PhD, leading to wasted time and money for the unachievable.

A further consideration for international applicants is the current political climate in the UK. The decision to leave the European Union in 2016, coming into force in 2021, will have considerable impact on UK immigration legislation. Most international students who enter the UK are now closely monitored by UK immigration services to ensure they are engaged in full-time studies. This is likely to become pervasive should EU students also be expected to account for their whereabouts and activities. For foreign applicants, navigating the various government departments and preparing visitor documents is another cost and time sink to factor into their application timeline. In sum, the challenge for international students applying for PhD status is far more complex than their UK counterparts. Significant planning in timing and resources is essential, requiring flexibility in the case of delays and discipline to meet all the requirements. Add to this the necessity to have a high standard of written and spoken English, all while preparing an appropriately academic and well-structured proposal.

Such challenges can be intimidating to the uninitiated. Anticipating problems and organising to overcome them is a crucial part of the international application process. Many UK universities recognise the challenges faced by international doctoral candidates and are pursuing different recruitment pathways to smooth the application process. Therefore, it is always useful to contact individual HEIs in the UK to determine what resources are available to support international applications. Contacting the national Department of Education in the country of origin is also a good idea, as they may be aware of doctoral schemes that support international candidates.

Some final words of encouragement

While this chapter focused on the challenges of doing a PhD application, it is important to remember why it is worthwhile investing so much time and effort. Doing a doctoral thesis can be a very fulfilling and rewarding experience, challenging you to attain research skills through your own endeavour. Being well prepared and clear in your thoughts about undertaking such a task will greatly facilitate these efforts and give you the confidence and self-belief to achieve a valuable outcome. While there are many hurdles to navigate, particularly for foreign candidates, once you start your doctoral studies you will become part of a vibrant and supportive research community, dedicated to high-quality research and study. To get the most out of this life choice requires commitment, hard work and, above all, a good foundation. This chapter provides you with many of the required tools for this task.

References

Denyer, D. and Tranfield, D. (2009). Producing a systematic review. In: Buchanan, D. A. and Bryman, A. (Eds.). *The SAGE Handbook of Organizational Research Methods* (pp. 671–689). London, UK: Sage Publications Ltd.

Dunleavy, P. (2015). *Authoring a PhD: How to Plan, Draft, Write and Finish a Doctoral Thesis or Dissertation*. London, UK: Macmillan International Higher Education, Red Globe Press.

Eco, U. (2015). *How to Write a Thesis*. London, UK: MIT Press.

Freeman, R. E. (1984). *Strategic Management: A Stakeholder Approach*. Boston: Pitman.

Freeman, R. E., Harrison, J. S., Wicks, A. C., Parmar, B. L., and De Colle, S. (2010). *Stakeholder Theory – The State of the Art*. Cambridge, UK: Cambridge University Press.

Higher Education Statistics Agency (2020). *Open Data and Official Statistics*. Available online at: <https://www.hesa.ac.uk/data-and-analysis>

Rugg, G. and Petre, M. (2010). *The Unwritten Rules of PhD Research*. Berkshire, England: McGraw-Hill Education.
Saunders, M. and Lewis, P. (2012). *Doing Research in Business & Management – An Essential Guide to Planning Your Project*. Harlow, England: Pearson Education Limited.

DAVID BOWEN

3 Completing a literature review

Preamble

Chapter 2 included a brief discussion on how to go about a literature review as part of the process of writing the academic proposal when formally applying for a PhD. The **aim of this chapter** is to delve into the purpose of a literature review and examine in greater depth the various considerations that will help you to complete a very worthwhile literature review. A literature review is an integral part of any PhD study. Except in very specific, rare circumstances, it is one of the critical elements that you need to develop before you engage in any empirical work in the field. Yet, the literature review is iterative and has a chameleon character as it generally needs to change its focus through the length of your PhD study. The contents of a literature review maintain their importance through to your discussion and articulation of a contribution to knowledge. With an allusion to a phrase used by the English poet William Wordsworth in his poem 'The Rainbow', also included in the vocals of various American music bands from the 1960s, the Child (literature review) is the father of the Man (the PhD thesis) or, as an alternative, the mother of the Woman. An outline of purpose and a classification of types of literature review are charted in the next section, with a focus on systematic literature reviews and traditional reviews. It is important to develop information literacy and gain an awareness of literature search methods, and those are discussed in the section that follows. The further sections examine critical reading, making notes effectively and critical writing, which build towards a conclusion to your literature review that is a springboard into the remainder of your PhD thesis.

Purpose and types of literature review

In Chapter 2 of this book, it is stated that the literature component of a PhD proposal, as submitted to gain a place on a PhD programme, needs to offer an overview of significant research material drawing on a range of potential sources, including but not confined to peer-reviewed academic journal articles, textbooks, academic conference proceedings, professional and trade articles, reports from government and others, and newspapers and magazines. It is added that there is a need to identify relevant theory or theories through which to examine your research topic and to offer a justified and well-evidenced critique of previous work. In essence that remains the basic purpose of a literature review after you have been accepted and enrolled on your chosen PhD programme, although obviously there is a need for extra depth, nuance and perspective based on exhaustive critical appraisal.

It is worth classifying types of literature review as that will help you gain a better idea of what is required of you (Thompson, 2012). Authors such as Grant and Booth (2009) in a science (health care) context state that there are upwards of fourteen variants of literature review. Their typology of reviews is interesting, not least because it highlights inconsistency and overlap in the definition of review types. That is a serious situation given the consequences for those commissioning reviews in health care and the subsequent effect on health care decisions. Arguably most reviews in business and management are not as important because for the most part their substance does not relate so overtly to life and death.

Grant and Booth (2009, pp. 95–96) use a framework to devise their typology based around a set method summarised in the acronym SALSA: search, appraisal, synthesis, analysis. Accordingly, placed in alphabetical order, rather than any other order, they distinguish between critical review, literature review, mapping review, meta-analysis, mixed methods review, overview, qualitative evidence synthesis, rapid review, scoping review, state-of-the-art review, systematic review, systematic search and review, systematised review and umbrella review. As a business and management PGR you will probably hear many of the terms used by peers and academics in an interchangeable way, as Grant and Booth (2009) also recognised in health care.

There is not sufficient space in this chapter to expand on all the types within the Grant and Booth (2009) typology. At the least you need awareness that there are different types of review. Thompson (2013) in a social science context draws on Jesson, Matheson and Lacey (2011) to make a distinction between two fundamental types: a systematic literature review (SLR) and more traditional literature review. That is useful as a framework here for further consideration of purpose and type.

Systematic literature reviews

With regard to SLRs, I choose initially to refer to a statement of intent by a current PGR, six months into her PhD, who is examining stakeholder engagement with the UK Corporate Governance Code (UKCGC) 2018. The UKCGC provides principles relating to how a UK company should be managed, directed and controlled. Here is the statement:

> To critically analyse literature, I will conduct a bounded systematic review to establish a range of journal articles on stakeholder engagement and to identify associated problems (Miles, 2015). The review is bounded by four filters. First, only academic journal articles will be considered. Second, only mainstream academic business journals will be considered covering the fields of corporate governance, business, law and finance. Third, the keywords of the articles must contain 'corporate governance' and either 'stakeholder engagement' or 'shareholder engagement'. Fourth, the review will cover the period from 2014 to 2022.

The essence of much to do with SLRs is contained within the statement above. It remains to be seen if the SLR will work because the PhD is not yet completed. However, the intention of the PGR is plain as she treads an early stage on the route to PhD. A particularly clear, informative explanation of the rationale for SLRs and a summary of the SLR process are contained in an SLR focused on entrepreneurial learning (EL) written by two more experienced and practiced academics (Wang and Chugh, 2014). As they state in their abstract (p. 24):

> Although EL research has gained momentum in the past decade, the literature is diverse, highly individualistic and fragmented, hindering the development of EL as a promising research area. In this paper, a systematic analysis of the EL literature is first conducted in order to take stock of the theoretical and empirical development and identify research themes and developmental patterns of EL research.

The process passes through a number of specific stages summarised in diagrammatic form and including the following elements (Wang and Chugh, 2014, p. 26).

- Setting the research objectives, for example, to identify key research themes and challenges for future research
- Defining the conceptual boundaries, for example, defining entrepreneurship and entrepreneurial opportunities
- Setting the inclusion criteria, for example, search boundaries, search terms, cover time-period
- Applying exclusion criteria, for example, articles primarily focussed on entrepreneurship but not the learning process
- Validating search results, for example, comparing the seventy-five final papers from the SLR with a Google Scholar search
- Data coding and validation (e.g. revisiting articles for recoding).

It is obvious that the inputs to the search process are crucial in determining the results. In order to mitigate a perceived problem of rigidity, Wang and Chugh (2014) introduce some flexibility into the process (e.g. the parallel Google Scholar search). In conclusion, they claim to identify three key EL research themes, three key research gaps and three challenges in the entrepreneurship literature. From that they justify the usefulness of SLRs as a way to take stock of theoretical and empirical development and identify research themes. Each of those elements is central to what is needed in the literature review of your PhD thesis. Moreover, from such a position it is a not a huge step to identify the specific gap that you intend to focus on and so locate your research within the wider subject field.

Finally, in this sub-section, for those of you further interested in how science approaches SLRs, maybe sparked by Grant and Booth (2009) above, you might like to refer to Moher et al. (2009) and from within that source the PRISMA checklist (PRISMA, 2009).

Traditional reviews

Although SLRs are popular, most PGRs use a more traditional approach and usually start with a sub-type of traditional review, what Thompson (2013) calls a scoping review. The scoping review also lays within the Grant and Booth (2009) typology and they describe it as a preliminary assessment of available research literature. According to the criteria set within their SALSA framework they indicate a number of its features. The completeness of search is set by time/boundary constraints; there is no formal quality assessment for inclusion or exclusion of material; synthesis is typically tabular with some narrative commentary; and analysis characterises the quality and quantity of literature and offers a review based around key features, including study design. In minor contrast, Thompson (2013) describes the scoping review in a slightly different way, but commonality of purpose is evident:

> This (scoping) review sets out to create an agenda for future research. It documents what is already known about a topic, and then focuses on the gaps, niches, disputes, blank and blind spots. It delineates key concepts, questions and theories in order to refine the research question(s) and justify an approach to be taken.

It needs to be noted that a scoping review differs from a final literature review, although many elements can and should remain. For example, tabular synthesis with narrative commentary is a succinct, powerful statement to a reader that you have spent due thought and energy on related published research. However, as Thompson (2013) continues, the purpose of the final review is not so much to create space for a research project, as in a scoping review, but to position a piece of research that is already undertaken. The final review emphasises what is necessary to understand the discussion and contribution in the later chapters of the thesis. That is why some alarm bells need to ring when a PGR states, in an Annual Progress Review (APR) at the end of the first or second year of study

(Chapter 8 of this book), that a literature review is complete. The literature review is iterative and needs to be relevant and maintain currency until the date of submission.

Sometimes, as you will hear from supervisors, the material that you leave out of a final review is as important as what you leave in. On occasion, a PGR is unable to let go of material built up from weeks or months of reading and writing, and hangs on to what is written *en bloc* in the final review. Alternatively, a PGR pares material down so that it loses its substance. I have seen an extensive literature, like consumer motivation, dealt with over one page of a PhD thesis. That is clearly unsatisfactory. Both occurrences above are not good and will worry your examiner. However, it may help you to let go of material if you make a pact to return to it after you have finished your PhD. Also, you can have a succinct section in your literature review that states what you left out and the reason for so doing.

Of course, traditional literature reviews are a staple part of academic journal articles. Sometimes, too, such reviews are an end in themselves, the sole purpose of an article. An open assessment of the method that lies behind many such reviews is provided in Cohen and Cohen (2019). They state that they sought to avoid a systematic, more structured approach and that their review is organic, creative, interpretive and so subjectively biased by their world views. Such an awareness of personal bias by Cohen and Cohen (2019) is one of the characteristics of criticality elaborated upon later in this volume (see Chapter 4).

In terms of the Grant and Booth (2009, p. 94) SALSA-based typology, Cohen and Cohen (2019) falls between 'critical literature review' and 'literature review'. Effectively most business and management PhDs will have a final review that is a melange of many of the types identified by Grant and Booth (2009) and all the sub-types that Thompson (2013) subsumes under the banner of traditional review: partly conceptual, examining related theories and issues, including appropriate commentary on methodology; partly state-of-the-art, examining the latest contributions; partly expert, with attendant subjective bias; partly initial scoping; and partly end-point reflection, including overt justified positioning and steering.

Information literacy and literature search methods

There was a time when both in common parlance and among educationalists there was much talk about the need to focus education on the so-called 3Rs (reading, writing and arithmetic). Two of those are at the core of this chapter. In a search for a relevant word containing the letter 'R' geographers, with their concern for understanding space and place, have advocated the need for the fourth 'R' of graphics. As far as I am aware, information literacy has not been added to the list of R-needs, but it is central to study today and that includes your PhD. As the literature review is likely to be the first activity that you engage in as a PGR, it is particularly relevant to highlight information literacy and literature search methods at this point.

Grant and Booth (2009) in discussing their typology of literature reviews, within the context of evidence-based health practice, point out the ascendancy since the 1990s of library and information sector workers, derived from their expert knowledge of information sources and high-level skills in retrieving information. Such knowledge and skills are important for you to tap into within your own university. Your university library will almost certainly invite you as a PGR to both introductory and follow-up workshops covering the potential of a modern library and how its staff can help you. The content of one such course is listed below and if you become familiar with the various components you will be on your way to gaining sufficient information literacy to make a good start on your PhD, specifically your literature review, and develop longer-term self-sufficiency and independence as a researcher:

> Demonstration of 'Library-Search': e.g. to find books, e-books, journals and full-text journal articles, and search libraries worldwide.
>
> Search of literature in the library's journal databases e.g. 'Business Source Complete', 'EconLit', 'PsycINFO', 'Emerald', Web of Science and advanced search techniques like 'Times Cited' etc.
>
> Outline of 'BrowZine' and 'Library Nomad'.
>
> Top tips for using 'Google Scholar'.

Introduction to the library research page including links to 'Open Access', 'Research Data Management' and where you can find published PhDs online.

Advice on correct referencing style, managing references and use of online referencing tools e.g. an overview of the capabilities of 'Endnote'.

The first step of a literature search starts with broad identification of your research aim(s), objectives, review questions and ongoing working topic. Any search around a working topic needs boundaries, such as publication type(s), for example, peer-reviewed journal articles; discipline or field, for example, economics or marketing; business sector, for example, banking; location, for example, EU countries; start and finish year, for example, post financial crisis 2008; and language of publication. You need to decide on those boundaries. That decision can be viewed as a second step. The boundaries can be wider or narrower than those listed above, for example, you may decide to search beyond banking to other service industries, or you may decide to confine your search to countries that joined the EU following its enlargement in May 2004.

As a third step, you will need to distinguish concepts in the form of keywords and phrases. If you have not studied for a while there are online tricks that you may need reminding about, for example, the use of truncation: $ or * on the root of a word picks up more potentially relevant material. Key concepts can be defined by use of Boolean operators OR, AND, NOT. OR retrieves records containing either terms; AND retrieves records containing both terms; NOT excludes record containing the second term.

The generation of keywords and phrases can come in a variety of ways. In Chapter 9 of this book we encourage you to talk about your research with peers, supervisors, other academics and beyond as often as appropriate. For sure, the literature review stage of your study is an appropriate moment to talk. You might well try and set up semi-formal or formal brainstorming sessions with peers at the same stage of the PhD as you, as that can bring mutual benefit. You can target an outcome, such as a hierarchical tree of keywords and phrases with connections.

Another way to generate keywords and phrases is to pay particular attention to any influential review paper that relates to your working topic. In every discipline or field there are some such papers. Your supervisors will be able to help in that regard. In one area of research focus among my own PGRs, tourist behaviour, I refer them to Cohen and Cohen (2012) updated as Cohen and Cohen (2019). A review paper that I published twenty years ago (Bowen and Clarke, 2002) still gets very regular citations, which suggests that there are PGRs and others using review papers in their literature searches.

As a fourth step you will need to select relevant databases that best reflect your subject area of business and management and related fields, such as those already mentioned in Chapter 2, and above. However, PGRs sometimes over-concentrate on keywords and phrases that they insert into databases. It is easy to ignore some of the trusted ways that have previously served the production of many fine PhD studies. There was a time when PGRs spent long hours in the library stacks turning the pages of journals, texts and various forms of grey literature: research that is either unpublished or has been published in non-commercial form, for example, government reports, policy statements and issues papers by companies and pressure groups, theses and dissertations (UNE, 2021). It is probably fifteen years since I have used such a method, but the principle can be adapted to an online environment. The use of keywords in databases is all very well as long as the authors of the literature sources have chosen keywords with due thought, and as long as relevant content is otherwise picked up on the database. However, that is not always the case, so I still advocate my own PGRs to spend time working through separate volumes and editions of chosen journals and other material. For example, at the start of a PhD I advise them to go back over the last three years of publication for particular journals, then five years and then ten years, skimming full-text PDFs of journal articles for abstracts and other components that can provide a quick but appropriate overview of content: sub-headings, figures and tables, introductions and conclusions. Such a suggestion sometimes meets with resistance but there is no doubt that serendipity can intervene to good effect such that relevant materials emerge, whether on substance, methodology or other aspects, that are not picked up by non-manual means. The process is a comparatively seamless way to search the literature compared to the time when hard-copy journals were sometimes deliberately squirreled away in obscure parts of a library by fellow students and/or particular articles were cut out and stolen from journals. To say that PGRs have never had it better in the search for literature is not completely true, because there are now so many sources with consequent information overload. That is why information literacy and good use of search methods are so vital.

Critical reading

In as succinct a review of critical reading as any other, Wallace and Wray (2011) outline the components that you need to think about as you engage in the long hours of reading that are the foundation of whatever type of literature review you write for your PhD. They specify that you need to be alert for what they call tools for thinking (concepts, perspectives, metaphors, theories, models, assumptions and ideologies) so that you can identify where they occur in each and every source that you read. They offer a relatively straightforward, pragmatic definition of each term. You might think that all PGRs will have a firm grasp of terms, but the reality is often different. I have seen some awkward *viva* moments when PGRs are asked to specify their use of any one such term, the consistency of its use or, even more challengingly, the way it is differentiated (e.g. theory and model). Therefore, check out the meaning of each Wallace and Wray (2011) tool for thinking before going too far with your literature review.

Wallace and Wray (2011) also draw attention to different types of knowledge: theoretical, research and practice-based, each represented by a different type of literature. Theoretical knowledge is the pulling together of concepts into a related system with identified connections. It is most evident in peer-reviewed academic journal articles though it also extends to some textbooks. Research knowledge is based on empirical evidence gathered through data collection and analysis. Again, it is most evident in peer-reviewed academic journal articles. Practice-based knowledge is personal experience or observed experience of others as evidenced in practice-based reports such as accounts of good practice by experienced professionals, for example, in professional journals. Wallace and Wray (2011) add policy literature as a further type of practice-based literature: the literature, most often in report form, of government, non-governmental organisations, business alliances, trade unions and charities, all part of the grey literature introduced in the section above. As indicated at the start of this chapter, the listing of literature can be expanded to include, for example, newspapers and magazines. Even in a changing media world there are still media outlets that support extensive research by journalists on business and management related topics.

The three types of knowledge are not necessarily as distinct as hinted above. For example, practice-based knowledge may overtly or non-overtly infiltrate peer-reviewed empirical research in academic journal articles when an author has first-hand working experience of the business and management research context. Likewise, the different types of literature may show some fusion. Policy literature may well be developed from empirical research gathered using sound academic method and rigour. Whilst it may not be subject to peer review of the kind associated with academic journals, it may well be subject to the scrutiny of a hierarchy of committees. In my own field of tourism, a report sponsored by the World Wildlife Fund (2008), updated ten years later by the Common Cause Foundation (2018), is crucial in any PhD research on environmentally friendly behaviour change.

Critical reading requires you to have an overarching awareness of the tools for thinking, types of knowledge and different types of literature (e.g. peer-reviewed academic journal articles, reports, newspapers and magazines). Within their schema, Wallace and Wray (2011) also call for you to take a view on the degree of certainty that can be assigned to the argument/claim that you are reading. Linked to certainty about a claim is the degree of generalisation, whether the claim extends to other contexts. Certainty is predicated on what is written in the form of a claim, or multiple claims, and the justification(s) for the claim *via* the evidence that is produced. It is worth dwelling on the claim and justification for the claim. Academic peer-reviewed journal articles are generally the source with the highest degree of certainty. For example, in an article based on empirical evidence there is a premium placed by journal editors and their public (academic researchers) on an underpinning of theory, a methodology that matches reliability, validity and other quality criteria (Lincoln and Guba, 1985; Tracy, 2010) and a stated match or mismatch of reality with theory. Academic journal articles will also feature the most cutting-edge research. Writers of textbooks, too, are drawn to journal articles for the theory and quality criteria that they represent. However, whilst there is a range of textbook types, from those targeted at a research community through to those targeted at undergraduate students, it is likely that textbooks will relax quality criteria to include details and ideas as expressed in the grey literature of reports and also media commentary and stories. Good media journalists working for reputable media outlets can also uncover information and add insightful commentary that may find its way into a literature review. However, there are many caveats that lower the certainty threshold that any particular claim is justified. It is invariably better to access and apply your own critical reading skills to publicly available data, rather than rely on the interpretation of data by journalists. Media journalists may emphasise specific data to represent the political or other stance of the media outlet that they work for or freelance on. There are also lazy journalists who lean on press releases and other shortcuts. In essence, whilst a variety of literature sources can add colour and currency, the balance of sources used in a PhD literature review in business and management is likely to be very heavily skewed towards peer-reviewed academic journal articles and also academic textbooks written for a research community. Practical awareness of that and other elements introduced in this section is essential for critical reading.

Wallace and Wray (2011, p. 109) introduce two lists of questions that can be asked in your critical reading. A mix of the questions from each list seems to capture the essence of the endeavour:

- Why am I reading this source?
- What review question am I asking of this source?
- What is being claimed that is relevant to answering my review question?
- How convincing is what the author is saying, including to what extent are claims consistent with my experience?
- In conclusion what can I make of this?

Making notes effectively

You need to accompany your reading with the making of effective notes, whatever type of literature review you write, whatever source your literature search reveals and whatever stage you have reached in your overall thesis.

That is because of the large quantity of material that you are required to read and the span of time over which your reading is likely to take place. However, it is also because the making of effective notes is closely related to critical reading and you need to be constantly on the alert for the components of the schema as summarised by Wallace and Wray (2011).

You need to assimilate what you read and that does not start at some indistinct time in the future but at the time that you are reading. You may remember back to your early years in high school, or even undergraduate study, when you probably spent much time and effort taking notes from various sources by adding copious amounts of highlighter to hard-copy or electronic text. You may have needed to read the whole text again if you wanted, sometime in the future, to jog your memory of its content. That is definitely not a technique to employ at PGR level. The sub-heading for this section is about making notes, not taking notes, and if you have not already devised a way to make rather than take notes you will need to do so as early as possible in your PhD study.

The ever practical Thompson (2013) suggests that you need to write the argument/claim of whatever source you read in three or four sentences. With some caveats, that is as good advice as you can get for making notes. I first observed someone doing that in my second year at university. The person concerned was reading for a degree in history but also training and competing in sport at a very high level. Time was at a premium and he emerged into the library for short, structured bursts of activity. Whatever he read was held, figuratively and literally, in the days of hard-copy, at a distance. He read fast and at the end of every article or book chapter wrote some very succinct notes. Driven by necessity, not enough hours in the day, he was making notes rather than taking notes. He gained a first-class degree, changed discipline and became a leading paediatric surgeon in London. He was an exceptional individual, but you can be that exceptional individual, too, at least as regards the making (not taking) of notes.

You may decide to structure your notes around the sort of elements that Wallace and Wray (2011) suggest, for example, succinct mention of particular concepts, perspectives, metaphors, theories, models, assumptions and ideologies, as appropriate, plus a comment on the argument/claim of the author(s) and degree of certainty that can be assigned. Or you may use the mix of questions at the end of the section above. Alternatively, you may devise other short-hand headings to keep in mind when developing your three or four sentences.

I have seen PGRs make use of various software programmes so that their succinct evaluative critique is captured in a structured, formalised way. I prefer to be more free-flow, but each of you as a PGR needs to think about devising what suits you best. Here is a note-making critique that I recently made on a peer-reviewed academic journal article (Guttentag, 2010):

> This is a star article. It is effectively a state-of-the-art outline. It is divided into two sections: virtual reality (VR) applications and implications for tourism. See the sections and sub-sections and see the conclusion. See also the definitions of VR and augmented reality (AR) and the distinction between them (p. 638). It appears that navigation and interactivity are crucial. See the comprehensive listing of devices (p. 638), most of which seem relevant ten years later. See how VR imports from medical advances (p. 640) and the link to authenticity (p. 645) and intellectual property (p. 646)

As you can observe there is a very clear judgement on what I think about the importance of the article. There are several references to theory and a note on currency, more than ten years after publication. Writing such short summaries requires discipline. It is easy to say to yourself that you are bound to remember what you read. You will not do so.

As an extra very technical note, I always add the full date that I complete any reading and summary. It is amazing how time passes and memory fades. With a record of the date, when I come to review my notes sometime hence I will be able to work out the stage of my knowledge and understanding at the time of reading and making notes (e.g. above on VR and AR). The content of articles can become more relevant with time. A simple record of the date gives a good clue whether there is a need to re-read a source *via* a different lens if/when your PhD takes a new tangent.

A number of programmes such as End Note, Zotero and Mendeley are also available to make sure that you capture the all-important details of your source. Such capture is a technical but essential add-on to note making. In the early days of such programmes PGRs spent much time setting them up and fighting with their various quirks. However, for the most part the programmes have now reached some maturity and are comparatively easy to manipulate. There are numerous freely available training videos that you can find through a quick search of You Tube. Some last for five minutes and some for upwards of an hour or two (End Note, 2016; University of Texas, 2020). It is useful to know, if End Note is completely new to you, that in five minutes you can learn the basics of how to collect, store and manage references. Your own university library will also have help-guides. Different providers require you to manipulate their systems in different ways, so here it is only worth pointing you to the overall capability of the systems that exist, rather than a more detailed account of any one system. However, although they are useful you do not have to use such technical props and there is no single programme that supports the needs of every PGR. You can do all of your collection, storage and management manually, as was done for all PhDs until 15–20 years ago. Just remember that an organised system is critical, whether centred on a downloaded programme or done manually. It saves time and effort in the long term. As with note making, that applies whether or not you have an excellent memory.

Critical writing: Organising the material and structuring the review

It is a truism of PGR study that it is never too early to start writing. However, you also need to write critically. The conditions for that are set by consideration of the purpose of a literature review, the specific or hybrid type of literature review that you intend to write, the level you have reached with your information literacy and literature search methods, the critical approach to reading and the development of your note-making capability.

Writing critically requires you to structure your writing with care. Thompson (2016) outlines five approaches that can help with that requirement: themes, canon/classic studies, chronology, wheel (hub and spoke) and pyramid. They are not mutually exclusive. It is possible to weave two or more together. I have seen all structures used well.

An approach that uses themes is the most common approach. My own PhD examined tourist satisfaction, specifically on long-haul tours (Bowen, 2001). One aim of the research was to identify whether consumer satisfaction with products and services was in any way reflected in tourist satisfaction. The literature review covered six major themes that the academic and practitioner literature highlighted as antecedents of consumer satisfaction: expectation, performance, disconfirmation (expectation in relation to performance), attribution (blame), emotion and equity (fairness). At various points in the literature review there were explicit explanatory notes to help the reader understand how my literature connected to the research aim/objectives/research topic. For example, as stated in Bowen (1998, 26):

> A range of core concepts are central to generic attribution theory. These are detailed below and, as elsewhere, explanatory notes have been added which are thought to be relevant to the tourism industry in general and long-haul tourism in particular.'

According to Thompson (2016) themes can also be drawn from methods and methodology, although in my experience that is comparatively unusual. However, it is possible to think of PhD topics that might use such an approach. For example, a PhD focused on the spatial movement of tourists in urban or rural environments might group literature according to changing use of techniques for gathering data: for example, from early attempts at physical tracking and observation (Hartmann, 1998) through to use of GPS (Global Positioning Systems) (Shoval and Isacson, 2007) and, more recently, Big Data (Salas-Olmedo et al., 2018)

The chronological approach lends itself to PGR studies in which there are clear stages in the theoretical development of a field or discipline. As an example, those of you researching services and service marketing may have come across a key work by Brown, Fisk and Jo Bitner (1994) in which they identify specific stages in the dynamic, early development of the services marketing field. Each stage is marked by particular arguments and formative contributions which Fisk et al. (1994) recognised and named as the crawling out period, scurrying about period and walking erect period. PGRs had the opportunity at that time to position their work in relation to those stages. A PGR today, studying consumer behaviour in services, for example, mobile phone usage and provider-consumer interactivity, might well develop a chronological review of mobile phone provider-consumer interactivity.

The canon/classic studies approach is similar to the chronological approach without the time element. It identifies particular arguments and formative contributions (theory, research, practice or policy) and weaves the PGR's aim, objectives and research topic around them. John (2015, pp. 66–108) researched factors that influence entrepreneurial intentions among undergraduates of South and South-East Nigeria. His abridged PhD contents page (below) illustrates a literature review centred on canon/classic studies that are drawn together with a conceptual framework. That is important because otherwise the canon/classic studies approach can lend itself to a list of literature rather than a critical review. Note, too, that John (2015) also moves beyond formative theory with a section on empirical research. In so doing he distinguishes between theoretical and applied study which of itself is a way to structure a literature review:

> Chapter 4: Review of related studies
>
> 4.1 Introduction..
>
> 4.2 Theoretical perspectives on entrepreneurial intentions and its influencing factors .....
>
> 4.2.1 Shapero's (1984) 'model of the entrepreneurial event' ....
>
> 4.2.2 Bird's (1988) 'model of implementing entrepreneurial ideas' ....
>
> 4.2.3 Robinson's et al (1991) 'entrepreneurial attitude orientation model'................
>
> 4.2.10 Elfving, Brännback and Carsrud's (2009) contextual model of entrepreneurial intentions ....

4.3 Conceptual framework on the factors that influence entrepreneurial intentions ....

4.4 Review of related empirical literature on factors that influence entrepreneurial intentions ....

4.5 Summary of the literature review …………..

The wheel approach, which I prefer to call the 'hub and spoke' approach, uses the metaphor of a spoked wheel to demonstrate structure. Various streams of literature from a field or sub-discipline, represented by the spokes, connect into a hub which is where the PhD research is situated. Accordingly, the PhD literature review is structured to illustrate in turn how each spoke supports the hub. Originality in the literature review comes from breaking down the barriers between otherwise disparate literature streams, so that the whole becomes greater than the parts. The application of literatures across fields and sub-disciplines in such a way can be very effective. For example, consumer behaviour PhD studies in tourism management have long drawn from and blended a variety of academic silos such as economics, geography, anthropology, sociology and psychology. Opportunities remain to pick up on literatures external to the field and apply the lens that they offer to well-trodden paths, for example, tourist emotions and neuroscience (Pearce, 2012).

The pyramid structure, or more precisely inverted pyramid structure, is based on a literature review that starts wide and then goes narrow. Large numbers of PhD studies and journal articles follow such an approach. At the apex of the pyramid you include the literature that is written on your particular research focus. Below is a very neat example that demonstrates such an approach. It is drawn from a PhD study researching business model innovation as employed by a traditional UK bank to enable adaptation and competitiveness within financial technology (FinTech) (Yeong, 2020, pp. 41–68):

Chapter 3: Theoretical underpinnings

3.1 Introduction ....

3.2 Background to the concept of innovation ....

3.2.1 Open innovation ....

3.2.2 Disruptive innovation ....

3.3 What is a business model? ....

3.4 The platform ecosystem perspective on business models ...

3.5 Business model innovation in traditional organisations ....

3.5.1 Defining business model innovation ....

3.5.2 Business model innovation as a response to FinTech innovations ....

3.6 The dynamic capabilities perspective on business model innovation ....

3.6.1 Defining dynamic capabilities ....

3.6.2 Dynamic capabilities and the resource-based view ....

3.6.3 Relevance of dynamic capabilities to the current study ....

3.7 Summary: research gaps in the existing literature ....

Effectively, each of the approaches above is a form of categorisation. There is almost unavoidable subjectivity in categorisation because categories are social constructions. Moreover, one may argue that every article within a specific literature is unique, and no category will do complete justice to every contribution and author. However, organisation and structure, with the inference that there are shared characteristics, helps understanding so that the reader is not overwhelmed and confused. As Steven Pinker (2002, p. 203) wrote:

> If it walks like a duck and quacks like a duck, it probably is a duck. If it's a duck, it's likely to swim, fly, (and) have a back off which water rolls ... (this) kind of inference works because the world really does contain ducks, which really do share properties.

Wallace and Wray (2011) summarise the characteristics of critical writing for a literature review. There is little to argue against the components that they highlight and many of them are already infused within what is written so far. According to Wallace and Wray (2011) there needs to be focus on a substantive, theoretical or methodological review question; discernment in choice of central sources; balanced, weighted viewpoints;

constructive not destructive criticism; convincing argument; accurate referencing; logical sequencing; and clarity of expression that takes the reader into good account. Wallace and Wray (2011) suggest that a convincing argument demonstrates the voice of the critical writer. Actually, each of the components builds such a voice. As with most lists the components overlap.

I used an extract from my own thesis earlier in this section to illustrate the use of themes. Explanatory notes in the text drew attention to how the themes connected to the aim / objectives / research topic (Bowen, 1998). As a final point on critical writing, organising the material and structuring the review, such signposting cannot be dismissed as a technical element of limited importance. I have long held the opinion that all writing, including the critical writing required of a literature review, loses verve without attention to signposting: for example, a clear and succinct introduction that highlights key components in the order that they appear; attention to the choice of headings and sub-headings, such that a skim-reader can fathom what the writing covers; and a final succinct recap. In other words, state what you are going to write – write it – state what you have written. The addition of visualisation, for example, in the form of a conceptual framework, is another prop that can help signposting.

Writing the conclusion

The conclusion of a critical literature review should always include a succinct summary of the literature, what is agreed and disagreed on, what is still ambiguous and the remaining gaps (niches, disputes, blank spots and blind spots) that are in need of exploration. The gap links to your aim and objectives, research question(s), and the conceptual framework or hypotheses that you produce. The conceptual framework and hypotheses greatly benefit from visualisation in diagrammatic form, tightly bound to the text. The visualisation can be a challenge to develop but it helps the reader and can act as an anchor point for conversation in your PhD viva.

The above aspects are demonstrated in most conclusions to literature reviews. An example of such a conclusion is shown in the abridged extract below from Younis (2018). Younis (2018) studied the internationalisation decisions of well-endowed rather than less well-endowed small and medium sized enterprises (SMEs). The literature review consisted of two chapters. One chapter focused on internationalisation and the second focussed on two relevant, selected literature streams: the so-called social capital theory (SCT) and the institutional based view (IBV). To understand the extract, you need to know that the slightly unusual term 'munificence' refers to well-endowed SMEs. However, you do not need to be an expert on internationalisation to gather the content of the literature review, its critique, stance and a considered identification of a gap (Younis, 2018, pp. 71–72):

> The literature review identifies a number of theoretical gaps which are relevant to the present research. Firstly, there is a plethora of research which over-emphasises the influence of specific categories of resource (such as management international experience, technology and innovation) over other resource categories to explain SME internationalisation (x 3 references, excluded in this abridged extract). Secondly, although decades have passed since Staw and Szwajkowski (1975) argued that environmental munificence is an important variable affecting organisations and that more research examining munificence is needed, studies that have emerged since then have captured munificence from strict market and financial perspectives, such as competitiveness or industry growth rates (x 5 references). Although useful only limited insights are drawn (x 3 references). Thirdly, the effect of informal institutional context remains an under-researched area in SME internationalisation (x1 reference). Fourthly, the extant literature extensively focuses on the role of international social capital in SMEs internationalisation and overlooks the role of SME's domestic social capital (x 2 references). Last, the existing literature offers limited insights and theorising on how SMEs' internationalisation decision is affected by resource-abundant rather than resource-constraint conditions, which is the main gap the present thesis aims to address. How this will be achieved is discussed in more details in the subsequent two chapters. Chapter 4 describes the national context of the empirical investigation while Chapter 5 is devoted in its entirety to research methodology and strategy.

The adapted excerpt above bookends a larger conclusion. Space here does not allow further expansion. The only element that Younis (2018) really misses out is a visual conceptual framework. However, the narrative is clear.

Of course, conclusions at the end of literature reviews are more or less obligatory within academic journal articles, too, albeit in shortened form compared to a PhD thesis. An example below, from a journal article on politics and tourism destination development (Bowen, Zubair and Altinay, 2017, p. 728), is illustrative of such a conclusion. You can learn a lot by paying attention to the way that various authors adapt a common template:

> Evaluation of the literature shows that politics and power are the focus of many studies in tourism that can be categorized in distinct streams. What has not been thoroughly investigated within the realm of tourism public policy is the evolution of power relations, with the shifting and shaping of power, in the form of power dominance, subservience, and decline. Given this research gap, this article responds to the following research questions:
>
> - Why and how have different stakeholders sought to gain, hold, and cede power in the tourism planning and development process?
> - How does power evolve, shape and shift?

Some final words of encouragement

One of the American music bands alluded to in the preamble to this chapter is *Blood, Sweat and Tears.* Completing a literature review normally requires unstinting effort: the meaning of the term blood, sweat and tears. As with all parts of your PhD thesis, all you can do is to try your very best. Hopefully, that will improve by picking up on what you are alerted to in this chapter. There are other practical ways to improve your critical reading and writing, so important in your literature review, such as looking for opportunities to write a review of any relevant new book related to your PhD topic, for example, for an academic journal or other outlet such as a blog (Chapter 9, this book). It is a good idea to prepare an email page with details of your PhD study and short bio-notes, so that you will be the first to reply when a book review invitation gets sent out by an academic, professional or practitioner group that you belong to. Or contact the driver behind a blog. Writing a book review is a great way to get to grips with emerging subject matter and, to borrow a phrase from Chapter 4, on criticality (this book), to place yourself on the battlefield of intellectual debate. I know PGRs who got a first spur for publishing from the acceptance of a book review in an academic journal. With that experience and motivation, you may attempt to get a shortened version of your PhD literature review published, during or after study for your PhD. That is the brightest of outcomes. At the very least, your literature review will be an important part of any empirical paper that you produce as a result of your PhD award.

References

Bowen, D. (1998). *Consumer Satisfaction and Dissatisfaction with Long-Haul Inclusive Tours*. Oxford Brookes University (PhD thesis).
Bowen, D. (2001). Antecedents of consumer satisfaction and dissatisfaction on long-haul inclusive tours – a reality check on theoretical considerations. *Tourism Management*, 22(1), 49–61.
Bowen, D. and Clarke, J. (2002). Reflections on tourist satisfaction research: Past, present and future. *Journal of Vacation Marketing*, 8(4), 297–308.
Bowen, D., Zubair, S., and Altinay, L. (2017). Politics and tourism destination development: The evolution of power. *Journal of Travel Research*, 56(6), 725–743.
Brown, S. W., Fisk, R. P., and Jo Bitner, M. (1994). The development and emergence of services marketing thought. *International Journal of Service Industry Management*, 5(1), 21–48.
CCF (2018). *Where Now for the Environment Movement: Weathercocks and Signposts Ten Years On*. <https://valuesandframes.org/resources/CCF_report_where_now_for_the_env_movement.pdf>
Cohen, E. and Cohen, S. A. (2012). Current sociological theories and issues in tourism. *Annals of Tourism Research*, 39, 2177–2202.
Cohen, S. A. and Cohen, E. (2019). New directions in the sociology of tourism. *Current Issues in Tourism*, 22(2), 153–172.
End Note (2016). *How to use EndNote in 5 minutes*. <https://www.youtube.com/watch?v=S3x06ZjBV6U>

Grant, M. J. and Booth, A. (2009). A typology of reviews: An analysis of 14 review types and associated methodologies. *Health Information & Libraries Journal*, 26(2), 91–108. <https://doi.org/10.1111/j.1471-1842.2009.00848.x>

Guttentag, D. A. (2010). Virtual reality: Applications and implications for tourism. *Tourism Management*, 31, 637–651.

Hartmann, R. (1988). Combining field methods in tourism research. *Annals of Tourism Research*, 15, 88–105.

Jesson, J. K., Matheson, L., and Lacey, F. M. (2011). *Doing your Literature Review. Traditional and Systematic Techniques*. Los Angeles, CA: Sage.

John, I. (2015). *Factors that Influence Entrepreneurial Intentions Among Undergraduates of South and South-East Nigeria*. Oxford Brookes University (PhD thesis).

Lincoln, Y. S. and Guba, E. G. (1985). *Naturalistic Inquiry*. Beverly Hills, CA: Sage Publications.

Miles, S. (2015). Stakeholder theory classification: A theoretical and empirical evaluation of definitions. *Journal of Business Ethics*, 142(3), 437–459.

Moher, D., Liberati, A., Tetzlaff, J., Altman, D. G. – The PRISMA Group (2009). Preferred reporting items for systematic reviews and meta-analyses: The PRISMA Statement. *PLoS Med* 6(7): e1000097. doi:10.1371/journal.pmed1000097

Pearce, P. L. (2012). The experience of visiting home and familiar places. *Annals of Tourism Research*, 39(2), 1024–1047.

Pinker, S. (2002). *The Blank Slate*. London, UK: Penguin Books.

PRISMA Group (2009). *PRISMA 2009 Checklist*. <http://www.prisma-statement.org/documents/PRISMA%202009%20checklist.pdf>

Salas-Olmedo, M. H., Moya-Gomez, B., Garcia-Palomares, J-C., and Gutierrez, J. (2018). Tourists digital footprint in cities: Comparing Big Data sources. *Tourism Management*, 66, 13–22.

Shoval, N. and Isaacson, M. (2007). Tracking tourists in the digital age. *Annals of Tourism Research*, 34(1), 141–159.

Thompson, P. (2012). Beginning the literature review – taking notes. <https://patthomson.net/2012/03/03/doing-your-literature-review-taking-notes/>

Thompson, P. (2013). *Not all literature reviews are the same*. <https://patthomson.net/2013/05/23/not-all-literature-reviews-are-the-same/>

Thompson, P. (2016). *Five ways to structure a literature review*. <https://patthomson.net/2016/08/29/five-ways-to-structure-a-literature-review/>

Tracy, S. J. (2010). Qualitative quality: Eight big-tent criteria for excellent qualitative research. *Qualitative Inquiry*, 16(10), 837–851.

UNE (2021). *Grey literature*. <https://www.une.edu.au/library/support/eskills-plus/research-skills/grey-literature>

University of Texas (2020). *End Note Basics (End Note X9)*. <https://www.youtube.com/watch?v=M4pdlnfBKf0>
Wallace, M. and Wray, A. (2011). *Critical Reading and Writing for Postgraduates*. London, UK: Sage.
Wang, C. L. and Chugh, H. (2014). Entrepreneurial learning: Past research and future challenges. *International Journal of Management Reviews*, 16(1), 24–61.
WWF (2008). *Weathercocks and Signposts. The Environment Movement at a Crossroads*. <https://d3bzkjkd62gi12.cloudfront.net/downloads/weathercocks_report2.pdf>
Yeong, M. W. (2020). *Financial Technology and Business Model Innovation: A Study of UK Banking*. Oxford Brookes University (PhD thesis).
Younis, H. (2018). *The Internationalisation Decision of the Endowed SME*. Oxford Brookes University (PhD thesis).

JASON BEGLEY AND GLAUCO DE VITA

4 The key attributes of an excellent PhD thesis

Preamble

Perfection is a lofty goal and, when it comes to thesis writing, some would argue an unattainable one. But if we chase perfection, we can catch excellence. So, what does an excellent PhD thesis look like? For all intents and purposes an excellent PhD thesis is one that examiners recognise as such. This begs the question, what are the key attributes or qualities that examiners look for in a thesis? The **aim of this chapter** is to elaborate on these qualities, namely, structure, originality, theory, criticality, rigour, data and clarity. The advice draws on our experience, opinion and practice, in our roles as supervisors and PhD examiners. It relates specifically to PhD theses in the disciplines of business and management and the social sciences though many of the issues discussed and recommendations put forward also apply to other subjects.

Structure

The importance of a coherent structure in a PhD thesis cannot be overstated. A clear structure offers a logical order in organising ideas, and order, in turn, helps understanding. We have already discussed the sequential way in which a well-designed PhD thesis would organise the material in Chapter 2 (see Figure 2.1) but it is worth reiterating that at its most basic, the core structure will entail:

- Abstract
- Introduction
- Literature review
- Conceptual framework
- Methodology
- Findings
- Discussion
- Conclusion
- References

It is worth reflecting further on the structure outlined above and offering greater detail on why the traditional thesis follows this process. The answer, simply put, is because it is logical to do so. Leaving the abstract (a useful summation for the reader) aside and starting with the introduction, the author of the thesis must provide a context and rationale for the study, outline the motivation for the research and set out clearly the aim and objectives for the work ahead. Following this wide-ranging overview, it is necessary to engage in research in depth. This is the literature review, a systematic, critical examination of leading journals and articles to ascertain the most recent and relevant research in the field and further refine understanding of the main research question.

At the same time the researcher will identify theoretical approaches used in complementary or comparable research that will inform the PGR's own approach to the research question. The literature offers understanding, while theory offers the instrument through which the research question can be answered. Theory will be captured within a theoretical framework at the end of the literature review, a selection of appropriate theoretical approaches. Literature and theory will then combine in the conceptual framework, where the PGR will justify the theoretical approach to answering the research question and then explain, often diagrammatically, how they intend to apply such thinking to the thesis. In other words, this section will contain the rationale for the research design and establish the basis for the ensuing steps to follow. This foundation will support the development of the methodology chapter.

The methodology chapter is the blueprint arising from the conceptual process, a step-by-step explanation of the intended activities the researcher proposes to pursue. Next, the researcher will undertake data collection and analysis, as informed by the conceptual framework and indicated by the methodology. Empirical data is an essential part of most PhDs and requires significant care in its accumulation, a point that needs to be made explicit in this part of the thesis. The findings from the data collection process and analysis will be captured over one or more chapters, before a thorough discussion and formulation of a set of recommendations is provided. Finally, the PGR will conclude with the answer to the original research question and how it informs both theory and practice, in other words, the academic and practical contribution.

Inevitably, there may be slight variations to this core, conventional structure. Such variations may depend, for example, on whether the PhD study employs a deductive or inductive approach. The former starts from theory with the aim of testing it, while the latter uses data to develop a new theory. Also, in some theses the literature review may be split into two separate chapters, one reviewing theory and the other existing applied/empirical work, culminating in the development of the conceptual framework, which can sometimes be presented as a separate chapter. Despite such variations, the process and the logic of the approach remain in evidence; contextualise, develop, review, adapt, apply, collect, analyse, report, resolve.

It is not coincidental that the core, conventional structure of a PhD thesis outlined above bears similarity with the structure one would expect of a journal article (more on this in Chapter 11) but it is worth pointing out that in recent years we have also witnessed the rise of PhD theses consisting of 'three papers' as an alternative format for writing up the results of three years' PhD research, now increasingly common in theses employing quantitative methods in the fields of finance and economics. Whilst variants exist also within this alternative way to structure the PhD thesis (see, e.g., the guidance from the Graduate School of the University of Reading),[25] the underlying idea is that the three papers are each free standing (in the sense that each can be read and understood independently) but, clearly,

---

25 This can be viewed online at: <https://www.reading.ac.uk/web/files/graduateschool/gradschwritingthesisascollectionofpapers.pdf>.

should be on related themes, each addressing an aspect of the main question investigated.

The three papers (of publishable standard), each constituting a separate chapter, should be preceded in the thesis by an introduction to the overall topic, which ought to contain essential background information, a rationale or justification for the study and a clear statement of aim and objectives, as addressed by the main body of work, that is, each of the three main chapters. There may also be a general literature review preceding the 'three papers' and a general chapter discussing methods and data used for the three distinct studies (though the latter can be subsumed as a study-specific section in each of the three 'paper' chapters). Unless stated otherwise by your institutional guidelines, it is a safer strategy to ensure that also within this alternative thesis format, you include a concluding chapter that summarises the main findings and contributions, policy implications, limitations of the study (or studies) and avenues for further research. As per the conventional format, all references may go at the end of the thesis, followed by appendices, possibly numbered in correspondence to each paper/chapter they refer to.

Originality

It has been our experience to date that the question of originality is something of a blind spot for many PGRs. In conversation with their supervisors many PGRs talk about the need for originality, but quickly place it low on their list of priorities as they instead fret about what they consider more pressing challenges, usually related to theory and literature. Typically, this stems from the PGR not understanding the importance of originality, but more frequently what is meant by an 'original contribution'. As Gill and Dolan (2015, p. 477) observe, *"while the concept of originality is undoubtedly specific to a discipline, it is arguably so nebulous that it is almost meaningless to most PhD students"*. This nebulosity stems from the lack of a single, definitive framework or definition to guide doctoral researchers (Gill and Dolan, 2015). This section of the chapter offers an important opportunity then, to stress the importance of identifying, from a very early stage, what is meant by originality and ensuring that a thesis makes an original or novel contribution. With this aim in mind, it explores differing interpretations, but more importantly points to several critical errors frequently made by PGRs in their search for originality. To start with, it is necessary to discuss the concept itself.

Most universities publish guidelines in their regulations explaining what the institution deems as an original contribution. Here at Coventry University, the guidelines state that a thesis will be considered to make an original contribution if it is *"rooted in original research which creates new knowledge or demonstrates originality in the application of knowledge"* (Coventry University, 2020, p. 79). This approach to guidance mirrors that of other UK Higher Education Institutions (HEIs) where regulations will be suitably wide-ranging thus lending themselves to a myriad of interpretations. What is perhaps lost in this generalist perspective is the difficulty of locating originality in a landscape already heavily populated by researchers; what PGRs will usually find is that the low-hanging fruit will have already been picked, leaving them with the more significant challenge of finding novelty in a packed field.

Phillips and Pugh (2010) extending Francis (1976) offer several suggestions on how to think about originality, an approach echoed by Saunders and Lewis (2012). These recommendations emphasise the collection and use of empirical data in new and novel ways, either by synthesising research material, discovering new data, using new evidence to offer new perspectives on an old issue, applying new techniques to existing data or applying cross-disciplinary perspectives and approaches to a research question. Although these suggestions have value, a more comprehensive explanation of what constitutes originality is supplied by the Research Excellence Framework (REF) criteria guidance document.[26] The REF guide states that research outputs that demonstrate originality may do one or more of the following:

- Produce and interpret new empirical findings or new material.
- Engage with new and/or complex problems.

---

26   The REF is the system for assessing the quality of research in UK HEIs and for distributing funding primarily by reference to research excellence.

- Develop innovative research methods, methodologies and analytical techniques.
- Show imaginative and creative scope.
- Provide new arguments and/or new forms of expression, formal innovations, interpretations and/or insights.
- Collect and engage with novel types of data.
- Advance theory or the analysis of doctrine, policy or practice, and new forms of expression.

It should be said that while the above offers a useful frame of reference, the expectations for doctoral studies are more circumspect. Rüger (2016) makes the invaluable point that it is depth not breadth that counts in doctoral research. The temptation to pursue a sweeping review of a discipline will inevitably end in tears, as such work is usually undertaken by teams of researchers, or by internationally renowned academics able to draw on decades of knowledge and experience. Doing doctoral research is as much about demonstrating the ability to do research as it is about doing original research. As such the expectations for originality do not extend to ground-breaking insights, or as Rüger (2016, p. 2) explains:

> Although one of the expectations of a PhD thesis is that it contains something novel as its centre piece, this is often confined to a narrow sub-area of a field. There is no need to spark off a new research field. The award of a PhD only documents the ability to carry out independent research to academic standards. A narrow area is normally sufficient for this.

Nevertheless, the more frequent encounters we have had with PGRs struggling for originality is of a different nature, those who promise far more than they can deliver, displaying too much ambition.

Dunleavy (2003) points to another frequent offence that occurs in the quest for originality, which he labels a super-trawl. Here the aspirant undertakes an enormous sweep of the literature, seeking increasingly rare nuggets from more and more unlikely sources, in the hope that the answer to the problem posed will arise from this process. Exhaustive searches through increasingly irrelevant literature only serve as a crutch. It will not provide the answer to the originality required. Tanggaard and Wegener (2016) also warn against forced novelty, but from a different perspective. In this instance the PGR, in a separate attempt to inject originality into the work, searches around until they find an interesting approach or concept and then tries to crowbar the idea into the work, regardless of its suitability to the research question. Rather than trying to impose a mismatched design into the research, the doctoral researcher instead needs to focus on the problem being tackled. While originality is important it should not come at the cost of the research itself.

Gill and Dolan (2015) also point to a very common mistake, namely claiming originality rather than demonstrating it. For example, PGRs will often refer to the fact that no one has done this type of research before. Notwithstanding the likelihood that this is probably naive, it doesn't actually explain what is original. Even if the statement were to be true, it does not show how the work adds to existing knowledge, how it extends or develops theory, it merely says, somewhat ingenuously, that there is a gap filled by the study. What occurs most often is that a PGR makes this claim while failing to realise that the topic they consider to be fresh and new has, in fact, already been developed, perhaps in a less obvious manner. This points to the need for a thorough literature review to identify work that may inform the research question or complement it without replicating it. You will also need to consider the value or *significance* of what is being proposed as 'original'. For example, no one may have thrown an elephant off a cliff to see if it can fly before, but that does not necessarily make it a worthwhile, novel research experiment. In short, there are gaps that are best left unfilled.

The flipside, of course, is when PGRs find research that appears to have completed what they have already decided they want to do. Some PGRs will studiously ignore the existence of this research, hoping no one will notice. Others might choose to underestimate the work itself. Rather than be intimidated by such research findings, it is far better to embrace them. Raise the issue with your supervisory team, discuss how the work impacts your own and determine if you can, without significant restructuring, incorporate the work into your own study and whether originality can still be found by building on this existing research output. Imagine if you had spent three to four years working on a research question only to eventually find that it had already been answered!

While originality and novelty will, usually, follow from the natural efforts of the PGR, there are several steps researchers can take to improve their efforts at making unique and valuable connections in their work. First and foremost, set aside time to evaluate ideas, map out concepts and connections and generally sum up and analyse the research you have read to date. This can be done alone, or in groups through peer discussion, or more formally through organised events using approaches such as the Delphi Technique to refine your ideas (Saunders and Lewis, 2012).

While these are useful suggestions, there is simply no substitute for digging into the existing bodies of research around your chosen academic debate and seeing what gaps are identifiable. Sometimes what is not appreciated by novice researchers is how the research field is slow moving and how research occurs carefully and incrementally. That leaves one final point to be made, which is to recognise and understand the limits of what can be achieved. Don't oversell what you can do or underestimate what can be achieved. Find a suitable compromise, with the support of your supervisory team, one that does not necessarily require changing the conversation, but instead adds to it.

Theory, theory development and theoretical contribution

Much has been written about theory, but what do we mean by it? Sutton and Staw (1995, p. 378) describe theory as follows:

> Theory is the answer to queries of why. Theory is about the connections among phenomena, a story about why acts, events, structure, and thoughts occur. Theory emphasizes the nature of causal relationships, identifying what comes first as well as the timing of such events. Strong theory, in our view, delves into underlying processes so as to understand the systematic reasons for a particular occurrence or non-occurrence.

Of course, within the broad church of business and management and the social sciences, the way in which theory is presented, utilised and extended in a PhD thesis may vary significantly, depending on the specific field in which the thesis is located. For example, a business law PhD thesis using as a theoretical lens Thomas Hobbes' social contract theory then applied to the context of environmental ethics and business behaviour, will look and feel very different from a purely applied economics PhD thesis aimed at revisiting John Maynard Keynes' theory of consumption. The latter will inevitably need to go through a process dictated by the traditional convention of testing economic theory also making use of mathematical economics and econometrics.

Let us briefly elaborate on the steps of the process of the latter example. The thesis will first need to unpack the original theoretical statement. Economic theory formulates hypotheses that are mostly qualitative in nature. Using the example above, Keynes (1936, p. 36) states:

> The fundamental psychological law ... is that men [and women too] are disposed, as a rule and on average, to increase their consumption as their income increases, but not by as much as the increase in their income.

Such a statement will need to be properly interpreted and qualified. In effect, here Keynes postulates that the marginal propensity to consume (i.e. the rate of change of consumption per unit change in income) is greater than zero but less than one, *ceteris paribus*. But although Keynes posits a positive relationship between consumption and income, he does not specify the precise functional form of the relationship.

The next task entails expressing Keynes' theory in mathematical form, through equations, to then allow an econometric specification to be developed for the purpose of empirical verification. Irrespective of the results to be obtained from testing Keynes' theory of consumption, it must be clarified that simply testing such theory would not constitute, in and by itself, an advancement or contribution to theory. Instead, the latter may be legitimately pursued by, for example, demonstrating under what conditions Keynes' theory of consumption is confirmed or refuted, possibly with an aim of extending it by accounting for the role played by, say, individuals' expected future income or individuals' life-cycle patterns of saving and borrowing. Such avenues, of course, have already been pursued by the likes of Milton Friedman and Franco Modigliani,[27] hence they no longer constitute a novel contribution as such.

---

27   Friedman and Modigliani were both recipients of the Nobel Memorial Prize in Economics, in 1976 and 1985, respectively.

Having elaborated on the important distinctions of how theory may be used in different subjects, it is fair to say that a typical business school PhD thesis, will contain a detailed literature review, capturing salient research as well as a theory section, which underpins the approach to be taken to the research topic within the thesis, in turn informing the creation of the conceptual framework. The literature review supports the selection of the appropriate theory to answer the research question posed at the start of the thesis. It is this theory development and subsequent contribution to knowledge, either through extending existing theory, utilising theory in a new or novel way or, in rare circumstances, creating new theory, that sets doctoral research apart from other postgraduate qualifications. It is also the most challenging part of the thesis to deliver. As Alvesson and Kärreman (2011, p. 1) explain:

> It is not so difficult to produce a description of what people do and say through interviews, observations and other methods, but to continue beyond that and suggest insights, concepts, explanations and other 'deeper' aspects that goes beyond the relevance of a particular case or a sample studied is not so easy.

Identifying the appropriate theory, to offer the most suitable lens through which to examine your research question and then integrating it as a research tool into your conceptual framework, is routinely cited as the principal problem encountered by doctoral candidates during their studies (see, e.g., Lings, 2008; Byron and Thatcher, 2016). It is probably worth reflecting that your own supervisors most likely went through the same challenges with theory development during their doctoral studies, experience that will manifest in their repeated emphasis on getting the theoretical aspect of the thesis as well-defined as possible, from a very early stage (Lee, 2008).

Lempriere (2019) offers an interesting way to comprehend the import of theory to a thesis, by imagining how the research problem would look without the requisite theoretical tools: a sprawling, unstructured research question, approachable from innumerable directions, offering no firm basis to successfully replicate the study, all understanding of the work being unique to the researcher alone. Theory, therefore, is the instrument by which research is pursued, that allows proven methods to successfully transfer from one task to another, offering the researcher the ability to focus on a specific question in a detailed and logical manner, each step clearly outlined and explained.

It is probably worth reflecting further on what we mean by the term 'theory', no simple undertaking. There is no single, accepted definition. However, most will agree on a general interpretation that views theory as a statement of concepts and their interrelationships that shows how and/or why a phenomenon occurs (Gioia and Pitre, 1990; Corley and Gioia, 2011). As unsatisfying as such a broad explanation may be, it serves to provide a basis of knowledge of what constitutes theory. Wilkins et al. (2019) offer several further definitions, themselves derived from business and management professors at leading research institutions, ranging from the view that theory is a "*vision of the world*" through to the more specific idea that "*theory is a causal argument or prediction that can be tested with empirical data and tools*" (p. 8). Perhaps the most telling contribution was captured in the following statement (p. 9):

> I don't think that there is a single definition of theory, rather there are several competing conceptions of theory, including theory as analysis; theory as explanation; theory as prediction; and theory as prescription.

In other words, theory is used to answer questions of behaviour or circumstance. For example, why consumers favour one product over another, or why one company is successful and another not. It is the lens through which these questions are examined. Perhaps more useful is to ask how we identify theory and, for the purposes of doctoral studies, how to determine what is a theoretical contribution (regarding the latter, please also refer to Chapter 11). Whetten (1989) states that theory should contain four necessary elements:

- Which factors logically should be considered as part of the explanation?
- How are they related?
- What are the underlying dynamics that justify the selection of factors and the proposed causal relationships?
- Who, Where, When? These questions set the boundaries and constitute the range of the theory.

These points helpfully frame our understanding of what a theory is, though critically offer useful observations rather than practical identification tools. It is a truism, and most unfortunate, that doctoral candidates are expected to grasp these concepts and engage with theory at a very early stage in their doctoral studies, despite frequently having limited exposure to such thinking. To resolve this challenge, supervisors will typically recommend wide reading and exposure to general theories, using this route to later identify more specific theories to be used in the thesis. Additionally, most UK PhD programmes now also offer a period of taught modules and training workshops for PGRs. These are frequently bespoke and discipline specific. For example, the Economic and Social Research Council, a key provider of postgraduate research funding in the UK, makes clear in its guidelines that it expects qualifying candidates to engage in master degree research training as a prelude to undertaking a full PhD, with either one or two years of core training spread across the course of their studies (ESRC, 2020).

A key aspect of these training modules is to help PGRs get to grips with the problem of theory identification and theory development. Closely related to the question of what constitutes a theory is the research approach, frequently discipline specific, that determines theory selection and allows the doctoral candidate to determine how to apply theory to a real-world problem.

Broadly speaking there are three recognisable categories of action undertaken as part of the research process: inductive, deductive and abductive research. Inductive research focuses on theory building, using real-world events as the building blocks for developing new theory. In contrast, deductive research approaches seek to use existing, well-established theory to explain real-world events. Abductive research borrows from both approaches, focusing on both existing theory and data interpretation to select the most appropriate explanation.

Complementing the research approach is the research philosophy or epistemology that underpins it. Epistemology is a philosophical concept that concerns itself with the study of knowledge, its nature, its validity and value, its methods and scope (Girod-Séville and Perret, 2001). Most significantly it makes a distinction between what can be proven and what is subjective opinion. Following the broad classification provided by Girod-Séville and Perret (2001), three schools of thought can be said to capture the essence of epistemological research questioning. Positivists advocate the principle of the objectivity, meaning the observed is not influenced by the observer. For interpretivists, observation influences action and understanding these interactions and relations is crucial. Constructivists go one step further, stating that understanding is constructed through shared knowledge, experiential learning[28] and reflection (ibid.). From a deductive perspective it is important for doctoral candidates to locate their own research approach and philosophical understanding when considering how they will select a theoretical instrument to answer their research question. It is only through this process that they will be able to envisage how to extend theory or use new theory to examine enduring questions. In other words, by immersing themselves in theoretical perspectives and allying them to the contextual understandings developed through the literature review, the theoretical gap will be identified, and the all-important theoretical contribution will emerge.

It is not enough just to list a series of theories. This mistake is routinely made by PGRs as they rush to complete a conceptual framework. Instead, theory should be selected with purpose, chosen because it explains relationships between what is being observed and has coherence and complementarity. This relationship is best described using a theoretical framework, normally appearing after the literature review. This should not be confused with the conceptual framework, which focuses on explaining, usually diagrammatically, how the concepts being explored as part of the research process relate to each other within the theoretical framework.

---

[28] Broadly speaking, experiential learning refers to the process of learning through experience. More specifically, 'learning through reflection on doing'. The modern conceptualisation of experiential learning owes much to David A. Kolb's development of the theory of experiential learning, which, in turn, draws on the experiential work of Kurt Lewin, Jean Piaget, John Dewey, Paulo Freire and William James. According to Kolb (1984), the impetus for new understanding and development is provided by new experiences, as he writes: "*Leaning is the process whereby knowledge is created through the transformation of experience*" (1984, p. 38).

Lempiere (2019) offers ten things to consider when developing your theoretical framework. The good advice is summarised below.

1. You need to have a solid grasp of your aims and objectives.
2. What theory/theories are you using and why?
3. Critically explain why you are adopting this particular approach.
4. Can the theories be broken down into different schools? Which one are you siding with and why?
5. A theory contains several concepts. Which will you be drawing upon? Why these ones? Have you defined them properly?
6. How do the concepts relate to your aims and objectives?
7. Have you clearly stated your ontological and epistemological positioning?
8. Are you the first to use this specific theory in this particular way? What benefits or drawbacks does that bring?
9. Can you spot any drawbacks with applying this theory?
10. How are your concepts related? Are you using them as hypotheses? Or as a model to make sense of the data?

For building theories inductively, Eisenhardt (1989) offers an example of theory development using case studies. First, formulate a tentative research question. Next, consider potential case studies or examples you might want to include in your research. Then craft instruments and protocols, for example, combining quantitative and qualitative data. Follow this step by engaging with data collection and preliminary data analysis. Then, once data are collected, further develop analysis, searching for cross patterns. From these steps, shape your hypothesis, enfolding your findings and explanations within a thorough literature review. What is evident from both these approaches is the central importance of knowledge of literature, empirical data and their relationship to existing theory.

Whether you are deductively using theory as a lens to peer at and explain relationships in observed empirical data or are attempting to develop theory inductively by sifting through data, should not matter. Theory reflects data, either by design or development (Alvesson and Karreman,

2011). Abductive reasoning combines both approaches, with the researcher seeking the most likely explanation among many alternatives in order to explain anomalies in the empirical data. To explain these irregularities the researcher can combine both, numerical and cognitive reasoning (Dubois and Gadde, 2002). This approach, though increasingly popular, is a challenging one and it is recommended that most doctoral candidates utilise the more traditional and well understood inductive or deductive methods for theory development.

It should be said that developing new general theory is usually considered beyond the reach of the average doctoral candidate. Instead, the theoretical contribution, a central aspect to a traditional thesis, is typically seen through the extension of a theory, the refining of a specific theory or the novel use of a theory, particularly from a complementary discipline, in a way that has not been seen before. Coincidentally, as further discussed in Chapter 11, what constitutes a good enough 'incremental contribution' is an area that remains a bit of a dilemma even for editors and reviewers of journal articles (see, e.g., Wright, 2015). Yet, we can say that a significant contribution usually has a narrow focus, on a specific research question in the area of business and social sciences research, with practical applications that have a real-world impact. However, replicating existing research, or reviewing it, would not be considered a sufficient contribution, and it is making this distinction that frequently causes PGRs substantial confusion.

Quite simply, a key aspect of theory development that underpins a theoretical contribution is a well-considered research question. If you wonder why this book relentlessly focuses on the importance of a carefully designed research question, it is precisely because everything flows from it. The research question informs the research objectives that, in turn, inform the literature and theory selection, which then establish the theoretical framework, the framework that the conceptualisation of the thesis intertwines with, all of which then inform both the academic/theoretical contribution as well as the real-world impact of the study. Everything fits together neatly, and if it is a well-crafted research question, then the task of identifying the theoretical contribution should flow naturally as part of the research process.

Criticality

Critical thinking or 'criticality' as it is now commonly referred to in academic circles (defined as the quality of being critical) is a cognitive approach that can be traced back to the ancient Greek philosophical tradition, particularly to the teaching practice and vision of Socrates 2,500 years ago. Socrates' method of probing, most notably known as the 'Socratic questioning' approach to disciplined and thoughtful dialogue, stemmed from the premise that we should never take knowledge and alleged truths at face value. We should always subject ideas, explanations and insights to critical scrutiny and evaluate their logical consistency before accepting them as worthy of belief.

Socrates emphasised the importance of gathering evidence, questioning reasoning and assumptions, analysing rigorously and tracing out implications of both arguments and actions. He also called for deep reflection to help us distinguish between beliefs that are reasoned, objective and rational and those that are driven by or are susceptible to biases, including biases stemming from our own preconceptions, native egocentrism or innate need for comfort. Critical thinking comprises of all these reason- and evidence-based evaluative and analytical dimensions. To this day, these dimensions remain at the core of the scientific research process. They also closely align to the more modern concept of 'reflexivity' (see Flanagan, 1981), which refers to the epistemological examination of how our own beliefs, culture, judgements and practices influence how we perceive and interpret the world around us, and hence the acceptance that the researcher is to some extent always part of the research (Finlay, 1998).

Criticality can be demonstrated in a variety of ways, but in academic debate and educational dialogue it will inevitably require a dialectic (thesis-antithesis) element in which alternative ideas, conceptions, framings, hypotheses or propositions are set against each other and comparatively analysed and evaluated in order to interpret differences and/or contradictions that need to be overcome or transcended. Criticality also necessitates a dialogical element where a more in-depth contextual conversation and/or inquiry is undertaken, leading to a logical synthesis.

Given all the above, it should be apparent why criticality is one of the main qualities PhD examiners look for in a thesis. Criticality is looked for and should be evidenced in the final discussion of findings and the capacity for synthesis of course, but also in the way PGRs engage and interact with existing literature. Critical thinking must pervade the review of relevant literature manifesting itself in every aspect of the literature review chapter, from making explicit the decisions about the boundaries of the debate under scrutiny (i.e. what literature was included and not included, and why) through to demonstrating the ability to *"derive and to explore ideas through literature rather than passively reporting it"* (Delamont et al., 1997, p. 66). Golding et al. (2014, p. 570) forcefully reiterate the message by arguing:

> Above all, examiners want to see critical engagement with the literature, rather than a list of who said what. To show critical engagement, a candidate might interpret, conceptualise, analyse or evaluate what has been written, supported with appropriate references.

That is further emphasised by Holbrook et al. (2007, p. 348):

> Even in a good, technically competent synthesis, they [examiners] also expect that the candidate will weigh up the literature and subject it to critical appraisal, ideally to lead to a new or interesting perspective. The lack of such appraisal casts doubts on the depth of the candidate's understanding of the sources, on their expertness in their chosen field, and certainly their scholarliness.

In their investigation of examiners' assessment expectations of 'the literature review' in PhD theses based on over 1,300 examiners' reports across five Australian universities, Holbrook et al.'s (2007) analysis of comments of such reports reveals that the area most wanting of PhD theses examined was precisely that relating to the critical appraisal, not only *"the lack of critique"*, but also the *"lack of discrimination in the use of the literature"*, leading the authors to conclude that (ibid., p. 348):

> There is a clear indication that examiners identify a critical perspective as an essential precursor to positioning a study and identifying its contribution in an informed and scholarly way.

Criticality in appraising the literature is about engaging with the key ideas and concepts of a debate while ensuring that they are exhaustively interrogated, probed and comparatively evaluated as part of the way the research is delineated and situated. This means that you must place yourself in the battlefield of the existing intellectual debate, mindful that in the presence of conflict or opposing views, taking the middle ground position purely for the sake of caution is likely to be the least correct. You must learn to *problematise* such ideas and concepts by not taking them for granted and by questioning assumptions and implications, premises and corollaries, inferences and conclusions. When problematising, 'less is *never* more'[29] and the optimal route between two points should never be the shortest one because problematising is, literally and unapologetically, about 'making problematic'. This includes asking questions that, retrospectively, deny other authors the freedom of not having explained 'why' they did (or did not do) something or 'how'.

As mentioned earlier, another important element of criticality relates to bias. We all carry biases and prejudices stemming from our experience, upbringing, culture, education and so on, which are very difficult to be consciously aware of, let alone eradicate. Such biases affect our perceptions and the way we process and interpret information thus also shaping the way we think, react to views and reach conclusions. Against this backcloth, engaging in a deliberate process of critical reflection and self-questioning on how such cognitive influences may act as a filter to our frame of reference in understanding and evaluating ideas, is of paramount importance. This is not just about engaging in higher level 'critical reflection' (rather than merely 'technical' or 'practical' reflection) of the kind advocated by Van Manen (1977, 1995), a level of reflection which goes beyond personal

---

29 This is itself a small example of *our* problematisation of the paradox 'less is more', enacted by turning the rhetorical device against itself: 'less is *never* more', we write. The original sentence uses two opposites to contradict one another, which is the beauty of the paradox. How can less be more? Despite the contradiction, the message it conveys is that something less complicated is often more appreciated. But, we argue, not when problematising! As we do here, by questioning the call for simplicity and minimalism to deliberately complicate things, and make you pause and think.

agency, takes into account the wider historical, cultural and political context, and embodies a political enterprise of emancipation and opposition against the *status quo*, but also about questioning oneself, reflexively, about one's own personal biases and subjective frame of reference.

This is especially important for PGRs involved in ethnographic-type studies and, in fact, in any research involving fieldwork where the investigator has a dual identity as both researcher and practitioner/participant. This is particularly common in the context of 'action research', that is, research whereby researchers and participants collaboratively link theory to professional practice to drive social change. For example, research in business education (e.g. research related to teaching and learning in business schools), which is usually conducted by authors who hold multiple roles, as lecturer, course/module leader and researcher. These research settings inevitably call for a reflexive stance to ensure an ethically acceptable position in which the researcher's actions and choices would be considered justifiable and sound. By way of example, I report below an extract of a PhD thesis on culturally inclusive pedagogies in business education in which the PGR (De Vita, 2006, pp. 35–36) discusses, critically and reflexively, his use of the 'anecdote' (a popular technique of the genre of narrative writing) as a powerful vehicle for the illumination of reality in the context of his own cultural identity positioning in the study:

> Admittedly, the narrative style embedded in this form of research scores low on the traditional standards of validity and reliability. But it is still unclear to the author why, in assessing the 'goodness' and 'credibility' of its methods, this tradition of educational research should be judged using positivists criteria of what constitutes good work and credible findings. The community of teaching practitioners, which this research serves, is more likely to be concerned with different aspects of 'credibility' such as whether the researcher has closely observed the phenomenon being studied and possesses wide knowledge and experience of the reality being talked about, as opposed to whether the results can be replicated. In this respect the author was in a privileged position of 'trustworthiness' in that he could offer the 'authentic' perspective of a practitioner who has been on both sides of the desk, first, as an international student, and then, as a non-English speaking background (NESB) lecturer. As suggested by Van Manen (1990), the raw data of a phenomenological study are personal experiences and what is important to know is how people interpret the phenomenological text.

Rigour

Rigour is another cornerstone of high-quality academic research, hence also a key attribute of an excellent PhD thesis. As boldly put by Morse et al. (2002, p. 13), *"without rigor, research is worthless, becomes fiction, and loses its utility"*. It should come as no surprise, therefore, that also the REF takes 'rigour' as one its three criteria for assessment of research quality (alongside 'originality' and 'significance').

Etymologically, 'rigour' derives from the Latin *'rigidus'* meaning rigid; a rigidity that in our research context is to be interpreted as an unyielding severity, strictness or exactitude of method that leads to valid conclusions. But it is important to emphasise that such exacting standards do not just apply to method or the reliability and validity of the results, issues we will return to shortly, but to all activities involved in the research process. For example, the REF for assessing output quality mentioned above frames 'rigour' as a construct meant to apply to a multiplicity of aspects, including the extent to which the purpose of the work is clearly articulated, an appropriate methodology for the research area has been adopted and compelling evidence presented to show that the purpose has been achieved. More specifically, the REF panel criteria and working methods state (REF, 2021, p. 35):

> Rigour will be understood as the extent to which the work demonstrates intellectual coherence and integrity, and adopts robust and appropriate concepts, analyses, sources, theories and/or methodologies.[30]

Another research activity where rigour should apply is the literature search which, as discussed in the previous chapter, is a crucial initial step to allow you to then conduct a comprehensive literature review to situate your research within existing knowledge. To be rigorous, a literature search must be thorough and systematic, with no notable omissions of significant previously published work. The subsequent review of identified literature

---

30 Online available at: <https://www.ref.ac.uk/media/1084/ref-2019_02-panel-criteria-and-working-methods.pdf>.

should itself denote a rigorous approach. One likely to entail the critical analysis and evaluation of often contrasting arguments, conflicting theoretical postulations and evidence, an appraisal of underlying assumptions and implications of alternative models or frameworks, and the identification of gaps that pave the way for the development of your own conceptual framework and 'thesis' (interpreted as your main argument) of how your work positions itself within the existing debate and adds to what has gone before.

But of course, in the context of the production of knowledge, rigour is most frequently discussed as an essential attribute of issues related to methodological standards and the trustworthiness of results and attendant knowledge claims. At its simplest, a method is a means to an end, one connecting a research question to a research answer. The scientific method aims to accomplish such task (finding answers, solutions or making discoveries) via activities such as systematic observation and experimentation, inductive and deductive reasoning, logical argumentation and the formulation and testing of hypotheses and theories. It is the rigour with which such activities are carried out that determines the validity of the method used given its appropriateness to answer the research question at hand. Finally, such an answer must satisfy the research community within which the question is considered as meaningful and needing to be answered.

Strictly defined, reliability refers to the extent to which confidence can be placed in the construct, approach or result, ultimately measured by whether the experiment and the result can be replicated, enabling subsequent researchers to arrive at the same conclusions and insights if they conducted the study along the same steps again (Denzin and Lincoln, 1994). Validity determines whether the research truly measures that which it was intended to measure or how truthful the research results are.

In quantitative research framed within the positivistic, empiricist 'observation and experiment' paradigm, especially that employing regression analysis, issues pertaining to reliability, validity and replicability, are typically resolved by a transparent protocol and a large set of available tests and procedures designed to offer reassurances as to the adequacy of sample sizes, reliability of coefficient estimates at customary statistical significance levels, the validity of the model estimated and the fulfilment of a number of other requirements to ensure the reliability of statistical inference and hypothesis testing.

Several such tests fall within the 'regression diagnostic' procedures used to appraise the avoidance of violations of the estimation method's statistical assumptions,[31] the appropriateness of the model specification and its overall 'goodness of fit'. For more detail on these tests, their accurate implementation and how they can help offer reassurances as to the reliability, validity, consistency, efficiency and replicability of the results obtained, we refer the interested reader to specialised research methods and econometrics textbooks and relevant journal articles. Suffice to say that PGRs using such quantitative methods are well advised to ensure they execute relevant techniques and interpret the results accurately, since it is not uncommon particularly in business and management PhD theses to find basic mistakes even in the use of the simplest types of descriptive or inferential statistical analyses.

In qualitative research framed within grounded theory, ethnography or phenomenology,[32] issues of reliability and validity are not as readily codified or standardised (Pratt, 2008). This is understandable given that the reliability and validity constructs are rooted in the positivist, empiricist paradigm (read again the thesis' extract reported at the end of the previous section in this chapter). It should not be surprising, therefore, that across the spectrum of qualitative data collection methods, from observation and interviews through to focus groups and surveys via questionnaires with open-ended questions, issues of validity, reliability, the trustworthiness of knowledge claims and especially replicability and representativeness, remain contentious.

---

[31] For example, in linear regression analysis, normality, homoscedasticity, the absence of multicollinearity, auto- or serial-correlation and measurement error.

[32] Grounded theory is an inductive approach for conducting qualitative research aimed toward theory development which is 'grounded' in data that has been systematically collected and analysed. Ethnography entails the immersion of the researcher in groups or organisations to study the affinity such cultural group share. Phenomenology entails the investigation of a phenomenon or event describing and interpreting participants' lived experiences.

This is particularly the case in observational studies that entail recording in field notes what the researcher has seen, heard or encountered, where different observers (investigators) may record different observations. So, whilst to be deemed appropriate at a preliminary or exploratory stage of research, 'observation' employed as the sole data collection method is a risky strategy, particularly in passing the rigour test. Moreover, it is difficult to conduct observational studies on large samples. Much better, therefore, if 'observation' is used as part of a multi-method involving two or more qualitative methods or even better, a mixed-method approach based on combining qualitative and quantitative methods.

Similarly, rigour is often seen as one of the main weaknesses of case studies. In an early rendition of the perils of the qualitative case study method, the article *Qualitative Data as an Attractive Nuisance*, Matthew Miles (1979) went as far as arguing that, within-case analysis was *"essentially intuitive, primitive, and unmanageable"* (ibid., p. 597). This means that PGRs using such methodology should go the extra mile in seeking to persuade examiners of the 'credibility' of methodological procedures (Siggelkow, 2007; Silverman, 2005, 2006; Yin, 1981, 1994). In excellent PhD theses, this persuasion is typically achieved by addressing issues of rigour extensively, laying open not only how aspects of validity and reliability were dealt with (and in which specific order), but also the problems that were encountered in doing so, and how such further challenges were resolved.

Indeed, a variety of strategies and techniques exist and should be utilised to demonstrate a transparent and robust protocol for all kinds of qualitative research, including the development of systematic coding schemes with the aid of computer programmes such as NVivo,[33] searching for deviant cases, and the use of established transcription techniques developed for conversation analysis aimed at improving the accuracy with which data are recorded.

A seminal contribution to understanding academic rigour in relation to qualitative (or naturalistic) social research was that made by Guba and

---

33 NVivo is a software programme used for qualitative data analysis that allows you to collect, organise, categorise, code, analyse and visualise unstructured or semi-structured text, including data from interviews, focus groups, surveys, social media and journal articles.

Lincoln (1982). They proposed four criteria for judging the trustworthiness of qualitative research and related methods. The first is the criterion of *credibility*, which they defined as the truth value of research findings. To achieve *credibility*, Guba and Lincoln suggested 'prolonged engagement', 'persistent observation', 'peer debriefing', methodological and theoretical 'triangulation', 'referential adequacy materials' and 'member checks' when coding.[34]

With respect to the extent to which the findings can be deemed applicable or generalisable to other context, Guba and Lincoln proposed the criterion of *transferability*, with recommendations to undertake 'theoretical/purposive sampling' and perform what Geertz (1973) termed 'thick description'.[35]

An additional criterion is that of *dependability*, which is meant to answer the question of the consistency of research findings. In place of strict replicability, Guba and Lincoln proposed 'stepwise replication' (via collaborative work) and the maintenance of an 'audit trail' to enable a 'dependability audit'. In later work (see also Lincoln and Guba, 2000), they contended that *'since there can be no validity without reliability (and thus no credibility without dependability) a demonstration of the former is sufficient to establish the existence of the latter'* (cited in Babbie and Mouton, 2001, p. 278).

Finally, to ensure the absence of researcher bias, the last criterion is that of *confirmability*, the satisfaction of which can be sought through 'triangulation', 'practicing reflexivity' and the use of 'confirmability audits' (Guba and Lincoln, 1982, pp. 246–248). Especially triangulation (see, also, Mathison, 1988), a procedure where the qualitative researcher searches *"for convergence among multiple and different sources of information to form*

---

[34] Once again, we refer interested readers to specialised manuals to dig deeper into specific methods. With respect to coding, we recommend Saldaña (2021), which offers a comprehensive treatment of functions of codes, and a selected repertoire of coding methods generally applied in qualitative data analysis.

[35] In the social sciences and related fields, thick description on human social action not only describes behaviours but the interpreted context of such behaviours. This is usually achieved by adding a record of subjective explanations and meanings provided by the people engaged in the behaviours.

themes or categories in a study" (Creswell and Miller, 2000, p. 126) has increasingly been seen as a valid technique to eliminate bias and increase the researcher's truthfulness of a proposition about some social phenomenon (Denzin, 1978).

The above criteria have sparked much debate over the past four decades and can be said to have been fundamental to the development of standards used to evaluate the quality and rigour of qualitative inquiry. For example, Morse et al. (2002, p. 17) argued that "*while strategies of trustworthiness may be useful in attempting to evaluate rigor, they do not in themselves ensure rigor*", primarily because they are applied only *post hoc*. Accordingly, Morse et al. (2002) place emphasis on *verification* as "*a process of checking, confirming, making sure, and being certain*" (ibid., p. 17). They propose several verification strategies as "*mechanisms used during the process of research to incrementally contribute to ensuring reliability and validity and, thus, the rigor of a study*" (ibid., p. 17).

The first such strategy is *methodological coherence*, to ensure congruence between the research question and the components of the method. In particular, the need to ensure that the research question matches the method, which matches the data and the analytic procedures. Second, the need to verify the *appropriateness of the sample*, which must consist of participants who best represent or have knowledge of the research topic and allow the researcher to obtain sufficient optimal quality data to account for all aspects of the phenomenon. Third, they suggest *collecting and analysing data concurrently*, to allow for an iterative interaction between data and analysis that forms a mutual interaction between what is known and what one needs to know. The final verification strategy they put forward entails *thinking theoretically*, meaning that ideas emerging from data are reconfirmed in new data; this ensures a gradual step-by-step development of theory, "*inching forward without making cognitive leaps, constantly checking and rechecking, and building a solid foundation*" (Morse et al., 2002, p. 18).

Despite continued controversy in the search for a fully codified and universally accepted set of criteria for assessing rigour appropriate to qualitative research, it can be safely argued that the original criteria traced out by Guba and Lincoln (1982) along with the verification strategies emphasised by Morse et al. (2002), have come to form a comprehensive blueprint of established, standardised norms for identifying core issues. The blueprint encompasses ways in which researchers involved in qualitative research can attempt to address those issues in order to increase the confidence in the approach employed, its transparency and the trustworthiness of resultant findings.

Data, data collection and data management

In doctoral research, data are the evidence that underpins the answer to your research question and can support the findings of your research project. Research data takes many different forms. They may include statistics, digital images, films, transcripts of interviews, survey data, artworks, published texts or manuscripts, or fieldwork observations. The term 'data' is more familiar to researchers in Science, Technology, Engineering and Mathematics (STEM), but any outputs from research can also be considered data. In the Humanities, Arts and Social Sciences (HASS) disciplines, for example, researchers might create data in the form of presentations, spreadsheets, documents, images, works of art, or musical scores. For PGRs in business and management related fields research data might take most of these forms, but it will most likely entail quantitative or qualitative data as discussed below.

As discussed in Chapter 2, data collection is a crucial part of your PhD. The distinction between primary and secondary data should already be well understood, with the literature review accounting for the most important secondary material. This section of the chapter focuses on primary data collection for doctoral researchers. Most PhDs will necessitate the collection of empirical data and, without well-documented, well-considered and, above all, careful collection of data in an appropriate and methodical manner, the thesis will serve little use. A considerable amount of your time in the first and second year of your studies will be spent ascertaining which data to collect, where and how to collect it and outlining how it will be used. The literature review, conceptual framework and methodology chapter are the building blocks of this process. Once you have those in place, care must also be taken in data collection and data management, allowing other researchers to examine your sources and replicate your processes, elevating your work from something that is stand-alone to a part of a greater body of knowledge.

Data quality is a complex and multifaceted construct, making it difficult to precisely define. Nevertheless, at its broadest, data quality refers to the requirements that the data are fit for their intended purpose, and that they have a close relationship with the construct they are intended to measure. The first thing to note is that the methods used should impact the manner through which you collect data and analyse it. Various methods are available and it is important to carefully select the appropriate one for your research topic.

There are two broad categories to consider. Quantitative research focuses on numerical data, or other data that can be converted into numbers, to collect and analyse information, make predictions, test relationships, identify patterns and so forth. The basic building blocks are statistics, and statistical techniques are used to interpret numerical data. For economics or finance PhD theses employing econometric analysis, data will be most likely to fall under the secondary data collection category of time series, cross-section or panel (longitudinal) data. Economic data are usually collected by national government agencies (e.g. the UK Office for National Statistics, ONS), international agencies (e.g. the International Monetary Fund, IMF) or private organisations. There are in fact a myriad of agencies and organisations collecting economic data for one purpose or another. But although there is an abundance of data available for economic research, this does not mean that the quality of such data is always good. The possibility of observational errors (by omission or commission), errors of measurement arising from approximations or round offs (up or down), missing values, sample selection and/or selectivity bias, are just some of the problems that should remind the researcher that the results of the research are only as good as the quality of the data on which they are based. This means that PGRs are well advised to devote considerable attention to discussing matters related to the quality of their data, their validity and reliability, even when such secondary data are obtained from well-established, publicly available databases.

Over the last number of decades 'big data' has become a critical component of quantitative research, as numerical data collected automatically has rapidly increased and brought new challenges for researchers. This has created considerable complexity not only in how such data are used, but also the methods of collection and, in particular, ownership of the data (Williamson and Johanson, 2017).

Qualitative research, in contrast, focuses on thematic issues, answering questions like how and why something occurs. This type of research tends to explore and tries to understand behaviours, rather than measure phenomena. Following Paradis et al. (2016), some common examples of the type of research approach used for qualitative research include:

- *Surveys or questionnaires* are used to obtain qualitative data, whose value lies in documenting attitudes, beliefs, etc. within a sample of individuals.
- *Interviews* also gather information from individuals, but in a more personalised, in-depth manner. These interviews are recorded and transcribed and then inputted to software such as NVivo to identify thematic concerns.
- *Focus groups* are used to gather information in a group setting, frequently from experts or people impacted by or close to the issue under review.
- *Observations* are used by researchers to gather information, to investigate and document daily behaviour, for example, observing how individuals undertake tasks or chores in a specific setting.
- *Textual or content analysis* examining written reports and other material such as diaries, official documentation, organisational changes and so forth, to identify key behaviours or activities.

Both approaches are quite distinct, offering different perspectives on behaviour and patterns. Quantitative work typically offers broader, aggregated findings, identifying overarching behaviour and delivering findings in more numeric and objective ways, often from a positivist perspective. Qualitative research is more nuanced, giving deeper insight into specific actions or behaviours, drawing on constructivist and interpretivist approaches (Patten and Newhart, 2017). Despite these differences, both, if properly executed, follow clear, logical processes, carefully developed plans and replicable and defensible research steps.

Alvesson and Karreman (2011) offer an excellent real-world example of how research methods influence data collection and analysis. In an account taken from a thesis using a qualitative approach, the PGR in question collected a substantial amount of material, including observations of meetings, interviews, records of conversations, etc. The result, as noted by the researcher was that he *"almost drowned in data"* (p. 9). By the estimates of the PGR he ended up using just 5% of collected material. However, as the authors note, this is not unusual in qualitative research. Continuing and detailed attention needs to be paid to the quality of qualitative data and the ways in which judgements are made about its content. What this points to, is the need to carefully record, manage and collate data as part of your research activities, choosing which data to use for evidence, but always offering access to the remainder of the collected data, in case it is requested for further clarification or verification.

Hence, an important part of data collection, whether using qualitative or quantitative approaches, is a Data Management Plan (DMP). As discussed in Chapter 1, this plan will state how you intend to collect, store and organise your data, thesis material, research notes and other supporting documentation for the duration of the research. Good data management is a necessity. Broman and Woo (2018) offer invaluable advice on good data collection techniques and procedures, specifically in relation to recording data to an electronic database. The first rule they stress is consistency in terms of naming, layout, variables, dates, key word use, phrasing, all across multiple files. This first point cannot be stressed enough, inconsistencies of record-keeping and collection make analysis and comparative actions overly complex. Furthermore, it makes replicating, verifying or re-evaluating data difficult. Other points to consider are keeping the raw data unsullied, instead making calculations and alterations in a separate file. Don't keep all your data in one, very large, electronic file (in case it corrupts). Instead, keep material organised into folders according to dates, themes, groups, interviews, etc. Create a data dictionary/index of all information and terms used. Routinely back up your files, particularly after a major revision or work session.

When collecting the data itself, there are key factors to consider. First, most doctoral research undertaken in UK business schools will require some form of ethical approval. Before this step can be undertaken, PGRs will need to know about the availability of data, its location and whether it represents a serious challenge to the researcher to collect the data, ownership of the data, whether it is confidential, what kind of permissions are required to access, record and disseminate the data. All this information will need to be determined before the researcher can even consider beginning to apply for ethical approval to gather data.

For example, gaining access to certain statistical collections in the possession of the UK data service,[36] requires not just specialist training, but also individual vetting and guarantees from the researcher's representative institution in how they will access, store and present data. Another example, from a qualitative piece of research a colleague was pursuing as part of her studies, was the necessity for Coventry University to give her ethical approval and permission to visit prisoners in jail. All the above, points to the need for careful investigation, discussion with team members and appropriate groups in your university, as well as frequent engagement with key data gatekeepers before data collection can occur.

Clarity

In this section we stress the importance of a clear, well-argued and, above all, logical progression within a thesis. Views on logic, of course, can vary greatly from person to person. One of the reasons we outlined the general structure of a thesis at the start of this chapter was to offer uniformity of understanding in terms of approach. However, clarity is somewhat different. It speaks to a PGR's ability to express ideas and understandings of research in a manner that can be easily understood, yet, maintains high academic standards in terms of writing.

---

[36] The UK Data Service is a national data service providing researchers with access to social and economic data collections such as census data, government surveys and business records.

But it is not just about the ability to write well. It is also about the difficult task of keeping the overarching theme of the research topic to the forefront of the thesis, even while writing a detailed sub-section of a chapter. Theses that fail to achieve this coherence can read well for pages and pages, but in a disconnected and/or tangential manner which serves only to confuse, disorient and discourage the reader from continuing. A traditional thesis is approximately 60,000–80,000 words of complex ideas interwoven into a single narrative about a research topic. The process of writing such a 'behemoth' is to break it down into smaller tasks, as we recommend throughout this book. However, such an approach can lead to compartmentalisation, leading to a disparate, uneven and/or fragmented piece of work unless the author repeatedly revisits and revises the work to ensure continuity and homogeneity of content and writing style.

It is this process of writing and re-writing a thesis that can be particularly dispiriting for a PGR, particularly during the writing up year when, not only have you had to focus on a task for a number of years, but now you have to revise the same chapters you have already written, often going through many successive iterations. There is, however, a very good reason for doing so; no one knows a thesis as well as the person writing it. That includes examiners. The doctoral researcher works to become a specialist in a particular topic after all. However, it does mean that when writing, the PGR can presume knowledge or understanding on behalf of the reader, which is a crucial mistake. As Golding (2017, p. 51) explains:

> To make your thesis a good read, you need to take a reader-centred approach to your writing. First work out what you want to say, but then change your focus and write it (or translate it) so it is clear, interesting and convincing for your readers.

As Golding premises, examiners of a thesis want to pass it, not fail it. But, like any normal reader, errors, disjointed writing, weak arguments or major omissions serve to distract them and give them a negative first impression. If, after that, the thesis is rambling and/or impenetrable due to a weak writing style, of course they will consolidate a negative opinion of the thesis. The most frequent conversation we have with PGRs, at all stages of their work, is the need for detail, clarity and signposting.

Explain individual roles, theoretical concepts, organisational structures and so forth with concise accuracy. Always tell the reader why you are about to write for three or four pages on a specific sub-theme; why is it important to this chapter, this section, or the overall thesis? If the piece is relevant to an earlier chapter or sub-section, say so. If you put a figure or table in, explain what it is saying and don't assume the reader will understand at a glance. Use quotes for impact or corroboration, not as a series of linked ideas that substitute for your own voice. Always explain, and if by doing so you are about to disappear down a rabbit-hole of detail, footnote with brevity instead. If you use footnotes, do it correctly though. Footnotes should be included to provide the reader with additional, relevant information about the content, possibly also to direct the reader to other sources.[37] If something is of interest but doesn't fit, put it in an Appendix (or Annexes). But make sure to state you have done so and what purpose it serves. Don't just use it as a dumping ground for any data you find.

Another point to reflect on is that the skills you will have developed will have changed your views on your own work. As you re-write, you will realise the naivety of some of your earlier thinking. Don't be too upset or embarrassed if you didn't fully understand an idea first time around; this, after all, is the purpose for revision. As you understand better, you will write better. More worrying is when you find research that contradicts your own. Some PGRs tend to panic, glossing over the work, or worse, obfuscating in the hope no one will notice. If you leave gaps in your work, they will be among the first questions asked at the *viva voce*. Don't hide or shy away from dissenting opinions. Catalogue them, engage with them and critique them.

Finally, write for purpose, write for coherence and write to the point. Reading and re-reading the work aloud helps enormously. You quickly

---

[37] Providing this additional information should be necessary but doing so in the main text could disrupt the flow of the writing. Hence the reason for using a footnote; just like the example of this one. Coincidentally, an anonymous reviewer of this book suggested to remove all the footnotes or, alternatively, incorporate them in the main text. We disagree. After all, footnotes have long been described as the hallmark of academic writing, primarily for the transmission of information, but occasionally to antagonise 'opponents' with arch rhetorical asides, as we do here.

discover a sentence is overly long when you have to pause to draw breath halfway through. Some PGRs seem to write to astonish their supervisory team, first and foremost. Don't over-engineer your work, it is a difficult enough task without adding layers of complexity to it for no purpose.

All the points discussed in this section are particularly true in the opening chapters when examiners are seeking to be reassured that the candidate knows and understands what is required of them. By the time examiners reach the end of the conceptual framework and begin to read the methodology section, most will have already formed an opinion that will influence their final grading of the thesis, as the opening sections of the thesis are the most complex and difficult parts to get right. That said, if the approach is flawed and the findings are not connected to the data and the research design, the work will also greatly suffer. This is the reason why consistency, coherence and clarity are vital.

Some final words of encouragement

If after reading this chapter you feel a little intimidated by the inherent challenges of writing an excellent PhD thesis, we should then say, *we have done a good job* with it. To appropriate an old legal adage, "*theses are like sausages, it's better not seeing them being made*".[38] But don't forget that despite the intrinsic complexities and difficulties of the task, doing research and writing the thesis should be fun. This chapter will have given you important insights into how to approach, design, develop and write your thesis. At first the task may appear daunting, especially when you realise you will need to write consistently and well on the same problem over several years. However, writing is training, the more you write, the better you get at it. There are few things more gratifying than seeing doctoral

---

38   The origins of the phrase "*Laws are like sausages. It's better not to see them being made*" is usually (and inaccurately) attributed to Otto Von Bismarck. An interesting discussion on the phrase by O'Toole (2010) can be found online at: <https://quoteinvestigator.com/2010/07/08/laws-sausages/>

researchers improve, and at great speed, not only how they scribe, but how they research, how they think, how they reflect and critique. This transformation is also one of the true joys of doing a PhD, one that makes it all worthwhile; the realisation that you are becoming an expert at something and thinking and writing to a level you may never have previously thought you could achieve.

References

Alvesson, M. and Karreman, D. (2011). *Qualitative Research and Theory Development: Mystery as Method.* London, UK: Sage Publications.
Babbie, E. and Mouton, J. (2001). *The Practice of Social Research.* South African edition. Cape Town: Oxford University Press South Africa.
Broman, K. W. and Woo, K. H. (2018). Data organization in spreadsheets. *The American Statistician*, 72(1), 2–10.
Byron, K. and Thatcher, S. M. (2016). Editors' comments: "What I know now that I wish I knew then". Teaching theory and theory building. *Academy of Management Review*, 41(1), 1–8.
Corley, K. G. and Gioia, D. A. (2011). Building theory about theory building: What constitutes a theoretical contribution? *Academy of Management Review*, 36(1), 12–32.
Coventry University (2020). Academic and General Regulations 2019/20. Online available at: <https://www.coventry.ac.uk/the-university/key-information/registry/academic-regulations/>
Creswell, J. W. and Miller, D. L. (2000). Determining validity in qualitative inquiry. *Theory into Practice*, 39(3), 124–131.
De Vita, G. (2006). Towards a culturally inclusive pedagogy in UK Higher Education: A business and management perspective. Oxford Brookes University (PhD thesis).
Delamont, S., Atkinson, P., and Parry, O. (1997). *Supervising the PhD: A Guide to Success.* Buckingham, UK: Open University Press.
Denzin, N. K. (1978). *The Research Act: A Theoretical Introduction to Sociological Methods.* New York: McGraw-Hill.
Denzin, N. K. and Lincoln, Y. S. (1994). *Handbook of Qualitative Research.* Thousand Oaks & London: Sage Publications.

Dubois, A. and Gadde, L. E. (2002). Systematic combining: An abductive approach to case research. *Journal of Business Research*, 55(7), 553–560.

Dunleavy, P. (2003). *Authoring a PhD – How to Plan, Draft, Write and Finish a Doctoral Thesis or Dissertation*. London, UK: MIT Press.

Economic and Social Research Council [ESRC] (2020). ESRC Postgraduate Funding Guide. Online and available at: <https://esrc.ukri.org/files/skills-and-careers/doctoral-training/postgraduate-funding-guide/>

Eisenhardt, K. M. (1989). Building theories from case study research. *Academy of Management Review*, 14(4), 532–550. Online, available at: <https://www.jstor.org/stable/258557?seq=1#metadata_info_tab_contents>

Finlay, L. (1998). Reflexivity: An essential component for all research? *British Journal of Occupational Therapy*, 61(10), 453–456.

Flanagan, O. J. (1981). Psychology, progress, and the problem of reflexivity: A study in the epistemological foundations of psychology. *Journal of the History of the Behavioral Sciences*, 17, 375–386.

Francis, J. R. D. (1976). Supervision and examination of higher degree students. *Bulletin of the University of London*, 31, 3–6.

Geertz, C. (1973). Thick description: Toward an interpretative theory of culture. In: *The Interpretation of Cultures: Selected Essays* (pp. 3–30). New York: Basic Books.

Gill, P. and Burnard, P. (2012). Time to end the vagaries of PhD examining? *Nurse Education Today*, 32(5), 477–478.

Gill, P. and Dolan, G. (2015). Originality and the PhD: What is it and how can it be demonstrated? *Nurse Researcher*, 22(6), 11–15.

Gioia, D. A. and Pitre, E. (1990). Multiparadigm perspectives on theory building. *Academy of Management Review*, 15(4), 584–602.

Girod-Séville, M. and Perret, V. (2001). 'Epistemological foundations'. In: Thiétart, R.-A. (Ed.). *Doing Management Research: A Comprehensive Guide*, London, UK: Sage Research Methods.

Golding, C. (2017). Advice for writing a thesis (based on what examiners do). *Open Review of Educational Research*, 4(1), 46–60. Online available at: <https://www.tandfonline.com/doi/pdf/10.1080/23265507.2017.1300862?needAccess=true>

Golding, C., Sharmini, S., and Lazarovitch, A. (2014). What examiners do: What thesis students should know. *Assessment & Evaluation in Higher Education*, 39(5), 563–576.

Guba, E. G. and Lincoln, Y. S. (1982). Epistemological and methodological bases of naturalistic inquiry. *Educational Communication and Technology*, 30(4), 233–252.

Holbrook, A., Bourke, S., Fairbairn, H., and Lovat, T. (2007). Examiner comment on the literature review in Ph.D. theses. *Studies in Higher Education*, 32(3), 337–356.

Keynes, J. M. (1936). *The General Theory of Employment, Interest and Money*. New York: Harcourt Bruce Jovanovich Inc.

Kolb, D. A. (1984). *Experiential Learning: Experience as the Source of Learning and Development* (Vol. 1). Englewood Cliffs, NJ: Prentice-Hall.

Lee, A. (2008). How are doctoral students supervised? Concepts of doctoral research supervision. *Studies in Higher Education*, 33(3), 267–281.

Lee, N. and Lings, I. (2008). *Doing Business Research: A Guide to Theory and Practice*. London, UK: Sage Publications.

Lempriere, M. (2019). *How to Structure a PhD Thesis*. Available online at: <https://www.thephdproofreaders.com/structuring-a-thesis/>

Lincoln, Y. S. and Guba, E. G. (2000). Paradigmatic controversies, contradictions, and emerging confluences. In: Denzin, N. K. and Lincoln, Y. S. (Eds.). *Handbook of Qualitative Research*. London, UK: Sage Publications.

Mathison, S. (1988). Why triangulate? *Educational Researcher*, 17(2), 13–17.

Miles, M. B. (1979). Qualitative data as an attractive nuisance: The problem of analysis. *Administrative Science Quarterly*, 24(4), 590–601.

Morse, J. M., Barrett, M., Mayan, M., Olson, K., and Spiers, J. (2002). Verification strategies for establishing reliability and validity in qualitative research. *International Journal of Qualitative Methods*, 1(2), 13–22.

O'Toole, G. (2010). 'Laws are Like Sausages. Better Not to See Them Being Made.' Quote Investigator. Online available at: <https://quoteinvestigator.com/2010/07/08/laws-sausages/>

Paradis, E., O'Brien, B., Nimmon, L., Bandiera, G., and Martimianakis, M. A. (2016). Design: Selection of data collection methods. *Journal of Graduate Medical Education*, 8(2), 263–264.

Patten, M. L. and Newhart, M. (2017). *Understanding Research Methods: An Overview of the Essentials*. New York: Taylor & Francis.

Phillips, E. M. and Pugh, D. S. (2010). *How to Get a PhD*. 5th Edition. Berkshire, UK: Open University Press.

Pratt, M. (2008). Fitting oval pegs into round holes: Tensions in evaluating and publishing qualitative research in top-tier American journals. *Organizational Research Methods*, 11(3), 481–509.

Research Excellence Framework [REF] (2021). 'Index of revisions to the 'Panel criteria and working methods' (2019/02)'. Available at:<https://www.ref.ac.uk/media/1084/ref-2019_02-panel-criteria-and-working-methods.pdf>

Rüger, S. (2016). *How to Write a Good PhD Thesis and Survive the Viva*. Knowledge Media Institute. Kents Hill, UK: The Open University.

Saldaña, J. (2021). *The Coding Manual for Qualitative Researchers.* 4th Edition. London, UK: Sage.

Saunders, M. and Lewis, P. (2012). *Doing Research in Business & Management – An Essential Guide to Planning Your Project.* Harlow, England: Pearson Education Limited.

Siggelkow, N. (2007). Persuasion with case studies. *Academy of Management Journal*, 50(1), 20–24.

Silverman, D. (2005). *Doing Qualitative Research.* London, UK: Sage Publications.

Silverman, D. (2006). *Interpreting Qualitative Data.* London, UK: Sage Publications.

Sutton, R. I. and Staw, B. M. (1995). What theory is not. *Administrative Science Quarterly*, 40(3), 371–384.

Tanggaard, L. and Wegener, C. (2016). Why novelty is overrated. *Journal of Education and Work*, 29(6), 728–745.

Van Manen, M. (1977). Linking ways of knowing with ways of being practical. *Curriculum Inquiry*, 6(3), 35–44.

Van Manen, M. (1995). On the epistemology of reflective practice. *Teachers and Teaching: Theory and Practice*, 1(1), 33–50.

Whetten, D. A. (1989). What constitutes a theoretical contribution? *Academy of Management Review*, 14(4), 490–495.

Wilkins, S., Neri, S., and Lean, J. (2019). The role of theory in the business/management PhD: How students may use theory to make an original contribution to knowledge. *The International Journal of Management Education*, 17(3), 100–116.

Wright, P. M. (2015). Rethinking "Contribution". *Journal of Management*, 41(3), 765–768.

Yin, R. K. (1981). The case study crisis: Some answers. *Administrative Science Quarterly*, 26(1), 58–65.

Yin, R. K. (1994). *Case Study Research: Design and Methods.* London, UK: Sage Publications.

GLAUCO DE VITA

5 Managing up, managing your time and managing your wellbeing

Preamble

Many postgraduate researchers (PGRs) embark on a PhD expecting to be managed by their supervisors, to have plenty of time to complete the thesis and to feel good about themselves throughout their doctoral journey. But anyone who has ever worked in academia knows all too well that for most PGRs this is wishful thinking. Any PGR working with a Director of Studies (DoS) who is disorganised, absent-minded or simply overworked (most academics easily fit at least one of these attributes) and who in the course of the PhD struggles to meet deadlines and feels increasingly unable to cope, appreciates how difficult it can be to figure out exactly what is expected of them, how to do more in less time and how to maintain sanity in the process. The **aim of this chapter** is to elaborate on several management strategies that can make a significant difference in cultivating a positive working relationship with supervisors, becoming more productive and coping better with the inevitable ups and downs by prioritising self-care.

Managing up

The term 'managing up' has become a trendy buzzword and is now commonly used in the leadership and management studies literature. Put simply, it refers to doing whatever you can to make your manager's job easier by essentially managing him or her in a way conducive to achieving your goals and delivering mutual satisfaction. It entails exerting straightforward influence, for example, by:

- anticipating problems and proactively working to prevent them.
- adjusting to your manger's style and approach to better meet their needs and fit their preferences.
- being flexible and willing to adapt in order to make your manager's job easier.

You may be wondering how the above relates to the PGR-supervisor relationship, asking yourself: 'Why should I care about managing up?', 'Isn't my PhD supervisor supposed to be the one who manages?' You should be caring about these skills because during your PhD the relationship with your supervisory team and DoS in particular will be vital to your research, your steady progress and your wellbeing. This is a strongly established finding in doctoral education research. Indeed, many empirical studies have found that a good relationship with the supervisor is associated with greater academic persistence, more satisfaction, fewer quit intentions and a higher likelihood of timely completion of the thesis (see, e.g., Ives and Rowley, 2005; Cotterall, 2013; McAlpine and McKinnon, 2013; Litalien and Guay, 2015; Leijen et al., 2016; Van Rooij et al., 2021). This relationship, therefore, really is at the core of PhD success. Hence, it must be managed, by you. Sverdlik et al. (2018) stated that your role in the PGR-supervisor relationship is just as important as your supervisor's. I would argue that that your role, by 'managing up', is *more* important. Managing up helps you to reduce communication barriers and, most importantly, to cultivate a strong, trusting relationship with your supervisors, allowing you to get the most from the supervision process and to get things done smoothly and effectively.

To manage your supervisor successfully you should have a very clear idea of your respective roles and responsibilities, where you both stand professionally and personally, and your supervisors' strengths, weaknesses and dislikes. You need to be acutely observant, perceptive and willing to adjust your behaviour to meet, ideally exceed, your supervisors' expectations. It is very much about ensuring you align your expectations to theirs.

Experience suggests that often PGRs have a different set of expectations from supervisors on how they should communicate with each other and what is the role of each. These different expectations are often the root cause of tension. Such tension can build up over time and degenerate into a rocky and, at times, unpleasant relationship.

In Table 5.1, I list the most typical cases of misaligned expectations between PGRs and supervisors on areas of critical importance for the relationship. Starting with 'intellectual support', this is a legitimate expectation by PGRs but let's be clear on what intellectual support means. For supervisors, providing intellectual support signifies challenging PGRs intellectually with an expectation that PGRs will accept constructive criticism and take feedback on board. PGRs should respond to these intellectual stimuli in a positive way, for example, by accepting they may have missed something or could improve aspects of the work accordingly. This doesn't necessarily mean that PGRs should treat everything supervisors say as gospel. They should probe the rationale of any advice given to them if there are aspects of this feedback that are not convincing or sufficiently justified. If there are any areas of your supervisors' comments that are unclear, by all means, don't be afraid to ask for clarification. But whatever you do, don't ignore supervisors' advice since, if acted upon, this is the way in which you can make the work better. No matter how negative or even demoralising feedback from a supervisor can feel, don't ever forget that this is meant to help you and your project. If your supervisor's criticism isn't particularly constructive or it is offered in a less than respectful manner, don't take it to heart; this says more about your supervisor than you. Still, try to consider if there is anything at all in those comments that may be worth taking on board. Ask yourself: '*Will this feedback ultimately enhance the thesis?*' I will never forget the sense of personal relief and admiration towards one of my past PGRs, when in an email in which he forwarded to me his first draft of the literature review, he wrote: "*Please, Glauco, be brutal in reviewing this chapter since I know I will need to raise my standard quite a bit and need specific guidance on how*". I knew then that we were going to get along just fine, in fact the chapter was pretty good anyway for a first draft.

An equally legitimate expectation of PGRs is to get 'emotional support'. Yet, far too often this translates into a constant seeking of approval,

Misaligned expectations	
PGR's expectations:	**Supervisors' expectations:**
• Intellectual support	• Able to accept criticism
• Emotional support/seeking approval/wanting to please	• Get excited about the work and value constructive criticism
• Telling you what to do	• Independence/initiative/ update us on what you found
• Proof-reading written work	• Properly presented written work
• Constructive environment	• Take responsibility for effective use of learning oppourtuntities, be pro-active and consult
• Patience/realxed pace/ 'marriage'	• Able to work under pressure/ fast pace/'move out'
• What are other PhD students or supervisors up to? Standard approach? Equal contact?	• Each PhD student and supervisor's needs and requirements are different

Table 5.1. Typical misalignment of expectations between PGRs and supervisors

desperately wanting to please the supervisor and getting excited purely for the purpose of praise. On the other hand, supervisors are mostly interested in the quality of the work. It is the research itself they want their PGRs to get excited about. Especially at the start of a PhD, many PGRs tend to be overly dependent on supervisors, expecting supervisors to tell them what to do and how to do it. While some general direction and guidance is a core responsibility of supervisors, at doctoral level, supervisors expect PGRs to show independence, original thinking and initiative in learning how to go about *their* study. Great PGRs are autonomous learners, who go to supervision meetings to update supervisors on what they found. In supervisors' minds, PhD supervision is more about lighting the fire than filling the pot and, consequently, any signal suggesting a tendency to want to be spoon fed is likely to be met with irritation and disappointment.

This irritation on the part of supervisors can be even more pronounced with respect to the input that may be expected of them on PGRs' written work. Some PGRs expect their drafts to be proofread, sanitised or even re-edited by supervisors, especially if the comments on the quality of the written work are not positive. On the other hand, supervisors expect to receive well presented, completed and polished drafts of chapters they are expected to offer feedback on. They are 'drafts' purely because they have yet to receive the seal of approval by the supervisory team but as far as supervisors' expectations are concerned, your 'draft' should actually be the very best work you can possibly produce, one that demonstrates full attention to detail, including a properly developed and double-checked list of references of all the sources cited in the text. The onus on supervisors is to explain, if there are any issues with your writing or content, what these issues are, be it frequent errors of grammar or syntax, a lack of critical thought or originality, an overly descriptive rather than inquisitive approach to engaging with existing literature, suspicions of plagiarism, etc. Any expectations of supervisors correcting such issues on your behalf is totally misplaced. Supervisors are there to point out such issues in the thesis, not to write it for you. For example, if you are aware the work needs proper proofreading, sort it out before you send your draft to your supervisors.

Another rightful expectation of PGRs is to work in a stimulating and nurturing environment. You are certainly entitled to it, especially given the hefty fees of doctoral degrees. But by the same token, you must take responsibility for your own development and for the effective use of the learning opportunities and resources that are made available to you within the university, faculty or department. These include participating in seminars, joining PGR reading groups, attending presentations by staff members or invited speakers and relevant training sessions and workshops, entering PGR thesis competitions, presenting at relevant conferences, etc. Time and time again, I have come across PGRs who express dissatisfaction about the lack of opportunities to receive additional feedback on their work but who nevertheless systematically fail to attend let alone present at seminars explicitly designed to provide such opportunities. Not good!

Some PGRs seek to work at a relaxed pace throughout the PhD, with patient supervisors, and tend to visualise the relationship with their DoS as a sort of 'marriage of convenience' that can last indefinitely. These expectations are the antithesis of what supervisors look for when taking on a new PGR. They expect their PGRs to be able to quickly learn to work at a fast pace, under intense pressure, to deliver on a deadline, complete the thesis and 'move out' after three years. Of course, they care about the individual they are looking after and probably will be as proud of their PGR's achievements as a parent would be. Nevertheless, they are conscious of the fact that the success of their supervision will also be measured by whether they can get their PGR to complete a high-quality PhD thesis within the timeline of the PhD framework, here in the UK, three years for full-time PhDs and five years for part-time ones. Hence, it is understandable that they, also for the PGR's sake, keep an eye on the clock and push their PGRs to make steady progress along the way. If you find yourself in a situation where your DoS needs to keep checking in and constantly worries about you delivering on time, chances are you are not doing it right. If so, the next section, on 'managing your time', is a 'must read'.

Finally, avoid entering a self-defeating and supervisor-deprecating mindset by focusing on what other PGRs are allegedly getting from their supervisors that you are not, how they are progressing, how frequently they say they have contact with their supervisors and how long their supervision meetings last. Each PGR, each PhD thesis and each supervisor is different, and different stages of a thesis present different challenges and call for different remedies. I have found myself in a position where, while I was desperately trying to push a PGR to make fast progress given the previous delays caused by difficulties of access to interviewees, I was, at the same time, urging another one of my PGRs to slow down. The latter had rushed through the estimation of her regressions and she seemed more concerned about completing the thesis early rather than paying due attention to the critical discussion of what the obtained results told her about the phenomenon subjected to empirical scrutiny. This was a time for her to reflect, and reflection takes time!

In addition to ensuring alignment of expectations, there are several additional behaviours that can help you take control of the relationship with your supervisors, make their and your life easier and get the most out of their experience and expertise.

Be proactive, initiate contact and be honest. You should take the initiative in maintaining regular contact with your supervisory team. At the very early stages of a PhD, formal tutorial meetings may even occur weekly, then monthly or even termly, depending on progress and requirements. Some PGRs expect too much contact and are overly dependent (remember that there is a time when help can only come from 'within'). At the other end of the spectrum, are those PGRs who lose contact altogether and disappear, forcing the DoS to chase them. Neither pattern is tolerable. Be sensible, and proactive in arranging regular meetings by emailing your supervisors while giving them plenty of alternative options of your availability in order to make it easy for them to find a suitable slot for you. The format and duration of these meetings, just like the preferred method of communication with supervisors, should evolve naturally based on mutual convenience and their preferences. It is advisable, therefore, to make sure you understand early in the relationship what those preferences are. Does your DoS prefer written emails or verbal discussion? Face-to-face or online? Does he or she prefer structured, formal meetings or informal chats? If your supervisors have a history of forgetting about scheduled meetings or being unprepared for them, send them a reminder the day before the meeting is scheduled to take place, with an agenda of what the key issues to be discussed are.

It is also good practice at the end of each meeting to take the opportunity to arrange a date and time for the next one. Shortly after the meeting, remember to send them some brief notes of what the meeting covered, a few bullet points should suffice, including any agreed follow-up actions to be completed by you (or them) by the next meeting. There may also be an institutional requirement for you, your DoS or both to keep an official record or log of such meetings. Try to be always punctual and well prepared for these meetings, making sure you have done all you had agreed to do at the previous one, and more. Indeed, don't feel constrained by just having to work to requirements. If you have the time, if you feel inspired by your reading and enthused by the progress you are making, aim to steam ahead while you can. This is *your* PhD and you are expected to take the lead in shaping your research and motivating yourself to move forward. Equally, if you are experiencing difficulties and realise you are falling behind, don't hide and, most important of all, don't lie about it. Calling off a meeting at the last minute, missing a scheduled one or going to a meeting with your DoS unprepared, without having made any progress and with silly excuses as to why, is very unprofessional and not helpful. If you are experiencing problems, if you feel stuck, if your motivation has dropped, if you have lost confidence, if you are going through personal issues that are inhibiting your progress, do let your DoS know. Being honest is, especially in these circumstances, crucial. It demonstrates good judgement, maturity, wisdom even. That said, don't ever forget your respective roles. Your DoS cannot be your counsellor, therapist or best friend. Nonetheless, the DoS should be made aware of obstacles that are hindering your progress or difficulties that are affecting your wellbeing, and they should make referrals when necessary.

Consider the message below I received from one of my former PGRs. The message is an excellent example of how to handle a potential problem by sharing candidly the reason for the delay and proactively proposing a possible solution, ahead of the crisis:

> Dear Glauco, we had booked a meeting scheduled to take place in 3 weeks to discuss your feedback for the chapter I am expected to email you in exactly one week (the agreed deadline was the 17th of June). I am sorry to say that my progress has been hindered by having to spend much time to plan for and arrange my wedding, and I can already see that if I force myself to meet the deadline, the quality of the chapter will suffer and end up being far from the standard we are both accustomed to. On this occasion, I feel I need more time to produce work I can be proud of. What I am asking, therefore, is whether it would be possible for you to grant me an extension for emailing you my completed chapter on the 24th (rather than the 17th) with a view to keeping our scheduled face-to-face meeting to discuss your feedback still on the 30th. Would one week or so be enough for you to read my chapter and send me your comments? If not, would it be at all possible to have the face-to-face feedback meeting postponed to the 15th, 16th or 17th of July (whichever suits you best, at 8:30am in your office as usual), i.e. the following month, after our respective holidays? (by the way, I would still be emailing you my chapter on 24th of June). Sorry for any inconvenience my request may cause. I know how busy you are and the importance of keeping to schedule, but it is precisely because I don't want to waste your time looking at a chapter that is not properly done to my very best ability that I am writing to you to make you aware of the difficulty I face and my extension request. Thanking you in advance, I look forward to hearing from you.

Needless to say, the extension was granted. In fact, I praised my PGR for his diligence, commitment and uncompromising attitude to placing the quality of his work at the forefront of our relationship without giving in to cutting corners. I also valued his mature approach to thinking ahead and making my job easier. He is 'managing up'. Coincidentally, look at the options for the postponed meeting and his concern about me having to read his chapter and provide feedback within one week because of his delay. His message denotes a clear awareness and sensible structure of how things can and should work between us. It also factors in any extended absences or holidays to help plan our respective schedules to help him stay on track. There is another twist about the example above that helps illuminate the notion of 'managing up' as a process. In a sense, every stride you take during your PhD journey is a micro-decision. But some decisions are more consequential than others and you – like my PGR above – need to recognise the importance of anticipating critical decisions, setbacks or delays and manage such events while ensuring your DoS is made aware of what is happening to you and how, as a result, your progress will be affected.

Of course, there will also be times when frequent, regular meetings are not needed. There will be periods when you as well as your supervisors know what you need to work on, with no impellent need for feedback or any steering from them. Just a matter of you continuing to move ahead with, say, your review of the literature or data collection. In such circumstances, say after a month during which there has been no contact, it may still be opportune for you to take the initiative by writing to your supervisors to update and reassure them that your silence is nothing to worry about, that you are well and are making steady progress.

Try to understand your supervisors, especially your DoS to navigate any differences between the two of you. Specifically, consider their strengths, their weaknesses and their likes or dislikes. Your supervisors' strengths should stem directly from their subject expertise, including publishing experience. Your DoS has the responsibility to advise you, offer guidance and support at every stage of your research, from the formulation of your main research question through to the post-viva revisions of the thesis, if any are required. They should know what a good thesis looks like, ideally having supervised many other PGRs to successful completion. They should be able to help you in anticipating serious difficulties ahead such as obstacles in accessing data, in obtaining ethical clearance or in conducting fieldwork. While you are delving into the depths and even minutiae of your topic, they should be wise in retaining their perspective on the bigger picture of the thesis, namely, where the significant original contribution of your work is likely to come from. They should also help you stay on track by keeping an eye on the clock and know, almost instinctively, when to ask you to accelerate and when it is wise to pull the breaks, pause and reflect, to ensure a timely completion of a high-quality thesis. Most importantly, you should place trust in them knowing what are 'good questions' and even 'good mistakes'. At times, as the research unfolds and the results of the project begin to appear, some unexpected insights may emerge that can quite significantly change the direction of the study that was originally envisaged. Many PGRs lack the necessary experience to be able to recognise, *prima facie*, unexpected golden finds they may have fortuitously stumbled upon, especially if emerging from unintentional exploration, 'happy accidents' or even mistakes in the approach or methodology. Great supervisors are percipient, prescient and foresighted, and have the ability to distinguish between tangents and unexpected discoveries that could be of real value to the project.

In managing up, it is even more important to *identify your supervisors' deficiencies*. There is no point ignoring them or trying to change your supervisors. Instead, try to compensate for their inadequacies to assist you in extracting as much value as you possibly can from the relationship. No matter how capable, experienced and well-read your supervisors are, don't assume they know everything. Great supervisors will recognise their own limitations and actively encourage you to interact with other senior scholars in the field about specific areas of your work where they know they are lacking. But if a supervisor feels threatened and doesn't explicitly encourage this approach, you need to take the initiative and seek out input from other recognised experts. This is also a way to build up your own personal research support network. As discussed in Chapter 6, this is an essential part of your development as an early career researcher. As you spend more and more time reading and learning about your topic, you will quickly become an expert of that topic and it may not be long before you probably know more about it than your supervisors. Hence, to ensure you get the most of your supervisors' thinking, you must be prepared to educate them on what you find, any new directions in the field or the latest thinking on your topic emerging from any new articles they may not have yet come across or had time to read.

Be empathetic. Academics are very busy people who routinely juggle many activities including teaching, administration, conferences, their own research, and who, in addition to you, most likely have numerous other PGRs they are supervising. Hence, they won't be able to offer you unlimited access, but they should be 'there' for you when you need them the most. So, ensure you make the best use of the time they can devote to you. To paraphrase the iconic line from the famous movie Jerry Maguire, 'Help *them*, to help *you*'. Also, avoid asking them to deal with things that fall outside their role, such as admin queries. Your supervisors probably dislike administration and bureaucracy as much as you do, if not more. For such queries, much better to contact PGR support staff. Supervisors are known to be very poor also at reading their PGRs' mind. So, make sure you raise important issues unbeknown to them, early, ahead of the crisis (when did Noah build the ark? Before the rain!). Supervisors are, on average, rather bad also at remembering specific issues that may be particularly important for each individual PGR they supervise. Hence, be proactive in spotting and reminding them of potential clashes ahead, bottlenecks, important events, critical follow-up actions expected of them, by alerting them well in advance.

Whatever you do, *avoid behaviours typically associated with the most common dislikes of supervisors.* PGRs who think they already know all that is required, who display lack of trust or, even worse, who question the competence of their supervisors, are unlikely to get supervisors to go the extra mile to provide help and support. But don't suck up to them or constantly tell them what you think they want to hear. Earn their respect through your commitment and the quality of your work. Finally, don't ever give your supervisors a reason to doubt your integrity or the credibility of your research (about your data, methods, etc.). If you are caught misleading them about even the smallest aspect of your project, you give them grounds to question your credibility also on the big and most important parts of your work, thereby putting at risk their as well as your reputation. Don't ever forget that integrity, to be interpreted as the practice of being honest and of adhering uncompromisingly to strong moral and ethical principles and values in research, is the cornerstone of the academic profession. A bad reputation within the research community for, in the extreme, data fabrication or academic fraud, can, therefore, destroy your academic career (see also the discussion on plagiarism, another form of academic misconduct, in Chapter 10).

The last definite 'no-no' is to go behind your supervisors' back in raising problems you blame them for. Any seemingly serious problem or dissatisfaction with your supervisors should be first discussed with them. It often happens that any confusion, misunderstanding or emotional tension that has been bothering you for a while could be resolved through a frank, five-minute conversation with them. But whether such a conversation would help clear the air or not, the point to note is that any difficulties or disagreements you may experience as part of the supervisory relationship must be raised *at the time of them occurring* directly with your supervisors in the first instance. If they are at fault, this would give them a chance to put things right. Only if failing to resolve such issues directly with them, you can then proceed to approach the relevant PGR Lead or PGR support structures within the department, graduate school or relevant doctoral college of your university as per institutional guidelines. These people and structures can help resolve any such issues through mediation and the involvement of a third party (usually a senior PGR tutor or the Director of the PhD programme) to the satisfaction of all, before the issues escalate and degenerate into formal complaints. But this process, which typically results in an official change of supervisors, is seldom smooth. It is likely to affect the sensitivities of all parties involved with usually a significant amount of grief and emotional upset by both the PGR and the supervisory team. It is for these reasons that PGRs should do some serious soul-searching, consider deeply and honestly their own reasons and motives, and explore every possible avenue to resolve amicably any differences before initiating requests for a change of supervisor or filing formal or informal complaints.

Managing your time

How can one 'manage' time? Strictly speaking, one can't. In effect, 'time management' is a preposterous construct, utterly absurd, since time itself – let alone the passage of time – is beyond our control; time flows in a fixed direction and is not reversible. That said, the term 'time management' is generally understood as the way in which we can monitor and influence *how we deal with time* (Eilam and Aharon, 2003), cognisant of the fact that time is a limited and hence precious commodity; free but priceless.

More specifically, going back to one of the earliest definitions in relevant literature (Lakein, 1973), time management refers to the process of determining one's needs, setting personal goals to achieve those needs, and prioritising and planning tasks required to achieve those goals. Thus conceptualised, time management is a critical skill that everyone needs to develop at some point in their life. For PGRs, especially those undertaking a PhD part-time alongside work, family and caring responsibilities, this skill is vital given their multiple commitments and overlapping deadlines dictated by a variety of personal and academic duties.

Indeed, in talking with the co-authors of this book, we uncovered that in over sixty years of collective experience in academia, we have yet to come across a PGR who has not, at least at some point in their PhD journey, felt panic-stricken by a fast-approaching deadline. It is fairly common to experience that overwhelmingly dreadful feeling of being unable to cope with a myriad of deliverables, while working simultaneously on, say, a publication, preparing a poster or presentation, collecting data, all on top of the inevitable administrative and/or logistical issues that need to be dealt with as part of research related activities. Not to mention the unforeseeable setbacks caused by unprecedented delays beyond one's control, which may leave PGRs even less time to complete tasks than originally envisaged. It is especially at those times that PGRs wish they had planned and managed their time better.

Of course, there is no single 'right' way to manage your time, despite a growing academic literature on the way people should plan their time effectively and the processes involved (see, e.g., Claessens et al., 2007). Different work environments impose different demands and can, therefore, determine how the concept of time is perceived. Cultural differences, too, can influence how we view time and time management (see, Brodowsky et al., 2008, among others). Moreover, how effective planning techniques are, often depends on the individual because people are different. Some need to feel the pressure of a fast-approaching deadline to start working in earnest while others fret at the thought and fold under pressure. Some are early risers, feeling that getting up and working in the early morning makes them more energetic throughout the day, helping them to accomplish more in a faster and more productive manner. Others prefer to do their research in the evening and can burn the midnight oil while enjoying the silence and lack of interruptions. Sure, people have different body clocks (circadian rhythms generated by our internal biological clocks can vary considerably from person to person) and what works for one individual might not work for another. But if you are experiencing difficulties in working effectively and efficiently, if you are frequently missing deadlines or are consistently falling behind and chasing your tail, then it might be a good idea to reflect on how you currently use your time and try to do things differently.

In what follows, I discuss some time-management strategies that you may want to try out to see what works for you. To complete your PhD in time and be a successful researcher, it is imperative that you make optimum use of the time available to you and that you find your best way for working as effectively and efficiently as possible. Effective time-management not only helps you visualise and achieve your goals, it reduces stress,[39] and helps you keep a healthy work-life balance thus making your research journey smoother and happier.

Essentially, the task of time management can be framed as the task of developing a clear, well-thought-out plan for spending our time in a way that allows us to make steady progress towards achieving our goals. In a nutshell, it is about deciding on 'things to do' given 'disposable time'. By disposable time I mean the time realistically available to us after deducting the time to be devoted *in primis* to our essential needs such as taking care of our personal hygiene, eating, sleeping, going to the dentist, etc. It is a

---

39 Without going into a detailed coverage of the definition and classification of stress, here the term is used to refer to any internal or surrounding influence that causes a disruption of our physiological or psychological equilibrium state. Although positive lessons can be gained via stressful experiences and a modicum of stress can help challenge and motivate people who perform best under pressure, too much stress or stress over a prolonged period is harmful and debilitative for learning and life.

task that inevitably requires us to *analyse*, *plan* and *prioritise* to make us more efficient. This process, in turn, effectively boils down to deciding what we should '**D**o now', what we should '**D**o later' and, of equal if not greater importance, what should fall into the category of '**D**on't do', also known as the three '**Ds**' of prioritisation. Establishing which activities fall into which 'D' is not always straightforward. In this respect, I have always found it extremely helpful to have internalised what has come to be known as the 'Eisenhower Decision Principle' (EDP),[40] according to which activities can be allocated to the 'Ds' above on the basis of the attributes 'important/unimportant' and 'urgent/not urgent'.

If you deem an activity as both important and urgent, it is a no-brainer you should give such activity the highest priority: '**D**o now'. At the other end of the spectrum, a task that is neither urgent nor important, is certainly one you should drop altogether ('**D**on't do'), thereby reducing the 'clutter' in your life to make 'space' (or 'time' as it were) for what really matters since there is no point in wasting time on 'unimportant activities'. In terms of how to deal with '**D**o later' tasks, I believe I personally owe much of my effective time management to my efforts to always try to do 'important' things *before* they become 'urgent', which helps me to avoid last-minute stress and stay ahead of schedule. If in doubt as to which 'D' the tasks related to your research progress are to be allocated, seek expert advice regarding what is urgent and/or important from your DoS.

Keeping a full schedule of the three-year PhD project plan (or five years for those enrolled part-time) can be most helpful. Many universities have it as a formal requirement. This requirement is often in the form of a Gantt chart (allowing to plot tasks scheduled over time), typically developed by the PGR in consultation with the DoS using a project 'back-casting' technique, that is, planning backwards from the end goal (PhD viva) to the current state of play (the present time). These schedules can and should be revisited by PGRs in discussion with their DoS on an annual basis to review progress and firm up plans for the following year. See Appendix 5.1

---

40   The Eisenhower Decision Principle derives from a quote attributed to former US President Dwight D. Eisenhower, "*I have two kinds of problems, the urgent and the important. The urgent are not important, and the important are never urgent.*"

for an authentic example of a Gantt chart submitted at her first Annual Progress Review (APR) milestone of the Doctoral Degree Framework of Coventry University, by one of the PGRs I currently supervise.

Of course, unpredictable delays due to unforeseen circumstances as well as stress itself are an unavoidable part of life. Hence, learn to be kind to yourself by accepting the things you cannot change or do anything about. But despite these occurrences, there is still value in keeping a schedule as a reference. As noted by Saunders and Lewis (2012, p. 68): *"Even if the inevitable happens and you find that you have some slippage in your schedule, at least you know what you are slipping from! Not having a schedule is simply unthinkable."*

Further practical tips that you may find useful in helping you to better manage your time and stay productive, are:

- *Raise your self-awareness and ask yourself difficult questions* such as 'What keeps me from doing what needs to get done?', 'How much of my time is controlled by others and how can I gain more control of my own time?', 'Which habits reduce my productivity?', 'What are my biggest time wasters and how can I cut them out?'.
- Create a *to do list*, to crystallise ideas on what you intend to do, get you to prioritise among listed items and make you accountable to yourself to get things done, a sort of self-contract.[41] But don't fall into the trap of spending more time managing your to do list than completing what's on it!
- Develop *healthy routines*, to be factored in around your work schedule. Go for a run or a walk, go to the gym, yoga classes, go swimming, bake a cake, watch a movie, play your favourite instrument. Whatever you enjoy doing, something that makes you feel good and you can look forward to, is a good activity to incorporate into your daily schedule. Try to keep healthy and fit, since it will also help your studies. As the Roman poet Juvenal wrote in the early second century AD, *"orandum est ut sit mens sana in corpore sano"* (Satire 10 of Book IV, verse

---

41   A self-contract is a kind of commitment one makes to oneself on what is to be accomplished, how and by when. While this strategy may not work as a motivator for all people, for some it does. I once had a PGR who went as far as specifying rewards for fulfilling her self-contract as well as penalties for breaking it.

356), from Latin, meaning you should pray for a healthy mind in a healthy body.
- Work in a *non-distracting environment* that helps you concentrate and get the work done. Distractions destroy purposeful action. Hence, whether you are in the library or your room, try to eliminate sources of interruptions, for example, turn off notifications from your mobile, social media and email account.
- *Fight off procrastination*. Ignoring or postponing an unpleasant or difficult task can end up in a habitual pattern of putting things off indefinitely and you can always find distractions if you are looking for one. But whether you turn to the right or to the left, your ears will hear a voice of frustration inside you saying: 'Oh my gosh, I still haven't done that!' This, in turn, can make you feel increasingly disillusioned with your work, disappointed in yourself, demotivated, guilty or ashamed. Hence, don't give in to the impulse of procrastination and schedule a full free day to start working on the task you dread the most in earnest. Focus your mind on the positive feeling of 'taking action'. As you make even small progress by finally tackling that section of the thesis that caused such apprehension, you will feel immediate relief and positive momentum will build up.
- *Be prepared to fight off negative thoughts that may arise during your PhD journey*. I would advise to do it the way top marathon runners do. Alex Hutchinson in his *New York Times* bestseller, *Endure – Mind, Body and the Elastic Limits of Human Performance* (2018), reminisces about his 1990s track team group sessions with a sport psychologist who introduced them to an incredibly powerful visualisation technique that I believe can be applied to a range of different contexts to help us perform optimally. The five 'Rs' self-talk technique for stopping quitting thoughts during a long-distance race, Hutchinson explains, are: Recognise, Refuse, Relax, Reframe and Resume. That's what you need to tell yourself when self-doubt starts creeping up about your PhD and you begin drifting off the pace.
- *Use a calendar*, to remind you at a glance of key deadlines for the week or the month, to help you avoid clashes and foresee potential bottlenecks in your schedule, ahead of the 'traffic'. You could even schedule in your calendar the dates of your booked holidays, as a motivational reminder of how long you need to sweat before your next well-earned break.

- *Break large tasks into smaller, more manageable parts*, even relatively small chunks of a larger project that you can complete in one (two- or three-hour long) sitting. Tell yourself: 'I may not be able to make great strides with my project today, but I will do small things in a great way.' Just like I did when working on this section of the chapter you are reading, which was 'the small item' in my own to do list of today, not the whole chapter. Indeed, avoid setting overly ambitious tasks over too tight a deadline. You will find it hard to complete them or complete them to the right standard, thus setting yourself up for disappointment. On this account, it is important to learn how to accurately estimate the likely duration of tasks.
- If you are not in the mood for writing or struck by writer's block, *don't be too harsh on yourself*. Give yourself permission to write badly, take the pressure off by doing something else from your to do list or take a break altogether. And be kind to yourself also when making mistakes you can learn from. If you have just walked through another blind alley in your research, don't despair. Rationalise it in the way Thomas A. Edison (often described as America's greatest inventor) did, when he said, "*I have not failed. I have just found 10,000 ways that won't work*". Remember, good judgement comes from experience and much of that comes from bad judgement.
- Accept that progress on the thesis is not necessarily going to be linear. Sometimes you must *be prepared to take one step back in order to then move two steps forward* (re-read Edison's quote above). Furthermore, stepping back can be vital to fully absorb or digest complex ideas, to reflect further on them and generate new propositions or approaches to tackle the task. It can also help you take stock of where you really are and gain a better perspective; you can't see the picture if you are in the frame. So, schedule time for such seemingly unproductive yet necessary phases.
- Plan some fun activities to *reward yourself*, something to look forward to while pushing ahead with work. Working non-stop on your thesis and often staying in the library until very late hours is not sustainable. It will drain you of both physical and mental energy, slow you down and be detrimental to your health (De Vita, 2021). Physical and mental energy are finite resources that run low if you use them too much for prolonged periods. Hence, don't fall into the trap of wanting to wear exhaustion like a badge of honour and seek to establish a healthy work-life balance.

Managing your wellbeing

The concept of 'wellbeing' is complex and multifaceted. Although a precise definition is still the subject of debate in relevant literature (Schmidt and Hansson, 2018), it is commonly understood as denoting a general state of comfort, wellness or happiness. Physical health, of course, might be said to be a constituent of wellbeing, but it is not taken to be all that matters. More comprehensively, wellbeing is expected to derive from the achievement of a balanced and fulfilling life across many dimensions. These include: a physical dimension, relating to our lifestyle and general state of health; a psychological dimension, based on our ability to cope with everyday life and how we feel about ourselves; a social dimension, relating to our need for acceptance from others; a spiritual dimension, to help us find meaning in life; an intellectual dimension, to expand our knowledge of the world around us; and a financial dimension, to enable us to support ourselves and feel sufficiently secure (De Vita, 2021). These dimensions speak for themselves as to why wellbeing is of great importance and why it is worth seeking and promoting.

PGRs are likely to face a variety of challenges across one or more of the above dimensions that may affect their mental health and wellbeing during their studies. Managing the relationship with their supervisors and managing their time on top of the pressure to produce high-quality research by a given deadline, are just some of them. Often PGRs face financial pressures, forcing them to do some part-time work alongside the PhD to support themselves, in addition to the typical stresses and strains of life, ranging from logistical issues to trying to maintain personal relationships at a time when they are still developing a sense of self and their new identity as a researcher. For PGRs coming from abroad, the challenges are compounded by adaptation issues that include being separated from family and friends for quite a long time and feeling homesick, the discomfort caused by culture shock and wider integration problems pertaining to adjusting to life in a different country (De Vita, 2021).

Given these challenges, it is not surprising that at some point of their doctoral journey, many PGRs experience mental wellbeing difficulties.

Indeed, existing research on doctoral candidates has consistently found high stress levels (see, *inter alia*, Kernan et al., 2011; Wyatt and Oswalt, 2013; Schmidt and Hansson, 2018), mental health concerns (e.g. Pallos et al., 2005; Hyun et al., 2006) and alarming physical health repercussions (e.g. Kernan et al., 2011; Juniper et al., 2012). Several studies have also found that financial stress, as indicated by higher education students' financial concern, is associated with mental health outcomes (see the review article by McCloud and Bann, 2019). In addition, a sense of belonging, disruption to the research programme and future employment prospects, sickness and additional caring responsibilities, can constitute particularly problematic issues for many PGRs. It is likely that social distancing measures, lockdowns and other restrictions related to the recent Covid-19 pandemic, including restrictions on travel, have amplified these concerns.[42]

Of course, anyone, PGRs included, has good and bad days. We all experience days when we are feeling a bit down, a little worried or not at our best. This is normal. I can attest to having spent many sleepless nights throughout my career being concerned about research projects I was working on. Something which, when it happens, usually makes me laugh in the morning because it reminds me of one of the funniest quotes of the Peanuts comic-strip character Charlie Brown, which goes, "*Sometimes you lie in bed at night and you don't have a single thing to worry about. That always worries me!*".[43]

But jokes aside, prolonged periods of low mood and self-esteem, of feeling anxious, fatigued, empty, very lonely or sad, overly worried or

---

42 I refer interested readers to the UK Council for Graduate Education (UKCGE) report 'Doctoral degrees and the potential impact of Covid-19 on current postgraduate researchers: What are the significant considerations?' (see <http://www.ukcge.ac.uk/article/covid-19-doctoral-considerations-guidance-note-456.aspxo>).

43 I apologise if my own way of exorcising an unquiet state of mind through humour may cause offence to some. Issues and questions linked to mental wellbeing are, indeed, serious and profound. However, in my defence, I point out that Ludwig Wittgenstein, considered by some to be one of the greatest philosophers of the twentieth century, has been quoted by Henry Dribble as saying: "*A serious and good philosophical work could be written consisting entirely of jokes.*" (Dribble, H., 2004, 'A View from the Asylum' in *Philosophical Investigations from the Sanctity of the Press*, p. 87).

stressed, especially if such feelings are affecting your day-to-day functioning, should not be taken lightly. They are tell-tale signs that something is not quite right, and you should immediately seek professional advice regarding your mental health and consult the relevant services available to you within the university. Do not suffer in silence and do not feel any sense of shame or embarrassment in needing or seeking help (De Vita, 2021).

While the Covid-19 pandemic has exacerbated mental health problems globally, an upside is that it has also brought the importance of mental wellbeing to the forefront, helping many organisations, including universities, to build a better understanding of mental health issues and explore new ways to support each other (De Vita, 2021). Coventry University, for example, launched a series of related initiatives, including a 'Time to Talk Day'. This is an annual event aimed at encouraging open conversations about mental health and wellbeing, and at highlighting how even small things such as a virtual message to a peer or a socially distanced 'walk and talk' can have the power to make a difference. In the UK, all universities have a 'Counselling Service' that offers a range of free and confidential services, often including individual therapy, group therapy, workshops on relaxation, self-esteem and mindfulness, and online self-help applications. Your university 'Student Services' may also be able to direct you to specialist support that is available to you locally.

Notwithstanding the importance of making sure you look for help when you need it, you should learn how to prioritise self-care in order to manage any stress more effectively and stay on top of your wellbeing. As noted in a recent Blog I wrote on the subject (see De Vita, 2021), strategies that have often been found useful in this respect, include:

- *Staying connected and avoiding isolation.* We are social beings and frequent contact with family, friends and peers, is important. So, schedule regular catchups with them, in person or online. Join student societies around recreational activities that are of interest to you, to socialise and make new friends. Study groups or reading circles, too, provide spaces for socialisation while offering further opportunities to enhance your learning and share experiences with other PGRs who may have similar concerns or face similar challenges.

- *Keeping active*, as discussed above, plays a critical role in both your physical and mental wellbeing. Sports and exercise are a great way to stay healthy, to take your mind off your research when you need a break, and to improve your mood and maintain motivation. Universities provide a myriad of opportunities to join different sport clubs.
- *Scheduling time to relax*. Despite its overuse, the old cliché 'a PhD is more like a long-distance run than a sprint' may still be said to convey a useful point. A PhD cannot be done in apnoea, solely focusing on submerging yourself into the thesis. To keep yourself from feeling like you are drowning, to be productive and stay healthy, you need to pace yourself and maintain balance in your life. Hence, schedule in your routines also activities that help you relax and recharge your batteries, including plenty of rest.
- *Developing self-awareness* of your wellbeing and learning to recognise the early signs of starting to feel a little out of kilter. Educate yourself by attending workshops or visiting the university webpages related to health and wellbeing. The latter offer useful resources, including advice about physical health, mental and emotional health, eating well, sexual health, alcohol and drugs, and safety.

Some final words of encouragement

There will be many lows as well as highs throughout your doctoral journey. You will experience moments of confusion, internal conflict and doubt, and go through a rollercoaster of emotions, including feelings of malaise and, at times, loneliness. It is important that you know from the outset that this is not abnormal. And don't lose sight of the fact that although a large part of your learning will be conducted through independent study, you are not alone, you are part of a community. Don't be afraid to look for help when you need it and ensure you prioritise your mental health and wellbeing. If effort, determination and endurance are the yin of pushing through to a successful PhD completion, looking after yourself is the yang. This is an important part of getting the most out of your university experience alongside sharpening many skills that will be indispensable throughout the rest of your life and career.

Appendix 5.1. PGR's GANTT chart of PhD schedule for second year

TASK	1	2	3	4	5	6	7	8	9	10	11	12
MONTH	Jan	Feb	Mar	Apr	May	June	Jul	Aug	Sept	Oct	Nov	Dec
Module 7010CRB: 'Introduction to Teaching and Learning in Higher Education'	▓											
Complete Chapter Three (Data collection) and Chapter Four (Methodology)	▓	▓										
Data analysis				▓	▓	▓						
Write up the results chapter; and, jointly with supervisors, draft a research paper for submission of publication to *Journal of Economic Studies*								▓	▓	▓		

TASK	1	2	3	4	5	6	7	8	9	10	11	12
MONTH	Jan	Feb	Mar	Apr	May	June	Jul	Aug	Sept	Oct	Nov	Dec
Submission of first publication from PhD with supervisors										▓	▓	
Prepare for the 2nd PRP and plan the detailed schedule of the 3rd year										▓	▓	▓
Further statistical software training and practice			▓	▓	▓	▓	▓	▓	▓	▓	▓	▓
Participate in many useful and interesting activities (such as reading groups), training workshops and events			▓	▓	▓	▓	▓	▓	▓	▓	▓	▓
PENDING (registered, currently on a waiting list)												
Participate in the FBL PGR poster presentation symposium												

Source: Ms XXXXX, 1st year PhD student (1st PRP at Coventry University, January 2020).

References

Brodowsky, G. H., Anderson, B. B., Schuster, C. P., Meilich, O., and Ven Venkatesan, M. (2008). If time is money is it a common currency? Time in Anglo, Asian, and Latin cultures. *Journal of Global Marketing*, 21(4), 245–257.

Claessens, B. J. C., van Eerde, W., Rutte, C. G., and Roe, R. A. (2007). A review of the time management literature. *Personnel Review*, 36(2), 255–276.

Cotterall, S. (2013). More than just a brain: Emotions and the doctoral experience. *Higher Education Research and Development*, 32(2), 174–187.

De Vita, G. (2021). Coventry University Research Blog: 'Postgraduate researchers, their mental wellbeing and Covid-19: A personal note', available at: <http://blogs.coventry.ac.uk/researchblog/postgraduate-researchers-their-mental-wellbeing-and-covid-19-a-personal-note/>

Dribble, H. (2004). "A View from the Asylum". In *Philosophical Investigations from the Sanctity of the Press*. Lincoln, NE: iUniverse, Inc.

Eilam, B. and Aharon, I. (2003). Students planning in the process of self-regulated learning. *Contemporary Educational Psychology*, 28(3), 304–334.

Hutchinson, A. (2018). *Endure. Mind, Body and the Curiously Elastic Limits of Human Performance*. London, UK: Harper Collins Publishers.

Hyun, J. K., Quinn, B. C., Madon, T., and Lustig, S. (2006). Graduate student mental health: Needs assessment and utilization of counseling services. *Journal of College Student Development*, 47(3), 247–266.

Ives, G. and Rowley, G. (2005). Supervisor selection or allocation and continuity of supervision: Ph.D. students' progress and outcomes. *Studies in Higher Education*, 30(5), 535–555.

Juniper, B., Walsh, E., Richardson, A., and Morley, B. (2012). A new approach to evaluating the well-being of PhD research students. *Assessment & Evaluation in Higher Education*, 37(5), 563–576.

Juvenal (1992). *The Satires*. Translation by Niall Rudd. Oxford, UK: Oxford University Press.

Kernan, W., Bogart, J., and Wheat, M. E. (2011). Health-related barriers to learning among graduate students. *Health Education*, 111(5), 425–445.

Lakein, A. (1973). *How to Get Control of your Time and Life*. New York: Peter H. Wyden.

Leijen, Ä., Lepp, L., and Remmik, M. (2016). Why did I drop out? Former students' recollections about their study process and factors related to leaving the doctoral studies. *Studies in Continuing Education*, 38(2), 129–144.

Litalien, D. and Guay, F. (2015). Dropout intentions in PhD studies: A comprehensive model based on interpersonal relationships and motivational resources. *Contemporary Educational Psychology*, 41, 218–231.

McAlpine, L. and McKinnon, M. (2013). The most variable of variables: Student perspectives. *Studies in Continuing Education*, 31(2), 109–125.

McCloud, T. and Bann, D. (2019). Financial stress and mental health among higher education students in the UK up to 2018: Rapid review of evidence. *Journal of Epidemiology & Community Health*, 73(10), 977–984.

Pallos, H., Yamada, N., and Okawa, M. (2005). Graduate student blues: The situation in Japan. *Journal of College Student Psychotherapy*, 20(2), 5–15.

Saunders, M. and Lewis, P. (2012). *Doing Research in Business & Management – An Essential Guide to Planning Your Project*. Harlow, UK: Pearson Education Limited.

Schmidt, M. and Hansson, E. (2018). Doctoral students' well-being: A literature review. *International Journal of Qualitative Studies on Health and Well-being*, 13(1), 1–14.

Sverdlik, A., Hall, N. C., McAlpine, L., and Hubbard, K. (2018). The PhD experience: A review of the factors influencing doctoral students' completion, achievement, and well-being. *International Journal of Doctoral Studies*, 13, 361–388.

Van Rooij, E., Fokkens-Bruinsma, M., and Jansen, E. (2021). Factors that influence PhD candidates' success: The importance of PhD project characteristics. *Studies in Continuing Education*, 43(1), 48–67.

Wyatt, T. and Oswalt, S. B. (2013). Comparing mental health issues among undergraduate and graduate students. *American Journal of Health Education*, 44(2), 96–107.

JASON BEGLEY

6 Making the most of training and development opportunities

Preamble

One of the motivations for this book was evidence of a rapidly changing landscape for doctoral studies, not just within the UK but also internationally. Postgraduate research, once the preserve of academia, has drawn increasing attention from a range of actors, particularly national governments seeking to upskill their labour forces. Growing stakeholder intervention, looking to broaden opportunities and diversify doctoral candidature, has seen more sophisticated approaches to developing researchers; where once PhD supervision was akin to a skilled craftsperson training an apprentice, this approach is now marked by greater standardisation of basic research skills allied to bespoke instruction in more advanced, niche expertise. Training and development, then, has taken on major significance for PGRs, most notably in the last two decades (Duke and Denicolo, 2017). However, this transition may not always be appreciated by supervisory teams or, more pertinently, PGRs still mired in traditional perspectives on the purpose and approach to PhDs. The **aim of this chapter** is to address this potential gap. The chapter starts by contextualising the changes that have occurred to doctoral research, focusing on the UK. Next, it examines training and development needs for PGRs from two perspectives, namely, during their doctoral studies and afterwards. Finally, the chapter focuses on changing mindsets around post-doctoral career pathways and the need to prepare appropriately in terms of skills learning, a theme further developed in Chapter 12 of this book.

The ongoing evolution of doctoral research

The nature of postgraduate research has greatly altered over the last two decades, not just within the UK, but internationally as well. No longer are doctoral studies just a means for accessing higher education (HE) work opportunities. Increasingly, a PhD is seen as a desirable qualification with employers outside the education sector, as well as within. As anticipated in Chapter 1, PGRs develop a wide range of skills as part of their studies and a vital part of their time as a doctoral candidate should be spent identifying their own strengths as a researcher, as well as training to complement or improve existing skills. It is crucial, however, to understand and appreciate why a doctoral qualification is so highly prized. Doing a PhD is not solely about acquiring specific, codified knowledge that can be easily documented and transferred. It is mostly about tacit knowledge, rooted in experiential learning, practice and values. Skills are honed and improved through working with mentors, socialising with peers and actively embedding oneself within the appropriate research environment.

As important, it should be noted, is the need to identify the skills that will be honed and developed as part of a researcher's doctoral studies and activities. It has been my experience in the past that PGRs, when being advised of the value of undertaking training and development during their studies, tend to hear training with a capital 'T' and development with a small 'd'. Their instinct is to seek out classes that will impart knowledge, giving them a perceived information edge in the market by adding value to their CVs. Rather than seeking elusive information that will reveal the secrets of being a researcher, training and development should be viewed as being akin to refinement, working to improve a strong base of skills to create a well-rounded, well-developed researcher. Training and development decisions should reflect this reality; filling explicit knowledge gaps where necessary but also continuously working to make the most of the abilities already in evidence. As repeatedly noted in this book, PhDs are a very specific task undertaken to answer a very specific question, but as a part of this process a doctoral candidate will need to demonstrate their learned skills as a researcher.

It is these skills, the ability to analyse, critique, structure a project around an argument and develop it through detail-oriented observation, that are increasingly highly prized in the private sector in a wide variety of activities, for example, research and design, management, new knowledge economy roles, etc. Research shows that doctoral students either underestimate or undervalue the appeal of these skills to employers (De Grande et al., 2014) This may in part be because the growth in demand for PhD holders in the private sector is still not fully appreciated. From an early stage the research doctorate was solely seen as a gateway to academia, serving as evidence of research capability. It impacted a relatively small number of students, usually those keen to pursue a career in HE, and its delivery was left to departments within HE institutions (Park, 2007; Barnes, 2013). Supervisors guided doctoral candidates down a specific research pathway and any training was specific to the PhD, sporadic and *ad hoc* (Fourie-Malherbe, 2016).

This began to change in the late 1980s in response to two emerging forces: a growth in the numbers undertaking research doctorates and a growth in demand for graduates with specific research skills (Gregory, 1995; Park, 2007). At the heart of the debate was the true purpose of a research doctorate, with those who warned against standardisation and dilution of doctoral research (Brown, 2001) set in opposition to those who believed that "*postgraduate research and study provides an opportunity for graduates to develop expertise and thinking skills that will be in high demand in parts of the knowledge economy*" (Matlay et al., 2014). Importantly, the latter group included policymakers, senior administrators in HEIs as well as inter-institutional bodies, for example, the Economic and Social Research Council (ESRC). By the beginning of the new millennium a surge of government reviews, driven by a desire to re-purpose the doctorate into a qualification with a broader appeal to employers other than universities, created a new emphasis on skills, skills training and career development with doctoral research activities[44] (Denicolo et al., 2016; Duke and Denicolo,

---

44 This trend was mirrored internationally, particularly in Europe where the Bologna declaration and the ensuing processes that emerged committed over forty-nine European countries to improving access, standards and support – in the form of training and development – to higher education, including postgraduate research.

2017; EHEA, 2020). Over the last two decades what has emerged as a consequence is a re-casting of the research doctorate as a vehicle for entry into high-skilled and highly paid careers in the private sector, with concomitant expansion of skills and training opportunities for doctoral researchers that focus on non-academic career pathways.

It should be noted, though, that many PGRs are still highly motivated by the desire to forge an academic career pathway. It is interesting to note that in the most recent Postgraduate Research Experience Survey 40% of respondents sought training in methods, while just 14% wanted training in transferable skills (Williams, 2019, p. 11). A comprehensive survey by Vitae[45] in 2013 showed that 44% of PGRs found employment in HEIs (Vitae, 2013, p.12). A complementary detailed survey of 266 postgraduate researchers by Matlay et al. (2014) noted that in terms of career intentions, the largest number of respondents (27%) wanted to remain in higher education for work purposes, with a further 16% hoping to perform research in the public sector, 16% wanting to be independent researchers and just 11% seeking private sector employment as researchers. More recent data on PGRs is more difficult to parse, as their returns are for all postgraduates, but they at least show that 79% of postgraduates were gainfully employed in high-skilled work in 2019 (HESA, 2019).

A look at statistical returns from HESA for doctoral degree recipients in 2019 is also illuminating.[46] Seventy percent of researchers completing their doctorate went on to full-time employment. Ten percent were engaged part-time, while a further 9% were engaged in 'employment and further study' according to HESA figures for 2017/2018. Only 2% were unemployed. Graduates with a known disability were more likely to be in part-time employment or voluntary work than graduates with no known disability. 2,220 of 12,660 PhD recipients were running their own business, self-employed/freelancing or developing a portfolio. However, only

---

45 Vitae is the UK leader in the professional development of researchers. It is part of the Careers Research and Advisory Centre, working with HEIs and government departments to improve researcher opportunities through innovation, training and resources, as well as events.
46 Latest year for which data are available at the time of writing.

Training and development opportunities 143

57% of PGRs were on an open-ended or permanent contract, with 40% being on some form of fixed contract (HESA, 2019). In other words, many PGRs don't immediately gain from receiving a doctorate. Instead they are at the starting line of their new careers and still have a vista of opportunities opening up before them.

This is, perhaps, the greatest misconception many PGRs have about their doctoral journey. They undertake it under the illusion that once they complete their studies, they will be so competitive in the job market that they will blow their rivals away and be a shoo-in for a job. Yet, the real value of a PhD is not that it makes doctoral graduates irresistible to employers (though, of course, it does make them highly desirable), rather it creates a range of new career opportunities that otherwise would not be open to them. However, these new opportunities are also much sought after and highly competitive. This point is crucial to training and development; PGRs need to understand that doctoral degrees are the entry requirement for the jobs they seek and they have to supplement their CV offer with a specific set of skills and training outputs that will make them more attractive to recruiters (for more advice on this, see Chapter 12).

What is encouraging from the evidence supplied by HESA is that having received their award, most postdoctoral researchers expressed high levels of job satisfaction. Only 7% of those receiving a PhD and entering full-time employment felt their skills were underutilised. Only 5% said their current work did not fit into their future plans. These figures were higher for part-time employees, 13% and 8%, respectively, and markedly different for voluntary workers (22% and 8%, respectively). Unsurprisingly, the highest dissatisfaction ratings were recorded by those who were not in employment, 56% and 57%, respectively (HESA, 2019). However, as noted earlier, the numbers of doctoral graduates returned as unemployed was very small (2%) which means that the vast majority of those receiving doctoral awards in the UK were following a career path of their choice and using the skills acquired as part of their doctorate training and development.

The data sources discussed above help show how perceptions are changing around doctoral degrees and their value beyond academic career pathways. Central to these changes are the new approaches to training and development that have emerged in higher education over the last two decades. Recognising this, key institutions and groups have acted to offer guidance to doctoral researchers around appropriate training workloads.

One further significant development in terms of the HEI's PGR training has been a greater sharing of resources and linking up of departments across universities, at least in the UK. For example, as pointed out by an anonymous reviewer of this chapter, in economics, it is not uncommon for smaller departments in universities outside the 'top 10', to share courses, library facilities, seminars and even faculty advisors across three or four different universities. These clusters (usually based on geographic location) have become more prevalent and important over the past decade. Along similar lines, Doctoral Training Alliance (DTA) programmes, centrally co-ordinated by the University Alliance (an alliance of UK universities) team on behalf of its partners,[47] combine DTA members and expert external trainers, to deliver a wide variety of discipline specific and professional skills training.

Skills and training guidelines for PGRs

UK HEIs have been tasked with providing training and development opportunities for doctoral researchers. Setting aside the question of the appropriateness of these changes to the purpose of the PhD, the major takeaway for prospective doctoral candidates is that training and development during their period of study has become a central activity for novice researchers. From a very early stage in their careers they need to be preparing for postdoctoral careers that include the possibility of non-academic work. This fact may not always be appreciated by supervisors who could still consider an academic route to work, often the only route they know, as preferable to all others. This may cause them to place too great an emphasis on academic concerns without the requisite urgency required to encourage their charges to think beyond the narrow confines of their own, immediate field of research. Despite this, supervisors remain an essential part of the

---

47   See full list of partner universities at: <https://unialliance.ac.uk/dta/partners/>.

PhD experience (Hockey, 1995) as they are both guides and gatekeepers to academic excellence. What has grown up around them is a whole raft of supporting services that require considerable skill for the uninitiated to navigate. A hybrid system has emerged where supervisors oversee academic learning and development, the central part of the research degree, but professional support services, often at faculty or school level, engage in inter/intra-institutional and interdisciplinary training of PGRs. Doctoral candidates are expected to self-assess their needs and identify skills gaps, which are then filled through bespoke training solutions.

Self-assessment can often be a tricky process that appears subjective if boundaries are not delineated. Thankfully, considerable guidance is on offer from leading research organisations. UK Research and Innovation (UKRI) is a governmental body in charge of allocating funding to UK Research Councils, as well as supplying guidelines on research activities and training. Seven Research Councils are captured under the umbrella of UKRI including the ESRC, the largest funder of social and economic research in the UK. The ESRC is particularly important for Business School doctoral researchers as a source of training and development support. For example, the Council published postgraduate training and development guidelines in 2015 (including a training and development strategy for PGRs from 2017 to 2023). A key takeaway from the document is the vision the ESRC has for future researchers:

> Research Organisations will be expected to demonstrate that their training will enable students to work in collaboration with a range of non-academic partners and to work effectively in an interdisciplinary environment. (ESRC, 2015)

These guidelines very much echo the overarching perspectives of UKRI which has also produced a statement of expectations for postgraduate training (UKRI, 2020). Here they explain their belief that researchers should be perceived as being skilled workers able to contribute across the entire national economy (ibid.). This goes far beyond the traditional aims for a research doctorate, the major focus of which, originally, was to contribute to a specific discipline alone. The recommended means to achieving the research vision of UKRI and the ESRC is through training cohorts. In other words, a move away from the craftsperson-trainee apprenticeship model and a move toward institutionally supported group activities, based on the understanding that researchers learn from their peers as well as beside them.

While this may appear to resemble closely undergraduate and taught master's methods of delivery, the understanding and reality are far different. In effect, as doctoral researchers, no matter how novice, the expectation is that you will be part of a research community, a network of peers working together to improve research skills, while working separately through guided supervision to answer specific academic questions related to a research topic. Again, this approach dovetails with earlier observations in Chapter 2 about doctorates needing to both demonstrate academic contribution, but also the research skills of the PGR. Supervisory teams oversee the academic component of PhDs, but increasingly PGR support services in HEIs are taking charge of the delivery of skills training through modules and workshops, as well as research development through seminars and career events, examples of which will be discussed later in this chapter. Sursock et al. (2010) observed the emergence of this services-centric approach to HE, stressing the growing importance of internal quality processes. As a consequence of these changes, Ward (2013) observed that broadly three models of PhD delivery have emerged that HEIs in the UK follow. They are:

- The apprenticeship model.
- The mentoring model.
- The administrative model.

The first two approaches are built around the supervisory team – differing mostly in the perceived role of the Director of Studies (DoS) – placing a greater emphasis on academic development and achievement. The administrative model is a more process-oriented pathway, focusing on transparency, an audit trail and stated objectives met at regular stages of the PhD.

The latter approach is favoured by national institutions and other education funding bodies. UKRI and the ESRC, for example, explicitly state a preference for the administrative model (Ward, 2013; ESRC, 2015). The Researcher Development Framework, discussed in the next section, is built around the concept of having multiple layers of support for skills training and development (Vitae, 2011). The major advantage of this approach is to remove the onus of general training and development from supervisory teams, offering a more standardised learning experience as well as committing considerably more resources to the support of PGR development. However, this can also lead to something of a disconnect between PGRs and their supervisory teams. For example, PGRs who value the close relationship of a supervisory team can sometimes feel disconcerted to be redirected elsewhere for their training opportunities. They can misconstrue this decision as evidence that training is a lower priority for a supervisor keen to offload more (perceived) mundane activities. Nevertheless, it is important to understand the advantages of this model of delivery, offering as it does consistent outcomes. A good way for both PGRs and supervisory teams to maximise the value of accessing multiple sources of training and development, is to sit down as a team, early on in the life cycle of an individual PGR, and discuss at length the training and development needs of the researcher, shaped by referencing the Researcher Development Framework.

Using the Researcher Development Framework as a training tool

At this point it would be useful to discuss what skills will be acquired and to identify the most useful and important development to pursue. One of the most useful tools that has grown in popularity amongst PGRs over the last number of years is Vitae's Researcher Development Framework (RDF). You will have seen the organisation of Vitae mentioned frequently throughout this book. It is one of the key organisations in the UK helping develop researchers at all levels, but it shines particularly brightly in the area of researcher career development and training. Over the last decade Vitae has been at the forefront[48] of work examining doctoral researchers' career pathways (Duke and Denicolo, 2017). In 2010,

---

48 Initially, this ran parallel to the work of research councils. For example, in 2001 the research councils issued a joint statement on skills training requirements for

Vitae released the first version of the RDF, which has since become the most popular tool for researcher development and skills identification. Its value lies in its widespread use, allowing a degree of uniformity to be adopted in terms of training approaches amongst units and organisations tasked with upskilling PGRs. The other major reason for the growth in use of the RDF, or the research development wheel as it is also called, is its simplicity.

There are three layers to the RDF, laid out in a circular formation. The inner circle contains descriptors used to identify excellent research characteristics, derived from empirical data and interviews with experienced researchers. These descriptors within the inner circle are divided into four domains, in a spoke and wheel design (Vitae, 2011):

- Domain A: Knowledge and intellectual abilities: The knowledge, intellectual abilities and techniques to do research.
- Domain B: Personal effectiveness: The personal qualities and approach to be an effective researcher.
- Domain C: Research governance and organisation: Knowledge of the professional standards and requirements to do research.
- Domain D: Engagement, influence and impact: The knowledge and skills to work with others to ensure the wider impact of research.

The middle layer of the RDF has twelve sub-domains, aligned to correlate with the inner circle's four domains. The outer layer of the RDF contains three to five phases associated with each of the domains and sub-domains, with each phase representing a distinct stage of development or performance related to research excellence. According to Vitae (2011) the descriptors encompass *"the knowledge, intellectual abilities, techniques and professional standards to do research, as well as the personal qualities, knowledge and skills to work with others and ensure the wider impact of research"*.

---

research students which would encourage the ESRC to publish annual missives on PGR training guidelines (ESRC, 2005). The Arts and Humanities Research Council has also produced a research training framework guide that can provide useful insights to interested doctoral candidates (AHRC, 2011; Ward, 2013).

Starting from the inner circle the researcher identifies the domains and sub-domains relevant to their research area of interest, as well as to their future career development. They are then able to identify their own skills gaps and skills training needs, though it is better to do so in consultation with supervisory teams and other PGR support services. Too frequently PGRs identify perceived personal failings they wish to address, rather than areas of greater relevance. Researchers are not expected to fully develop all domains to the same level. Instead they are expected to identify areas of growth and development they wish to encourage, or areas they find interesting or enjoyable to engage with. The RDF also helps researchers understand the key skills they are developing and that employers will find attractive. Then, with the support of their supervisory teams and support services within their institution, develop an action plan, that is, a timeline of training activities they wish to pursue, to flesh out their already ongoing development as part of their doctoral studies. Vitae also provides an action planning tool to support this exercise.

By tailoring training, PGRs gain a better understanding of their own strengths and weaknesses, enabling them to accurately identify and promote their own abilities. Furthermore, since support services are well versed in the use of the RDF, they will also be very capable in helping design a bespoke action plan. Increasingly PGR support services are delivering training solutions closely aligned with the RDF descriptors. Moreover, supervisory teams are also able to work closely with PGRs on RDF descriptors development, removing some of the challenges around self-assessment of skills and training needs. Furthermore, having a stated career goal from the beginning will also greatly benefit this process. Of course, one size does not fit all and sometimes PGRs can find they are not a perfect fit to the RDF descriptors. Or, they begin to change their ideas around career and training development as they begin to better understand their own specific skills and research project topic. In this case they should again work with their supervisory teams and support services so as to develop a plan that suits them best. The important thing is to use frameworks such as the RDF as a useful tool for training and development, but not to be bound by them.

The skills you should acquire as a postgraduate researcher

It is probably best to consider acquiring two sets of specific skills; those required to complete your specific research project and those that will add value to you as a researcher. Of course, it is imperative as a PGR that you adequately equip yourself to complete your PhD first, so it makes sense to concentrate on the immediate training and developments skills to meet this task at the beginning. At the opening of this chapter I observed how many PGRs treated training and development opportunities as a means to learning skills they felt would strengthen their CV, rather than develop them as researchers. In my experience this tendency usually manifests when they eagerly seek out software training, such as SPSS, NVivo, etc. They impatiently dismiss general skills training, move quickly past research philosophy and instead seek out specific packages that will provide evidence to an employer they are well versed in a wide range of useful computer applications. For some, it is a form of reassurance, something they can point to as proof that they have made advances in their time as a doctoral candidate. It is certainly true that there is a need for this type of upskilling, and it would be remiss to ignore the opportunities for this type of skills training during your time as a PGR.

However, such focus alone, albeit necessary, will not be sufficient to sway employers, academic or otherwise. Particularly in the private sector, employers are seeking workers with more than just a rote ability to use software. If that was all they wanted they would merely send their own staff out for the same type of training; it would be complete in a few weeks and they would have saved a lot of money on bringing in a new employee. What they are looking for from PGRs are employees with a deeper understanding of research and the philosophies that underpin it. As an example of what I am describing here I am reminded of my early days as a research assistant when I was asked to undertake some SPSS training. It wasn't my area of expertise and I presumed I would merely learn to use the software for a specific project I had been tasked to support on. Instead, I was sent to the maths and statistic department to learn about the concepts that underpin the program; my line manager at the time already had a useful guide to using SPSS I could refer to anytime. What he wanted me to appreciate and understand was not which buttons to press, but why I would be pressing them. For me this is the distinction between training and development; training is to learn the skills required to, for example, manipulate and analyse data effectively, development is to acquire the means of understanding these processes. To be effective as a researcher, both should be pursued in tandem. It is worth reflecting on the importance of both practices using an analogy. Airline pilots need bespoke skills training to fly specific aircrafts, yet they also have to pass rigorous theoretical knowledge exams to obtain their licence before getting their 'wings'. Who would want to board a plane knowing that the pilot lacks a proper understanding of even rudimentary aerodynamics relating to lift generation, drag or, even more terrifyingly, the aerodynamics of stalling?[49]

Many universities now frontload training, preferring to upskill PGRs in their first year, giving them more time for data collection and writing up in their second and third year. Furthermore, PhD programme management teams will require PGRs to manage much more than just data collection and writing. Most PGR programmes in universities will expect doctoral researchers to spend much time on project management, data management and ethics training. This can be frustrating for some as they view such training as generic and unchallenging. They are eager to see the 'next level' knowledge they hope to attain and fail to appreciate that a PhD requires that basic skills such as project management and data training are done exceptionally well. The phrase 'The devil is in the detail' (an idiom intended to convey that seemingly simple things can be more complicated than appreciated on first viewing) is particularly true for doctoral research, where small mistakes can have major repercussions. As such, this kind of training, though unexciting, is necessary. Such training is usually delivered by professional services, those involved in the administration of PGR

---

49   As an example of the implications of a pilot's lack of understanding of the aerodynamics of stalling, consider the fatal crash of a Bombardier Dash 8 Q400 near Buffalo (NY, USA) in 2009. It has been reported in the media that the accident occurred because the aircraft speed was allowed to drop on approach, and the pilot then reacted wrongly to the onset of a stall by persisting with a manual nose-up pitch attitude.

programmes and tasked with ensuring that doctoral researchers comply with the various rules and procedures laid out in University regulations. This is usually the first training a PGR will undertake by way of induction and introduction to their PhD programme.

The next set of training will usually be academic in content, delivered by a range of lecturers and research staff across the faculty, school or department. An example of a typical module of activity is described below. In this instance, the example refers to the Research Methodology Course delivered by Coventry University Business School in May 2021, for new PGRs starting that month. Run over a two-week period, the various workshops came under three categories: research skills, methodology and software skills. Research skills included generalist sessions on the research environment, the philosophical foundation of research, research design and interdisciplinary research. This set the context for future classes, provided important insights for the attendees, but also served to point to the critical element of researcher development that plays a key part in postdoctoral careers and research pathways.

While the opening sessions offered an important over-arching narrative to the training and development of PGRs, the second part of the course was much more targeted and aimed to support specific needs of doctoral candidates. Topics included economic analysis (including, e.g., interaction models in econometrics, frontier approaches to estimating and computable general equilibrium modelling), panel data analysis, time-series analysis and qualitative research methods (e.g. questionnaire design, case study design and learning to use Qualtrics). PGRs were encouraged to attend sessions that corresponded to their research needs for their projects, as well as other complimentary areas that they wished to strengthen as part of their personal development. These types of tailored solutions are typically encouraged at this stage; after a widely attended series of introductory sessions, these workshops were much smaller and intimate in delivery/attendance by comparison.

The final part of the programme of activity focused on learning the basics of various software packages that corresponded to the methodology workshops, for example, SPSS, STATA, Excel and NVivo. However, these workshops only dealt with the hands-on operation of these packages.

PGRs were expected to undertake further, self-directed learning aimed at improving these basic skills. These were supported by a range of further training opportunities routinely offered and advertised by the faculty or other support services around the university. For example, Coventry University's library services deliver a SIGMA statistics workshop annually, covering topics like multiple linear regression and analysis of covariance. In parallel to their first blocks of training, PGRs were expected to develop a personalised, bespoke agenda of training and development activities using tools such as SAGE projects. This was done in consultation with professional services and their supervisory teams.

Skills that can be developed through other channels

Outside of the classes and workshops described above, there are also opportunities for PGRs to identify and pursue training that would require outside support from other agencies. For example, in 2018 I was contacted by a then PGR, who has since completed his PhD and entered full-time employment in the private sector. His question to me was about opportunities for General Data Protection Regulations (GDPR) training, PRINCE 2 (a project management certification), as well as other project management certificates ('PMP' in this instance). His email was frank and to the point:

> I had a quick question about two areas that I am looking to do some formal training in, and obtain a certificate from, as I have noticed that they would be very useful in the job market.

Although we were unable to help him with his project management certification, we did point him to appropriate agencies to help with his other information requests. What was most important about this exchange is that two years before completion, this doctoral researcher was already thinking ahead to the next stage of his journey; life after graduation.

One area of training and development that most PGRs will undertake and is, in fact, largely underappreciated, occurs as a natural part of their data collection activities. An essential part of gathering empirical data involves significant amounts of networking with private sector or government representatives. Indeed, many PGRs in Business and Management and related fields will, frequently, need to develop good relations with key individuals embedded within companies or organisations to enable access to information, whether it be for surveys, archives, or documental evidence. Engaging in this process facilitates the creation of valuable connections that will underpin empirical data collection, for example. Frequently these same groups will be eager to see the outcomes of doctoral research and in some cases will, in fact, be sponsoring it. Establishing these links requires considerable skills development that will provide PGRs with valuable tools throughout their careers. Furthermore, networking activities can often provide employment routes into industry or other comparable agencies after doctoral studies are completed. A quote from one PGR who recently completed their studies at Coventry University is illuminating:

> In the course of my PhD I have made connections with lots of researchers and lots of companies in the Midlands area, so I am hoping that when the time comes for me to be seeking work myself, I will have built a coalition of people that will be able to assist me further my career.

In a globalised world of work, where labour is highly mobile and frequently changes jobs or even occupations, developing networking skills that build relations and social capital with employers is a valuable competence. However, it is a skill PGRs often neglect or underestimate (de Janasz and Forret, 2008). Networking, in a narrow sense, involves individuals' attempts to develop and maintain relations with other individuals who they perceive as being potentially beneficial to their future work or career (Forret and Dougherty, 2001). While this interpretation, on the surface, may seem cynical, perhaps even deceptive, it is best viewed as a two-way street, where both parties mutually benefit from a relationship. Perhaps a broader interpretation is one that views networks as important conduits of social capital, offering shared access to valuable information, resources and opportunities, for example, the tacit knowledge created and transferred by organisations (Nahapiet and Ghoshal, 1998).

Many times, PGRs seem fearful of engaging in networking, worried that their brashness will be poorly received, perhaps even disdained as a form of begging. What is not always appreciated by PGRs is how their enthusiasm and drive can bring a freshness and vitality to an organisation, a group, a research centre, wherever their interests lie. Sometimes, overwhelmed or unnerved by the seniority of the person they are dealing with, they struggle to recognise how their own innate passion for research can invigorate those they are networking with. Experienced and knowledgeable persons, whether in academia or the private sector, will recognise and understand this, and will always be on the lookout for talented early career researchers to add their own energy to work projects. As wisely noted by one of our colleagues (an Emeritus Professor) who kindly reviewed and commented on one of the early chapters of this book:

> Something that I have never seen addressed in books in this area is how to relate to other senior scholars in your PhD topic area. This was immensely important to me in my doctoral study [..] I was actively encouraged to interact with other senior scholars. I've always talked about this in research methods workshops and participants have often told me later that it turned out to be very helpful advice. [..] I have developed several very rewarding relationships with young academics whose supervisors suggested that they talked to me about specific areas of their work in which I was recognised as expert and I learned a great deal from them - hearing about their work often keeps me up to date.

Understanding the significant benefits of these potential relationships at an early stage of doctoral study and creating personal networks that go beyond the mere transfer of data, data collection and analysis is also an important step for later career opportunities.

Another valuable way for PGRs to hone both networking and other research skills, based on tacit rather than codified learning, is frequently realised through work experience. In the past, teaching in particular, was treated as a useful source of extra income by staff and doctoral researchers alike. Opportunities were infrequent and often only extended to a very small cadre of top-performing PGRs. Teaching classes were highly sought after, viewed as they were as a key to opening the door to academic employment once doctoral studies were completed. In more recent years, research project work has become more plentiful and more important, offering alternative benefits to teaching classes in terms of the skills developed. In contrast, teaching has declined in importance for PGRs, offering less assurances of academic employment, but still an important chance to improve key skillsets. Universities are also keen to offer more work opportunities for PGRs as well, particularly project work in part-time research assistant roles. That is not just as a financial incentive to PGRs, but to put into practice the skills they have been developing during their years of study. This makes training and development decisions that PGRs take in the early part of their doctoral studies even more impactful.

Some final words of encouragement

Doctoral research has undergone significant change over the last two decades, becoming more embedded within national discourses around training and development. The perception of a PhD has evolved from that of a purely academic qualification to an award with greater utility, demonstrating advanced skills and abilities that are particularly desirable in sectors such as the knowledge economy. With more attention being received from national policy units dedicated to research and innovation, a plethora of guidelines have emerged on maximising a doctoral candidate's time in terms of upskilling and career development. HEIs and leading education groups like Vitae have responded to these inputs by investing significantly more resources into support services dedicated to identifying training possibilities and encouraging self-directed growth. For PGRs this presents a whole new panorama and a wider set of opportunities for personal and professional development. Their immediate prospects on completing their thesis have expanded considerably, no longer limited to academic job openings alone. From an early stage PGRs, with the support of their supervisory teams and institutional professional services, should be creating a training and development plan that looks beyond the immediate goal of completing their research. Those PGRs that do will reap the rewards at the end of their studies, whichever career pathway they choose to follow.

References

Arts and Humanities Research Council [AHRC] (2011). Research Training Framework Guide. Available at: <https://ahrc.ukri.org/documents/guides/research-training-framework-guide/>
Barnes, T. (2013). Higher doctorates in the UK 2013. UK Council for Graduate Education. Available at: <https://docplayer.net/1736073-Higher-doctorates-in-the-uk-2013-dr-tina-barnes.html>
Brown, D. (2001). The social sources of educational credentialism: Status cultures, labor markets, and organizations. *Sociology of Education*, 74, 19–34.
Coventry University [CU] (2019). Studying a PhD with the Centre for Business in Society. Available at: <https://www.youtube.com/watch?v=qAmAqeYeNNQ&feature=emb_logo>
De Grande, H., De Boyser, K., Vandevelde, K., and Van Rossem, R. (2014). From academia to industry: Are doctorate holders ready? *Journal of the Knowledge Economy*, 5(3), 538–561.
De Janasz, S. C. and Forret, M. L. (2008). Learning the art of networking: A critical skill for enhancing social capital and career success. *Journal of Management Education*, 32(5), 629–650.
Denicolo, P., Duke, D., and Reeves, J. (2016). Researcher development and skills training within the context of postgraduate programs. *Education*. Available at: <https://www.oxfordbibliographies.com/view/document/obo-9780199756810/obo-9780199756810-0174.xml>
Duke, D. C. and Denicolo, P. M. (2017). What supervisors and universities can do to enhance doctoral student experience (and how they can help themselves). *FEMS Microbiology Letters*, 364(9). Available at: <https://academic.oup.com/femsle/article/364/9/fnx090/3796317>
Economic and Social Research Council [ESRC] (2005). Postgraduate Training Guidelines. Available at: <https://esrc.ukri.org/files/skills-and-careers/doctoral-training/postgraduate-training-guidelines-fourth-edition-2005/>
ESRC (2015). Postgraduate Training and Development Guidelines – Second Edition 2015. Available at: <https://esrc.ukri.org/files/skills-and-careers/doctoral-training/postgraduate-training-and-development-guidelines-2015/>

European Higher Education Area [EHEA] (2020). European Higher Education Area and Bologna Process. Available at: <http://www.ehea.info/index.php>

Forret, M. L. and Dougherty, T. W. (2001). Correlates of networking behavior for managerial and professional employees. *Group & Organization Management*, 26(3), 283–311.

Fourie-Malherbe, M. (2016). *Postgraduate Supervision: Future Foci for the Knowledge Society*. Stellenbosch: Sun Press.

Gregory, M. (1995). Implications of the introduction of the Doctor of Education degree in British universities: Can the EdD reach parts the PhD cannot? *The Vocational Aspect of Education*, 47(2), 177–188.

Higher Education Statistical Agency [HESA] (2019). Higher Education Graduate Outcomes Statistics – UK, 2017/18. Available at: <https://www.hesa.ac.uk/news/18-06-2020/sb257-higher-education-graduate-outcomes-statistics>

Hockey, J. (1995). Change and the social science PhD: supervisors' responses. *Oxford Review of Education*, 21(2), 195–206.

Matlay, H., Smith, K., Williams, D., Yasin, N., and Pitchford, I. (2014). Enterprise skills and training needs of postgraduate research students. *Education and Training*, 56(8/9), 745–763.

Nahapiet, J. and Ghoshal, S. (1998). Social capital, intellectual capital, and the organizational advantage. *Academy of Management Review*, 23(2), 242–266.

Park, C. (2007). *Redefining the Doctorate*. York, UK: Higher Education Academy.

Sursock, A., Smidt, H., and Davies, H. (2010). Trends 2010 – A Decade of Change in European Higher Education (Vol. 1). Brussels: European University Association.

UK Research and Innovation [UKRI] (2020). Statement of Expectations for Postgraduate Training. Available at: <https://www.ukri.org/wp-content/uploads/2020/10/UKRI-211020-StatementOfExpectationsPostGradTraining-Sep2016v2.pdf>

Vitae (2011). Vitae Researcher Development Framework (RDF) 2011. Available at: <https://www.vitae.ac.uk/vitae-publications/rdf-related/researcher-development-framework-rdf-vitae.pdf/view>

Vitae (2013). What Do Researchers Do? Vitae. Available at: <https://www.vitae.ac.uk/vitae-publications/reports/what-do-researchers-do-early-career-progression-2013.pdf/view>

Ward, A. E. (2013). Empirical study of the important elements in the researcher development journey. *Knowledge Management & E-Learning: An International Journal*, 5(1), 42–55.

Williams, S. (2019). Postgraduate research experience survey 2019. Advance Higher Education, 5. Available at: <https://www.advance-he.ac.uk/knowledge-hub/postgraduate-research-experience-survey-2019>

JASON BEGLEY

7   Strategies to deal with difficulties and major crises

Preamble

In my role as academic director of a PhD programme, I am faced daily with a variety of problems, ranging from the highly unusual, such as supervision during a pandemic, to more frequent, mundane issues of administration and miscommunication. Each one has the potential to derail postgraduate researchers' (PGRs) workflow, sometimes for weeks on end, leading to further problems as deadlines loom. Some of these issues are both unfortunate and unavoidable. Others, with careful planning and forethought, can be solved quickly and efficiently. The **aim of this chapter** is to unpack the most frequent and concerning problems brought to my attention by PGRs that can cause great anxiety for the uninitiated and offer helpful advice on how to deal with them. Special attention is given to added challenges for international, part-time and first-generation PGRs, PGRs with a disability and those who also work as staff members. Issues of discrimination, not belonging, isolation and doing doctoral research during a global crisis such as the Covid-19 pandemic, are also given ample coverage.

The challenge of getting over the line

I have sat in numerous intervention-like meetings with supervisory teams and their PhD candidates and carefully explained to them that the one thing I care the most about is getting the struggling PGR over the line;

that is to finish, submit and defend their thesis. I make no apologies if this singular frame of mind colours much of what I write next, but it has largely been my experience to date that all other issues are merely sublayers of the central concern of getting a PGR to complete. Anger, despair, blame, resentment all only serve to deflect from this core issue of completing a PhD. When the PhD sails smoothly towards a natural conclusion, most individuals will put up with whatever problems they encounter to achieve a shared goal. It is only when they are diverted from this path that problems intensify and escalate. Sometimes the problems have been there from the start and have, over time, spiralled out of control. Other times life intervenes in the most inconvenient of ways. Yet, it is always the fear of losing years of work and effort that creates a crisis. In this chapter, therefore, the focus will be on the issue of how crises emerge or evolve, and how to manage them when they do.

The chapter focuses on a range of concerns broadly captured under institutional challenges and individual barriers. The term 'institutional' is used here to refer to the wide variety of difficulties associated with pursuing a PhD ranging from the culture shock of undertaking a doctorate in a foreign country right through to the complexity of 'occupying the hyphen' (Drake and Heath, 2010) as an insider-outsider 'staff member' pursuing a doctoral qualification. Topics that will be covered in this first part include international candidates in a foreign system, part-time research challenges, pursuing a PhD while having a disability, discrimination and what it can mean for a PGR, and doctoral expectations. The second part of the chapter will be more focused on the individual, discussing a range of problems that are frequently encountered by PGRs during their studies. These include fatigue, impostor syndrome, time constraints, balancing work and study, difficulties of data collection, isolation and the challenge of researching during a global crisis. Cutting across these categories will be the central role of the supervisory team and the importance of the relationship between the candidate and their supervisors which determines the smooth functioning of the whole. The chapter, as the other chapters in this book, draws on many years of tacit knowledge garnered through 'experiential learning' and 'reflection on doing' and uses examples to both explore the challenges and offer suggestions as to how to overcome such problems.[50]

Cultural and institutional challenges

International PGRs

As discussed in Chapter 2, the challenge for international candidates is not immoderate. In that chapter we noted how cost, language, culture and regulatory barriers were all significantly higher for non-domestic applicants trying to gain entry to the much sought-after PhD programmes in the UK. On being accepted onto doctoral courses, international candidates face a substantial range of additional impediments related to cultural and institutional differences. The UK HE system, unsurprisingly, is strongly influenced by the society it is embedded in, reflecting Western, and in many instances, Christian values (Durepos, 2016). Individuality, egalitarian principles, informal collegiate relations, all are frequently in evidence and can surprise or even unsettle the unprepared. One simple example is of an Indonesian candidate who refused to shake hands with a female supervisor. For him it was a mark of respect, but it served to surprise and discomfort the educator who was unused to such a custom.

Perhaps more serious than a simple misunderstanding are the expectations of international postgraduates set against the realities of the institutional culture in the UK. Many international candidates, particularly those from the Far East, often have a highly hierarchical view and expectations of the relationship between student and supervisor, where senior figures are rarely criticised.[51] Often, such PGRs' expectation is that they will be

---

50 These examples will protect the identities of the individuals involved by changing several details about the case, though the point will still adhere to the essence of the event.
51 In their critique of the cross-cultural validity of the student-as-customer metaphor and its pedagogic implications, De Vita and Case (2003) highlight the clash between the student–teacher relationship embedded in the Western model of

instructed, will receive strong direction from staff, including even identifying material on behalf of the PGR and writing tracts of their work.

In the UK education system, the doctoral researcher is left very much to their own devices, the belief being that they need time and space to self-manage their research and take responsibility for their work. For some, newly arrived into a foreign country with a different language and social character, this can prove very confusing and disorientating at times resulting in a sense of detachment and isolation. This sense of solitude can be mitigated by embedding within existing groups or organisations, familiar cultural or linguistic characteristics frequently found in university settings. This approach, however, carries the risk of the PGR becoming remote or secluded from the very environment that the international candidate had made such efforts to enter. Perhaps then engaging with groups that address skills gaps for PGRs, such as improving written or spoken English, can help overcome engagement barriers, for example, through discussion with those who have previously encountered or still share the same challenges (Robinson-Pant, 2010).

On occasion, cultural differences can manifest within the supervisory environment. For example, several years ago I was approached by an international PGR. He expressed concern over the alleged in-fighting he perceived within his supervisory team. Different views served to confuse him, as he expected a harmonious discussion and univocal direction from his team. He was unprepared for what is standard amongst UK-based academic institutions, the healthy cut-and-thrust of debate and the expression of a wide range of views and ideas to help him explore his research topic from a variety of perspectives. He had to sit down with his team and discuss the roles of the various supervisors within his group and his expectations of each. It was necessary to clearly outline his own views on supervision and to find out how they matched with the actual approach his team would take.

Often PGRs arrive to the UK with certain expectations from sponsoring home institutions, organisations or government funders. For

---

education and the spiritual model purported by the Vedic theory *"where teachers are not only facilitators, but moral and inspiring examples as well"* (p. 390). They go on to note that in other religious educational models too, *"the vertical relationship between the teacher and the disciple is central"* (ibid, p. 390).

example, Neumann and Rodwell (2009) discuss the challenge of ethics procedures for international researchers, as most UK institutions will, for instance, insist on specific processes, noting:

> In cultures where the relationship between researcher and the researched is based on trust - and where access is negotiated verbally rather than through written documents – our UK research governance procedures appear legalistic and may disrupt longstanding relationships between the researcher and her/his participants. (Neumann and Rodwell, 2009, p. 56)

The concern for international PGRs is that the final piece of work may seem to stand at odds with the norms and values of colleagues in their home institutions. The most frequent problem perceived among international PGRs stems from a lack of understanding of what a UK thesis entails amongst non-UK funders. Often their expectation is that their sponsored candidate is undertaking specific research into policy problems, ignoring the all-important academic component, particularly in terms of the essential contribution to academic theory. This requires careful investigation by PGRs before they arrive in the UK, but also frequent communication with their home organisations, particularly those funding the research. It also requires UK supervisory teams to understand the constraints under which their charges operate so they can explore best possible solutions that keep all parties satisfied.

Part-time researchers

Another major group that encounters a differing set of challenges in terms of pursuing a PhD are part-time researchers. Unlike international PGRs, however, part-time researchers arguably receive less attention from institutions. Neumann and Rodwell (2009) believe that those engaged in part-time studies are overlooked in policy and research terms to the point of invisibility (p. 55). Watts (2010) concurs with their assessment, noting that "... *the image of the lonely part-time student who is not a full participant within the academic community remains difficult to dislodge*" (p. 123). He further bemoans the emphasis within UK institutions on guiding full-time PGRs through three to four years of intense study, with little thinking of those with a longer-term role.

The biggest challenge facing part-time PGRs is that of time management (a topic we amply discussed in Chapter 5). The perception that part-time studies are somehow easier and less stressful is both widespread and completely misplaced. First, UK universities have very clear regulations, strictly enforced, about the amount of time to be spent on part-time (PT) study. This usually equates to half the time that would be spent in full-time (FT) study. The thesis is often expected to be finished within four to six years compared to three to four for a FT PhD. In other words, the time constraints are tight leaving very little room for slippage. Phillips and Pugh (2010) believe that this research structure creates a dichotomy for PT PGRs, forcing them to switch from their job to PhD research day after day, which can prove mentally draining, and so aiming to work on the thesis during evenings and weekends while holding down a job. The challenging task requires significant support from friends and family to accept that someone they care about is effectively going to be unavailable for months, if not years, as one tries to balance a hugely difficult workload.

Mature (older) PT PGRs can be particularly vulnerable. Assumptions are often made that mature researchers will handle the pressure better than younger ones due to life experience. But while this may be indeed be the case, it is equally true that mature researchers returning to study after a long period away from higher (third level) education may have to relearn all the skills they had acquired before, as well as gain new ones related to technology, online databases, ethics procedures, etc. Additionally, they are more likely to have families who depend on them, creating even more stressful scenarios, particularly if financial factors are or become an issue. Considering that most PT PGRS are self-funded and pursue their research over six years, fees and finances can become very problematic for many part-timers (Neumann and Rodwell, 2009).

One memorable example for me was the case of Annette (I am using a pseudonym). She was pursuing her FT PhD when family life intervened and forced her to become a FT carer for her parents. Unwilling to leave her studies behind, Annette chose to switch to PT research. The result was an increasing sense of isolation and a very challenging workload as she split her days between caring for her close relatives and engaging with the research community. Thankfully, the Director of Studies (DoS) offered continual advice and support. Her DoS also frequently liaised with the leads of the PhD programme in the institution, highlighting where further supporting action was required by the university. Mostly though it was down to Annette herself to remain driven and focused despite the difficulties. Not everyone is as fortunate as Annette to have this mental fortitude and resolve, though there are several approaches that can be taken to help the creation of a positive mindset.

First, it is important for PT PGRs to make a clear demarcation between work, research time and rest. As highlighted in Chapter 5, setting aside weekends and time off for family and friends, for rest and relaxation, is incredibly important. Too often I have seen PGRs trying to push through their research in a rush of energetic dynamism, only to quickly run out of steam or reach the point of burnout. Fatigue, frustration, irritability and apathy, are all hallmarks of mental strain and exhaustion created by over-zealous enthusiasm. Closely linked to a lack of a break is the problem of poor time allotment. Frequently PGRs, but especially PT PGRs, set themselves unreasonable milestones and deadlines. When they miss them, they become frenzied and overdo the next stage of their work, leading to exhaustion and slowdown in the following stages, inevitably spiralling downwards. Flexibility is key; if you do not meet a self-imposed daily deadline, draw a line under that day and concentrate on the good work you did, not what you failed to achieve.

It is also important to look outside your supervisory silo for inspiration. Part of the isolation felt by many PT PGRs stems from the low level of engagement with their institution or even with networks outside their university. With less time and fewer opportunities to attend events than their FT counterparts, PT PGRs need to be more surgical in identifying useful seminars and conferences, both internally and externally, to improve their research understanding as well as to promote their work. Universities are increasingly aware of the challenge for PT study and are increasingly offering more tailored solutions to support this kind of activities. Of course, as Cain (2013) observed, not everyone is keen to plug in to busy events and public discourse. But even for the focused introvert, discussing the PhD research with small, tight knit groups of friends and family can be surprisingly refreshing as well as helpful in terms of firming up one's own understanding of the work.

Postgraduate researchers with a disability

2017 was an important year for PGRs in terms of reporting on their mental health and wellbeing. The Higher Education Authority (HEA) included new questions on mental health in their annual Postgraduate Research Experience Survey (PRES). This included returns for those with a disability. The results were disturbing. 48% of PGRs with a disability had considered leaving their programme of study, compared to 24% for PGRs without (Slight, 2017).[52] Perhaps then the most difficult pathway lies in front of those PGRs with a disability who undertake research. The UK Equality Act 2010 defines a person as having a disability if he or she has a physical or mental impairment and the impairment has a substantial and long-term adverse effect on his or her ability to carry out normal day-to-day activities (HM Government, 2010). The act gives further guidance on timing, limitations and activities that would come under this Act, but they are suitably broad to cover a very wide range of issues, both mental and physical. Suffice to say that such health problems are debilitating in the normal range of daily activity, undertaking doctoral studies at the same time, with all the stresses and pressures that go with them, are even more so.

How are disabilities approached? The UK government is aware of this challenge and has committed to widening participation for those who come under the definition of having a disability according to the 2010 Act. They have made a financial support package available to all students from the UK called the Disabled Students' Allowances. Under this scheme a PGR can currently get up to £20,850 a year for specialist equipment and a carer's support, details of which and how to apply can be found at their website (HM Government, 2020). Since 2015/2016 Higher Education

---

52   The same question was not repeated in the 2019 survey.

Disability	Female	Male	Other	Total
A specific learning difficulty	360	370	0	730
Blind or a serious visual impairment	15	15	0	30
Deaf or a serious hearing impairment	20	20	0	45
A physical impairment or mobility issues	40	35	0	75
Mental health condition	195	130	0	325
Social communication/Autistic spectrum disorder	20	40	0	60
A long-standing illness or health condition	110	95	0	205
Two or more conditions	95	60	0	155
Another disability, impairment or medical condition	85	65	0	155
No known disability	6,960	7,170	5	14,135
Total	7,895	8,000	10	15,905

Table 7.1. UK domiciled qualifiers by disability and sex, postgraduate research
Source: HESA, 2019, <https://www.hesa.ac.uk/data-and-analysis/students/table-35>.

(HE) providers have been given greater responsibility for providing specialist equipment and onsite support for those with disabilities (HESA, 2020a). The result of the efforts of the UK government and HE providers to improve circumstances for disabled PGRs has been a small increase in representation since 2015/2016, according to the Higher Education Statistical Agency. This includes those attending universities in receipt of an allowance (HESA, 2020b). For example, in the science subject area at least, the numbers of PGRs completing with a known disability increased from 64 % to 68 % from 2014/2015 to 2018/2019 (ibid.).[53] Table 7.1 above shows a breakdown of all UK-based PGRs completing with a recorded disability in 2018/19.

Table 7.1 shows the variety of challenges facing those with a disability, but also their minority share within the overall group of PGRs. What should hearten those with comparable conditions, is the growing recognition that disabilities are not an impassable or insurmountable barrier to completion. From the same source, a breakdown of completion rates for PGRs with disabilities for each HE institution (HEI) in the UK can be gleaned. This information can provide some early guidance to prospective PGRs, and readers are encouraged to go to the links provided in the reference section and examine this information for themselves. Linked to this

---

53 Latest figures available. Also, only science subjects were made available by HESA.

observation is the important point about the need to undertake preparation if you have a disability before embarking on a PhD. An essential first step is to contact support services at your institution of choice to determine the availability of specialist equipment, trained staff and specific solutions to specific disability needs. Sometimes the best institution is not the highest ranked but the one that offers the most tailored support. What is further encouraging is the increasing awareness of the need for such services amongst most if not all HEIs alongside the growing list of actions being taken at governmental and organisational level to address them.

Vitae, a key UK organisation supporting the professional development of researchers, provides substantial resources for disabled researchers to exploit, including through their ongoing Premia project. This work draws on case studies of disabled PGRs and their supervisors to identify key challenges and offer recommendations (Vitae, 2020a). In these case studies the following issues were identified as the most challenging for PGRs with a disability (Vitae, 2020b):

- The need for long periods of concentration.
- The need to organise large amounts of material and retrieve relevant information.
- Long periods of reading or sitting.
- Meeting targets and managing time while making allowances for bad days, bouts of illness and/or regular hospital visits.
- Heightened feelings of isolation, over and above the experience of other PGRs.

The major recommendation from Vitae is to contact preferred universities and within them existing research networks for those with comparable disability challenges. Leaning on and learning from their experience can provide enormous benefits. Again, most if not all universities will have some means of facilitating such efforts (ibid.). The other point that Vitae strongly advocates is careful financial planning. So, consider not just the cost of your studies but also possible additional expenses a disabled researcher may need to incur.

Dealing with discrimination

Higher Education Institutions (HEIs) in the UK have always prided themselves on supporting inclusivity, multiculturalism and diversity. That is not to say, however, that PGRs from a multitude of backgrounds and ethnicities will find their research pathways completely smooth. The research world remains a difficult one for many from certain backgrounds, though this is more likely due to ignorance (of others), rather than conscious intent. Discrimination and harassment still occur, but they tend to be firmly dealt with when detected. One obvious example that springs to mind was a prospective PGR who explained early on in his interview that he refused to work with researchers from a neighbouring country due to perceived cultural differences and rising national tensions. He was given short shrift by the university and ultimately not recruited to the PhD programme. But the example serves to highlight the challenges still encountered by certain minority groups within HEIs.

Discrimination can occur directly at individual level in terms of race, gender, sexual orientation, religion, culture, etc., or indirectly, when policy or practises create barriers for certain groups or people. All HEIs will have a code of practice in place to address such issues which, when encountered, particularly at an individual level, should be reported to the appropriate units within the institution. However, some forms of discrimination can be more pervasive and difficult to navigate. For example, Durepos (2016, p. 32) refers to "... *an intensifying masculinist entrepreneurial discourse that hegemonically defines what counts as a successful academic career*".

Doubtless, UK Business Schools are becoming more corporate and profit focused, which may strike a note of discord for some PGRs. The issue of gender and HEIs as raised by Durepos (2016) is also a matter of ongoing concern that may impact some doctoral candidates. A 2016 report of gender representation in research by Vitae (2016) observed that across the European Union only 41% of academic researchers were female, while just 21% of full professors were female. This raised the spectre that women might view the research environment as one that was unwelcoming for female researchers and discourage their participation (ibid.). In the UK, the latest numbers for research staff show a more representative picture than seen in the rest of Europe a few years ago, but the problem persists. Here, although the majority of undergraduates completions were by women, in terms of working in third level only 45% of managers, directors and senior officials were female, 46% were classed as having a professional occupation and only 45% were engaged in associate professional and technical operations (HESA, 2020c). This was despite the fact that the number of women undertaking a first degree had actually increased from 56% in 2014/15 to 57% in 2018/19 (HESA, 2020d). These same numbers for those undertaking PG research, were 47% and 49%, respectively (ibid.). The sharp decline in female representation from UG to PG was not as evident from postgraduate to staff, but was apparent, nonetheless.

It is difficult to explain this fall in female representation, especially from UG to PG research. Traditional views of women as carers and men as earners may play a part. It might also be that life moves forward and at least some of these women voluntarily enter traditional carer roles in society once completing their degree. However, Lester (2013) cites at least two examples where a HE provider failed to support a doctoral candidate with a family-oriented policy. The first case was that of a doctoral student who became ill and was forced to abandon their teaching assistant role as policy did not extend to supporting the families of sick PT workers. In the second, equally troubling example, a female doctoral candidate was explicitly told by a colleague not to pursue a faculty job for fear her desire to have a family would impact on her teaching responsibilities. In my experience such cases are unusual but require vigilance to ensure they don't become commonplace and are typically dealt with in a punitive manner to stop them recurring. Perhaps more divisive was a recent case brought to my attention. Geraldine had decided to marry once her PhD was complete. However, she underestimated the length of time required for her thesis and, despite successfully navigating her *viva voce*, suddenly found her wedding day arriving mid revisions. The university regulations were unrelenting, and Geraldine was forced to re-arrange her wedding day to allow her time to complete her thesis.

On the one hand Geraldine should have put greater thought into her planning. On the other hand, the unsympathetic inflexibility of the institution's regulators chimes with Durepos' earlier observation about the increasing entrepreneurial mindset evident in UK business schools; the unseemly haste to have her finish allied to an unwillingness to make exceptions is very much in step with the increasingly manufactory processes in evidence around their PhD programmes. Vitae offers ten recommendations for institutions to improve equality and diversity for research staff and I recommend supervisors and PGRs alike to read them (Vitae, 2020c). In the main, they point to the need for top-down, well-resourced, continuous actions with both supervisory staff and PGR engagement. All universities in the UK are committed to facilitating such improvements. However, HEIs act slowly and are hard to steer. For those candidates who find life goes on around their studies, it is important to plan far ahead, offer plenty of notice of upcoming changes to your work/life situation and give supervisors and administrators ample opportunity to find ways and means to help where life throws a curveball.

Pursuing a doctorate as a staff member

One specific group that has, to date, received limited attention in literature dedicated to doctoral research is that of staff members undertaking a PhD while simultaneously working within HEIs. Yet, of the cases I have worked to support in the past, none have been more challenging than those that involve staff members working on PhDs part-time. A good teacher doesn't necessarily make a good researcher. The example of Mark still stands fresh in my mind.

Mark had completed his Masters (a taught Masters) and successfully applied to the university to become a temporary lecturer. At that time not having a PhD was not the serious impediment to advancing down the academic path as it is today and, as Mark was a good teacher, he eventually became full-time in his business school. However, a change in policy at the university meant that Mark was now required to undertake a PhD or risked losing his job. So, he agreed to do one, and time was set aside for his research. I remember vetting his application and wondering whether he was being overly ambitious. But his DoS, who also happened to be his line manager, was confident; Mark was a good teacher and would, therefore, make a good doctoral candidate. Such a *non sequitur* frequently bodes ill in my experience and so it came as little surprise to me (though causing considerable concern) when our Faculty tutor approached me to discuss the sudden 'crisis' with Mark. His descent had been rapid, unable to balance work and research study, leading to mental stress and eventual breakdown. What had been particularly painful for all concerned was the fracturing of the relationship he had with work colleagues who were also part of his supervisory team, as Mark's inability to pursue one field of activity impacted negatively on the other. It is this case, more than any, that prompted me to include this section in the chapter.

The latter point, the imposition of work life on the separate sphere of research, is an inherent risk to PT PGRs who are also members of the Faculty. Drake and Heath (2010) refer to this relationship as the 'insider-outsider conundrum'. They define insiders as those practitioners that draw on their work experience to inform their research question. For staff in HE, this can lead to a blurring of the lines of work and research as colleagues, sometimes more junior, are tasked with switching from a support role to one of critical supervisor. There is the potential embarrassment of having your work dissected and comments made as to the need to sharpen writing skills and thesis structure, and of 'losing face'. As Drake and Heath (2010, p. 25) observe:

> Other university staff undertaking their studies alongside junior colleagues said that their colleagues had great difficulty in viewing them as anything other than their 'line manager'. Even on study days and in researcher action learning sets, conflict between being a practitioner and being a researcher was problematic for some.

What is required is the 'occupation of the hyphen' as the authors refer to it. In other words, a careful balancing of the two roles; the 'insider' role of the teaching staff doing informed research and the 'outsider' role, that of a doctoral candidate pursuing a PhD. From an early stage the candidate must make explicit that there is a clear distinction for them between doctoral research and supervision, and their daily workflow. Making this demarcation would be greatly facilitated by the choice of supervisory team. It makes good sense to look outside the Faculty, perhaps even your institution, for additional independent support. If the expertise can only be found within your immediate circle, it would be beneficial to identify a neutral, experienced person to also sit on the supervisory team who can offer insight and act as a counterweight to the familiar relationship between work colleagues.

The challenge for the individual

Mental health and wellbeing

As stated earlier, the Postgraduate Research Experience Survey 2017 showed some very worrying results for PGRs with a disability. But the problems of stress, anxiety and mental suffering occur in high instances for all PGRs. The most recent PRES 2019 goes into even greater detail on PGR mental health and general wellbeing in its Section 12. The numbers remain consistent, from 2017 to 2019, on average, 26% of PGRs consider quitting their studies. Of the reasons given, the three most important that accounted for the bulk of responses were 'Family, health or personal problems' (15%), 'Financial difficulties' (14%) and 'Difficulty balancing commitments' (13%). Other major reasons offered included a lack of support for research (11%) or just a realisation that a PhD might not be suited to their needs (9%). Perhaps the most telling set of data came from questions around life satisfaction, with PGRs, on average and compared to the rest of the UK population, being significantly unhappier. In fact, PGRs were more likely to be anxious than the general UK populous by 27 percentage points (Williams, 2019). Although awareness of the stress of being a PGR has been growing over the last decade, largely in response to reports by supervisory teams, it is only in the last few years that more and more resources are being deployed by universities to combat these issues (Vitae, 2020d). While no one factor can explain the presence of such anxiety amongst researchers, several issues can be considered as contributing factors.

In part, the nature of the work involved in being a PGR lends itself to higher stress levels. De Lange et al. (2004) highlight the link between high job demands and anxiety while Levecque et al. (2017) makes this point explicit in the case of PhD candidates. Doing a PhD is arduous not least because you are expected to focus on solving the same problem for many years. The initial enthusiasm, therefore, can give way to fatigue and boredom. Worse, once the doctoral candidate begins to realise the scale of what they are attempting, some may find fatigue and boredom give way to fear, loathing and not a little panic. Approaches to deal with such issues have already been outlined in Chapter 5 of this book, so we refer the interested reader to that chapter.

Another challenge for PGRs can be the repetitious nature of the work. Scrutinising responses from questionnaires in excruciating detail or re-running econometric regressions, over and over, can wear down even the most determined PGR. Focusing on singular aspects of the work and meeting smaller targets can be both rewarding and offer respite. However, it is important to identify suitably appropriate goals. Failing to meet self-imposed and unrealistic targets can also initiate a slide into frustration and a sense of defeat. It is important to discuss your plans with your supervisory team and agree a set of sensible, achievable goals. It is also important to listen to the voice of experience. If your supervisory team are telling you that you are over-ambitious, it is not a good idea to ignore their sage advice. I have lost count of the number of first year doctoral candidates who have explained to me their plans to finish their thesis in less than three years, only to be struggling to meet deadlines by year four. The usual pathway here is a rushed literature review, conceptualisation and methodology, followed by months of revisions; and looking for shortcuts is only destined to lead to greater problems down the line.

Spending an appropriate amount of time on the 'Literature review', arguably a very challenging and important part of the thesis, is a necessity. Without the appropriate foundation of specialist knowledge and critical evaluation of 'what has gone before' in your literature debate, it is impossible to identify the knowledge gap and subsequent academic contribution. A critical review of relevant literature is also essential to the 'who' and the 'why' of the conceptual framework, which, in turn, leads into the 'how' of the methodology section. The reason these elements are frequently rushed is because nervous doctoral candidates are unsure of what they will need to have completed by the end of their first year of studies and, in their planning, err on the side of abundance. As a colleague memorably jested to me, on receiving over 25,000 words of a literature review after three months: 'Never mind the quality, feel the width.' It might be appropriate here to give some broad suggestions at what might, feasibly, be a series of reasonable goals for a PGR and their supervisory team aiming to finish an 80,000-word thesis within three years. Using the template outlined in Figure 2.1 in Chapter 2, we can offer the following approximate guidelines:

> **Year 1.** A well-constructed critical review of relevant literature of approximately 10,000 to 20,000 words leading to a cogently justified, theory-based 'Conceptual framework' that synthesises the gaps to be filled, objectives to be addressed and/or hypothesised by the analysis/investigation to be undertaken. A blueprint or, even better, an early draft of the methodology to be employed, with a justification as to why this specific methodological approach is chosen, would also be expected.
>
> **Year 2.** A polished and updated literature review chapter and, in addition, a completed draft of the methodology chapter (of approximately 10,000 to 16,000 words). Collected empirical data (whether secondary data or data from questionnaires/survey/focus groups). An early draft of the results and provisional findings.
>
> **Year 3.** Writing up year, when the earlier chapters are revised and the later chapters examining different aspects of the research questions and research objectives, discussion, recommendations and conclusions are completed.

I would stress that it is exceedingly unusual to find PGRs who complete this quickly and when they do, they usually have had a head start by preparing much of the groundwork in advance and, of course, top-notch supervision. The one area that is frequently underestimated by PGRs is the phase of data collection, to be discussed later in the chapter.

Work avoidance

As Charles Dickens (2009) memorably observed in his nineteenth-century literary masterpiece David Copperfield, *"Procrastination is the thief of time. Collar him!"*. One of the greatest sins that is committed by PGRs is falling into a pattern of work avoidance tactics. I know this sensation only too well, having found myself spending a day designing the most ostentatious of excel charts rather than undertaking an unpleasant task looming large in my email inbox; that's self-indulgent procrastination for you.

Angelle et al. (2010) identify a more serious issue for PGRs who are unwilling to move their research forward however, referring to a procrastination cycle of 'work avoidance'. In this cycle the researcher realises the scale of the challenge ahead. Intimidated and filled with self-doubt, they proceed to work around the edges of their research, rather than engage fully with the task. The result is escalating fear and panic, as they fail to meet deadlines which, in turn, leads to further procrastination. Lacking motivation and fearing humiliation, they drop out of their studies, believing that they were never capable of doing them in the first place, despite never actually engaging fully with the work. To avoid the build-up of these emotions, it is important to reduce the task to a more manageable size (see related advice offered in Chapter 5). Important too will be the guidance and actions of the supervisory team. They should create a framework of activities to guide PGRs, so that they understand where to start and how to progress. Enthusiasm and confidence are also built by the supervisory team. Too frequently we forget to praise the candidate for what they have achieved and instead focus on trying to make right what they have completed so far. This tendency is a trap many supervisors fall into. The single-minded desire to make better a diamond in the rough often can overwhelm our sense of what is needed for the individual. It is worth remembering that if supervisors want to help fix a piece of work, it is only because they believe it is worthwhile to fix it in the first place. If we sometimes forget, please, remind us.

Not belonging

Closely linked to the issue of self-doubt is the sense of 'not belonging', of feeling as an 'impostor'. Interest in understanding why some academics become dissonant with feelings of inadequacy has emerged in the literature since the late 1970s. Clance and Ames (1978) were the first to observe what they identified as an impostor phenomenon among female academics. In their study, one subject professed to believing: "*I'm not good enough to be on the faculty here. Some mistake was made in the selection process...*". Her colleague observed, "*Obviously I'm in this position because my abilities have been overestimated.*" This form of self-doubt can be paralysing. It encourages sufferers to underrate their own abilities and produce tepid, conservative work when they have the capability to do much more. In my experience no one accidentally slips through the system. I constantly remind PGRs they deserve to be doing what they do, that they have skills that have brought them to where they are now.

More recent research has identified two groups of PGRs that are particularly susceptible to being overwhelmed by the belief they are impostors. Chapman (2017) examined a group of mature doctoral researchers who professed to such feelings of inadequacy and disassociation. Chapman argues that isolation and their feelings of being outside the institution cause the issue to foment, leading them to believe that they do not belong in HE level education. She writes:

> … for those with Impostor Syndrome [it] is associated with fear: fear of judgement, fear of failure and ultimately fear of exposure and being 'found out'. This was a genuine debilitating emotion for some of the students who found it difficult knowing 'where to start'. (Chapman, 2017, p. 114)

It is important for these mature doctoral researchers to become part of the research environment, from their first year. A case that occurred sometime back was that of Deirdre, a PT mature candidate who threw herself into her studies with some gusto. It did not appear she was having any problems, but in chance conversation with her over a coffee, she mentioned how she felt intimidated by her younger peers who all appeared to know exactly what to do. After a little probing, I began to realise she was feeling removed from the research community and was, in fact, doubting her own ability. I encouraged her to attend our monthly reading group, for a more informal forum to discuss research. While the meetings usually began with a discussion around a journal article, they often touched on a range of issues faced by PGRs. Being able to openly discuss research in friendly surroundings was helpful and so was realising her peers had their own challenges and concerns.

Another group highly susceptible to cultivating feelings of deficiency and detachment is that of first-generation researchers. Much has been written about first-generation students, but comparatively less about PhD candidates. For those whose parents did not receive a degree and are in effect pioneering new (intellectual) territory, it is widely understood that they have more barriers to progress than those coming from a background where third level education is considered a normal undertaking (Terenzini et al., 1996; Pascarella et al., 2004; Gardener and Holley, 2011). For doctoral researchers this also remains true, but with a higher likelihood of manifesting for female and black doctoral candidates self-identifying as first-generation researchers (Gardener and Holley, 2011). These PGRs are frequently highly motivated and driven by a desire to succeed (Próspero et al., 2012). When these first-generation researchers encounter barriers to progression, they typically internalise the problem and try to resolve it without support. When that fails, problems can occur.

Gardener and Holley (2011) in a series of interviews with first-generation researchers identified a range of issues, the most challenging of which was their belief that they occupied two worlds, as one interviewee described it:

> In a way I'm kind of caught in between these two groups: the working-class group and the world of academia. I don't fully belong to either group anymore. I kind of have one foot straddling that line. (Gardener and Holley, 2011, p. 84)

As a first-generation doctoral researcher myself, I can relate to this strange sense of being neither fish nor fowl. My own research studies took longer than my peers simply because my first year was spent in splendid isolation as I struggled to grasp the concept of what a thesis truly entailed. Self-doubt gripped me and I truly felt as if I was in an alien environment. What made it much more difficult was being unable to explain to friends and family what I was experiencing. How could they understand? They had no point of reference. They could only offer support, but as this was based on their belief in me and nothing evidential, it only served to add further pressure. I would love to be able to say I had a single breakthrough moment, but ultimately it was a long hard slog. Given enough time and considerable patience by my supervisor at the time, I was able to overcome the deep torpor I sank into, to achieve, by sheer persistence, the outcome desired.

Many texts point to the value of peer support, supervisory support and Faculty support. This is true. It is important to discuss your work and the challenges inherent to it with as many academic colleagues as possible, to help frame the route through to completion. But ultimately it is my belief that strong-willed persistence is the key. The willingness to keep beating at the mass of raw material and data until the work begins to take shape. The only words of advice I can offer here for the first-generation researcher suffering from paralysing uncertainty is not to be distracted by the progress of others. Too frequently I have seen PGRs be derailed in their work by, what appears to be on the surface at least, the smooth sailing progress of those around them. Worried they are not also achieving the same outputs they begin to think they are falling behind. Or worse, they begin to wonder if their supervisors are wrong and they need to be doing more. As we stressed in Chapter 5, different people work at different paces and in different ways. They work at different times on different aspects of their work. Don't be distracted by others, believe in yourself, believe in your team and keep working at the problem.

The pursuit of perfection

The final point worth making in terms of work derailment is the laudable yet dangerous pursuit of perfection since no thesis is ever perfect. This ties closely to concerns you may have over your own abilities. Particularly true of first year PGRs, but frequently in evidence in later years as well, is the researcher who will keep revisiting work trying to hone it to absolute perfection. While attention to detail and improved iterations of each thesis chapter is central to good research, these candidates fail to progress as they draft and redraft early sections or chapters of their thesis, indefinitely. This can happen because the PGR is unable to progress to the next stage of their thesis, so they end up putting the thesis in a holding pattern as they go back and revisit older material, rather than forging ahead with new work. It can, therefore, signal insecurity and self-doubt. This should be seen for the work avoidance technique it actually is (and be discouraged by supervisors if it repeatedly occurs). Specifically, sending small sections of work to supervisors over and over, seeking endorsement for minute changes, only serves to discourage everyone involved in the supervision. Take responsibility for your own work and if you must have someone proofread it, ask a trusted peer, don't impose your time-wasting anxieties on your team. Significantly, try to view perfection as a construct to aim to gravitate towards (rather than an achievable goal to be pursued obsessively) and make your search for excellence a habit.

More worrying is when the pursuit of perfection arises not due to procrastination and delaying tactics, but because the doctoral candidate has lost confidence and is unable to take a step forward without the approval of supervisors. Most often this occurs after the first piece of their work is critiqued by the DoS. Clouded by self-doubt and rocked by the many mistakes and/or changes required, inexperienced doctoral candidates can find themselves spending their first year desperately trying to make their work gleam. This has less to do with getting the work right and more about self-validation. For supervisors it is important to be supportive about the first piece of work that you hand back to your charge. Make sure it praises what has been done well alongside criticising, constructively, what has been done poorly, contextualising such feedback as a stepping off point to later, better chapters.

For PGRs who find they are suddenly spiralling out of control and cannot arrest their descent into self-recrimination, I recommend pausing, and reflecting. No thesis was finished in the first few months of study. It is better to be clear now on what is expected than to spend three years oblivious only to find out at the *viva*. More importantly, focus on all the messages being given to you by your supervisory team. Don't just focus on the negative comments but try to fix them. You are not trying to please your supervisory team. You are not trying to impress your peers. You are focusing on correctly and accurately completing a research process. Be guided by your supervisory team and focus on the measurable and the achievable. And don't obsess about perfection in an unhealthy desire to prove you belong.

Further critical concerns

Data management and data collection

In the final section of this chapter I want to touch on two areas that have the potential to greatly impact research and research outcomes, the topics of data management and data collection, as well as the connected challenge of undertaking research during a crisis such as the current Covid-19 pandemic, which can create enormous difficulties when it comes to data collection.

Empirical data underpins the thesis and when it proves impalpable or unobtainable it can bring research to a complete halt. A case from several years ago demonstrates the seriousness of the problem when it arises. Connor had moved successfully through the first phase of his studies and went into his second year ready to begin data collection. However, getting the data proved difficult. The companies he approached did not want to waste time on his surveys. He appealed for help and his supervisory team tried to utilise their contacts. Some data were obtained, but it was not substantial enough. As time passed, Connor became increasingly desperate. It is unclear exactly what happened next. Initially it seems that Connor tried to make the data stretch further than it could, but this was rejected by the supervisory team who told him he would need much more data to back up his arguments. A sudden surge of material only served to confuse the matter, as it appeared that Connor may have begun to falsify information. When his team requested to see the raw returns, Connor broke under the pressure. He suddenly claimed that due to serious personal problems he was unwilling to disclose, he had decided he would withdraw from the PhD programme. He did.

A particularly sad case for everyone involved, particularly as the overriding emotion was that more could have been done if only Connor had disclosed at an early stage the true depths of his predicament and his despair. Moreover, the problem surfaced far too late, at the beginning of the fourth year of FT PhD, for anyone to do anything about it. However, it does serve to highlight some important points about data collection. Early engagement with sources is crucial, there is no point developing research questions and objectives if the empirical data to evidence them cannot be obtained.

An early survey of available sources and their accessibility should be a priority during the application stage, as emphasised in Chapter 2. In the first year of your studies the temptation is to focus on theory and context, accepting data records at face value without delving deeply into their veracity, reliability, location or how they will be accessed. Good academic research will always leave a clear trail of actions to save future researchers duplicating effort. Especially as you work on your literature review, you will need to make notes on sources of data. Set up a separate folder and make detailed records of what other researchers have done and, more importantly, any obstacles they have encountered or caveats about the quality of the data used. Not only is this a great labour-saving device (saving you a second trawl through the literature in year two) but also good practice for your own research writing.

By the end of your first year you should be in the position to discuss with your team your proposed empirical data collection and data management plans. This will include any revisions you might want to make to your original sweep, as you will have learned new data sources and issues with existing ones. Once your team has agreed any changes and advised on what approach to take, this new knowledge will inform the conceptualisation and methodology of the thesis. It is important when building timelines to give ample time for interviews, archive dives, even data manipulation. Remember, the world does not march to your drumbeat. Just because you are in a hurry to get work done, doesn't mean others will be as eager. Build in buffers for interviews, to give subjects ample opportunity to meet you. Stress test questions to ensure you are getting the information needed. You will often only get one shot at an interview and steering interviewees in the direction required is often difficult. Don't go seeking the answers you want to hear but the answers that the subject (interviewee) wants to tell you. This will frequently change expectations, even understanding of a subject. Be prepared to change your views and material supporting them for what the evidence shows rather than bemoaning the lack of expected results. This is what research is about, after all.

Strategies to deal with difficulties and major crises 183

If you are doing surveys, give yourself enough time to develop and circulate them, as well as a feasible date to have them returned by. Telling recipients that you need results by the following week for a progress report will not work. Equally, if you are dealing with quantitative data, give yourself time to verify and analyse the data and record it. Getting used to accessing databases is time consuming. Keep detailed records of where data were obtained from, as you will frequently want to return to and look through such data sources. Be prepared for gaps and breaks in the data. Organisations present data in the manner they perceive as most useful to their audience, not necessarily your research. There are few things as frustrating as realising the information is there, just not available in the format you need, requiring significant effort on your part to produce a small piece of information that few will appreciate, other than in your immediate field of research.

A colleague of mine frequently complains that when he presents his work he will put up a graph that has taken him weeks to complete, only for his audience to largely ignore it, treating it as something to be expected rather than admired. If you have spent a considerable amount of time correcting a gap, this should be demonstrated in both your data management section and in your discussion of findings. Explain why it took so long to complete one small section of the work. A recent example that springs to mind occurred in a mock *viva* where the candidate casually mentioned he had done a shift-share analysis of both regions in his case studies. Despite the time and effort invested, it had revealed only what he had expected, so he dismissed it. Again, when doing data collection, record your work including the minor achievements.

If you find yourself in the unfortunate position of not having enough data collected, don't try to stretch your store as Connor did. No academic contribution is worth your integrity. Instead, discuss the problem honestly with your supervisory team to look for solutions. They might suggest proxies for existing information or might feel that the collected data will suffice for a less ambitious piece of work. Let me give you a concrete example by way of explanation. Veronica[54] was a PGR that I supervised to successful

---

54   Name changed to avoid identification.

completion. Her area of interest was stakeholders in a specific industrial sector and how they interacted in times of economic difficulty. Veronica wanted to examine the entire supply chain, but after her second round of interviews she had enough data only for producers and not suppliers. The choice was to go back for a third attempt or, instead, offer greater detail on the producers. Because Veronica had excellent contacts with the producers, the decision was made to shift the emphasis of her work to the producers only, with an annex offering further information on the suppliers, the difficulty of obtaining their views and what the next possible steps were for researchers following her pathway (as a profitable avenue for future research). The important point that Veronica learned was that her work was not perfect. But remember, no PhD thesis is. What was important was to garner sufficiently new and important evidence that would inform both academic understanding and governance of the sector, using a research process that was robust, replicable and thorough. Veronica was able to defend her approach because she had been scrupulous and transparent in her empirical data collection, even if her ambitions for the material fell short due to real-world obstacles.

Research during a global crisis

The final part of this chapter reflects on the current crisis that is afflicting countries as well as researchers worldwide. The pandemic of 2020, caused by the virus Covid-19, has been unparalleled in modern times in terms of the speed of its spread allied to its contagious properties, which compelled draconian actions by governments globally. Millions were forced to isolate curtailing movement and interaction. The scale of the pandemic has brought into sharp focus the role of closely intertwined global networks that support the flow of goods and services, logistics, travel and work practices. In the UK the outbreak of the virus offered a significant challenge to the education sector, leading to a range of solutions that allowed HEIs to remain open and research and teaching to continue apace. However, this was not a painless transition and what is captured below is a reflection on this process, at each stage of the doctoral journey, and the lessons that can be taken by researchers who may still be impacted by the pandemic or are facing a similar challenging event of their own.

The response to the pandemic by university senior managers was to lockdown campuses across the UK and seek alternative means to deliver supervision. Those who were due to travel to the UK for study were either deferred or encouraged to start their studies from their home countries until such time as the risk of travel and transmission had receded to more acceptable, safer levels. The first area that was greatly affected was PhD applications. Many who had made careful plans for the start of their PhD suddenly found themselves delayed by three to four months, depending on enrolment cycles at their institution of choice. The result was a huge flurry of activity for admissions teams, followed by a glut of applications for the next enrolment period as deferrals and normal numbers of applications came together, overwhelming administrators, some of whom were already dealing with illness on their teams. Mistakes were almost inevitably made and in one memorable example in our university a new starter was threatened with deportation due to an outdated document in their application. Only for a timely intervention by our university's authorities at the UK immigration office, the candidate avoided being forced to return home and reapply for his visa. If time is not a constraint for you as an applicant, consider deferring for a longer period beyond the next enrolment cycle to avoid such issues occurring at exceptional times such as this one.

If you have been already accepted onto a course and are fearful of the dangers of travel due to contagion, contact your new institution to request permission to pursue your studies remotely from home. If in receipt of a grant or stipend it may be necessary to renegotiate some of the terms of your agreement with your university. Most HEIs will be much more flexible about regulations during these events and will understand the problems facing those travelling for purposes of doctoral research. On arrival to the UK from abroad, international candidates may be expected to quarantine for a fixed period. During this period, using online resources and contacting your supervisory team in an online forum will allow an early start to be made during isolation.

Ultimately, access to key resources will be of key concern to researchers, domestic and international. Many UK universities have a range of supporting services and resources to draw on, for example, by making laptops and critical software available offsite. Information on what is available will be displayed prominently on the main university site and you should contact those in charge of overseeing these resources to find out what applies to you. This is particularly important for those with a disability who may be even more disadvantaged than others during this period. For some, isolation will be too great a challenge. To combat this universities will frequently supply safe spaces on campus for purposes of work and research. These will need to be booked but can provide an important change of pace and scenery. Supervisors can also meet PGRs face-to-face in these designated areas but whilst adhering to the strictest social distancing measures and with facial protective equipment, though the preference would be for online engagement as much as possible.

The biggest challenge, of course, is to those PGRs seeking to do data collection during a pandemic. Previously I discussed the import of empirical data collection and the associated problems of failing to gain access to relevant data. During a pandemic, when travel and face-to-face interviews become problematic, researchers will be forced to alter expectations and their research methodology. The first step should be to contact your supervisory team to discuss the implications for your work. Alternatives should be discussed, including, for example:

- Substituting face-to-face interviews with phone interviews or online surveys.
- Reducing the number of required interviews for your research and elaborate on your increased constraints as a result of the unforeseen circumstances at the end of the thesis as part of your acknowledgements of limitations.
- Contacting archives to source electronic records or have physical records copied and sent to you.
- Your University should also be contacted to see how much financial support they can offer for these additional tasks resulting from crises not caused by you.
- Rearranging workshops and meetings for a later period, again with the permission and support of your institution in terms of timing.
- Contacting firms and organisations to investigate the possibility of limited or controlled access using safe travel and safe location options *en route* and/or on site.

Failing these steps, PGRs must give some thought to suspending their studies, particularly if they are paying fees. Again, HEIs will be supportive of such decisions in a period of crisis.

In terms of writing up, it may appear at least that isolation and immobility would be the least of a doctoral candidate's worries. But in an extremely stressful period, the inability to distract oneself with a relaxing trip, just for a change of scenery, can be mentally draining. Fatigue grows quicker with fewer release valves available to the PGR. Regular team meetings with supervisors can help, if only to let off steam. But it is also important to take frequent breaks and set aside tasks if frustration builds. The major concern is that fatigue may lead to procrastination, deadlines will be missed and the mental wellbeing of the candidate spiral downwards. It may seem counterintuitive, but most universities will understand the pressures of writing-up during a pandemic and do their best to support PGRs including allowing the option of suspending temporarily, if requested.

The final point to consider is that of doing a *viva voce* online. Having chaired several, I can testify to their unusual nature. While I have been extremely lucky to date in having had largely trouble-free sessions, I would certainly not recommend an online environment, particularly for an expected-to-be difficult *viva*. In the first instance, they take a much longer time to perform. There is also considerable difficulty making sure all internet connections are good and without interruptions. The timing and etiquette of asking questions is still something of an unknown. Ultimately, I would argue that online is no real substitute for just sitting in a room and discussing your work with knowledgeable peers. If you are involved in an online *viva*, read the suggestions offered in Chapter 10.

Some final words of encouragement

Writing a PhD thesis is not easy. It is an enormously challenging task that requires a wide range of skills including project management, data collection, critical analysis, organisational abilities and a holistic understanding of research. While it requires a level of intelligence and ability that is uncommon, it is much more about being able to persist in pursuing a singular task over an extended period with an overarching perspective allied to detailed and careful work practices. It prepares you to pursue research projects, both small and large, by training you to, step by careful step, put together a well-structured, well-thought-out piece of work that demonstrates knowledge of the discipline and contributes to it in a meaningful way. It is not a passport to success, or the final test in a person's education. It is, instead, a process that both teaches you how to research, but also contributes to research knowledge of the world around us. Debunking the myths that persist around doing a PhD, understanding what it is you as a doctoral researcher are actually achieving, should be of solace to you, offer you succour and encourage you to push ahead and attain your goal.

References

Angelle, P., Agnello, M. F., Amlund, J. T., Caffarella, R. S., Chance, P. L., Edmonson, S., Fulmer, C., Gonzalez, M. L., Gooden, M. A., Henderson, J. E., and Jacobson, S. (2010). *The Doctoral Student's Advisor and Mentor: Sage Advice from the Experts*. Plymouth, UK: Rowman & Littlefield Publishers.

Cain, S. (2013). *Quiet: The Power of Introverts in a World that Can't Stop Talking*. New York: Broadway Books.

Chapman, A. (2017). Using the assessment process to overcome Imposter Syndrome in mature students. *Journal of Further and Higher Education*, 41(2), 112–119.

Clance, P. R. and Imes, S. A. (1978). The imposter phenomenon in high achieving women: Dynamics and therapeutic intervention. *Psychotherapy: Theory, Research & Practice*, 15(3), 241–247.

De Lange, A. H., Taris, T. W., Kompier, M. A. J., Houtman, I. L. D., and Bongers, P. M. (2004). Work characteristics and psychological well-being. Testing normal, reversed and reciprocal relationships within the 4-wave SMASH study. *Work and Stress*, 18(2), 149–166.

De Vita, G. and Case, P. (2003). Rethinking the internationalisation agenda in UK higher education. *Journal of Further and Higher Education*, 27(4), 383–398.

Dickens, C. (2009). *David Copperfield*. Ebook, Project Gutenberg. Online available at: <https://www.gutenberg.org/files/766/766-h/766-h.htm>

Drake, P. and Heath, L. (2010). *Practitioner Research at Doctoral Level: Developing Coherent Research Methodologies*. London, UK: Routledge.

Durepos, G. (2016). Early Career Reflections on Discursive Pressures in Business Schools. In: Prasad, A. (Ed.). *Contesting Institutional Hegemony in Today's Business Schools: Doctoral Students Speak Out*. London, UK: Emerald Group Publishing.

Gardner, S. K. and Holley, K. A. (2011). "Those invisible barriers are real": The progression of first-generation students through doctoral education. *Equity & Excellence in Education*, 44(1), 77–92.

HESA (2019). UK domiciled qualifiers by disability and sex; Postgraduate (research). Online available at: <https://www.hesa.ac.uk/data-and-analysis/students/table-35>

HESA (2020a). Widening participation summary: UK Performance Indicators 2018/19. Available online at: <https://www.hesa.ac.uk/data-and-analysis/performance-indicators/widening-participation-summary-1819>

HESA (2020b). What are HE students' progression rates and qualifications? Available online, available at: <https://www.hesa.ac.uk/data-and-analysis/students/outcomes>

HESA (2020c). Who's studying in HE? Available online at: <https://www.hesa.ac.uk/data-and-analysis/students/whos-in-he>

HESA (2020d). Who's working in HE? Available online at: <https://www.hesa.ac.uk/data-and-analysis/staff/working-in-he>

HM Government (HMG, 2010). Equality Act 2010: Guidance. Available online at: <https://assets.publishing.service.gov.uk/government/uploads/system/uploads/attachment_data/file/570382/Equality_Act_2010-disability_definition.pdf>

HM Government (HMG, 2020). Help if you're a student with a learning difficulty, health problem or disability. Available online at: <https://www.gov.uk/disabled-students-allowances-dsas>

Lester, J. (2013). Family-Friendly Policies for Doctoral Students. In: Holley, K. A. and Joseph, J. (Eds.). *Increasing Diversity in Doctoral Education: Implications for Theory and Practice: New Directions for Higher Education*, No. 163. London, UK: John Wiley & Sons.

Levecque, K., Anseel, F., De Beuckelaer, A., Van der Heyden, J., and Gisle, L. (2017). Work organization and mental health problems in PhD students. *Research Policy*, 46(4), 868–879.

Neumann, R. and Rodwell, J. (2009). The 'invisible' part-time research students: A case study of satisfaction and completion. *Studies in Higher Education*, 34(1), 55-68.

Pascarella, E. T., Pierson, C. T., Wolniak, G. C., and Terenzini, P. T. (2004). First-generation college students: Additional evidence on college experiences and outcomes. *The Journal of Higher Education*, 75(3), 249–284.

Phillips, E. and Pugh, D. (2010). *How to get a PhD – A Handbook for Students and their Supervisors*. Berkshire, England: McGraw-Hill Education.

Próspero, M., Russell, A. C., and Vohra-Gupta, S. (2012). Effects of motivation on educational attainment: Ethnic and developmental differences among first-generation students. *Journal of Hispanic Higher Education*, 11(1), 100–119.

Robinson-Pant, A. (2010). 'Internationalisation of higher education: Challenges for the doctoral supervisor' *in* Thomson, P. and Walker, M. (Eds.) 2010. *The Routledge Doctoral Supervisor's Companion: Supporting Effective Research in Education and the Social Sciences*. London, UK: Routledge.

Slight, C. (2017). Postgraduate Research Experience Survey 2017. Higher Education Authority (HEA). Available online at: <https://s3.eu-west-2.amazonaws.com/assets.creode.advancehe-document-manager/documents/hea/private/hub/download/pres_2017_report_0_1568037544.pdf>

Terenzini, P. T., Springer, L., Yaeger, P. M., Pascarella, E. T., and Nora, A. (1996). First-generation college students: Characteristics, experiences, and cognitive development. *Research in Higher Education*, 37(1), 1–22.

Vitae (2016). Women in research: The latest developments in gender equality. Available online at: <https://www.vitae.ac.uk/vitae-publications/guides-briefings-and-information/vitae-women-in-research-2016.pdf>

Vitae (2020a). Premia: Supervising disabled doctoral researchers. Available online at: <https://www.vitae.ac.uk/doing-research/supervising-a-doctorate/supporting-disabled-doctoral-researchers>

Vitae (2020b). Doing a doctorate as a disabled researcher. Available online at: <https://www.vitae.ac.uk/doing-research/every-researcher-counts-equality-and-diversity-in-researcher-careers/resources-and-support-for-disabled-researchers/doing-a-doctorate-as-a-disabled-researcher>

Vitae (2020c). Equality and diversity: Actions for all. Available online at: <https://www.vitae.ac.uk/vitae-publications/guides-briefings-and-information/vitae-equality-diversity-actions-for-all-2015.pdf>

Vitae (2020d). Researcher wellbeing and mental health. Available online at: <https://www.vitae.ac.uk/doing-research/wellbeing-and-mental-health/vitae-mental-health-web.pdf/view>

Watts, J. H. (2010). Supervising part-time doctoral students: Issues and challenges. In: Thomson, P. and Walker, M. (Eds.). *The Routledge Doctoral Supervisor's Companion: Supporting Effective Research in Education and the Social Sciences*. London, UK: Routledge.

Williams, S. (2019). Postgraduate Research Experience Survey 2019. Higher Education Authority (HEA). Available online at: <https://s3.eu-west-2.amazonaws.com/assets.creode.advancehe-document-manager/documents/advance-he/AdvanceHE-Postgraduate_Research_%20Survey_%202019_1574338111.pdf>

DAVID BOWEN

8 Annual progress reviews

Preamble

Throughout the course of a PhD, whether part-time or full-time, you will be required by your university to submit an annual update of your doctoral work in the form of a written review and subsequently discuss its content verbally, most often with one or more academics from outside your supervisory team. Often, although not invariably across countries and institutions, such written review and discussion is known as an Annual Progress Review (APR). Readers will know the precise terminology that applies to their own university. The **aim of this chapter** is to discuss what is likely to be required of you in order to pass through and benefit from the APR process. Unless otherwise specified, mention of the term APR will refer to both the written and verbal component.

APR overall function and structure

Function

The key function of an APR is to review progress made through the year as part of overall progress towards PhD submission. That includes reference to the previous year or years, as appropriate. However, an APR is also a projection onward into any subsequent year, or years in the form of a justified plan. The APR, therefore, is both retrospective and forward looking. When you submit an APR, you are effectively defining a position in the development of the PhD. It is a marker in time.

Your audience for the APR (written and verbal) will be a single generalist academic with extensive experience of PhD research or, more likely, an APR panel consisting of a generalist plus a specialist academic with knowledge of your theory and/or methodology. Other combinations may make up the APR panel as deemed appropriate by your faculty or university. Some universities involve an academic from outside the faculty onto the APR panel. One or more supervisors, too, are sometimes invited either as active participants or observers. However, we know of some universities where supervisors are not allowed to take part. It is worth noting at this point that members of the APR panel are not 'supplementary supervisors' but their advice should be taken seriously nonetheless and discussed further with the supervisory team. Often too it is left to the APR panel to make the critical decision to allow the PGR to proceed or to recommend terminating their enrolment. Contact between the APR panel and the supervisor is of paramount importance to avoiding misunderstandings but where that does not happen or in cases where the Director of Studies was not present at the APR, the PGR should brief the supervisory team on what was said at the APR.

The APR panel may be set up in a very formal way or may be comparatively informal. In some institutions it may involve a presentation of specified length, either timewise or in terms of the number of presentation slides.

APR written review

Typically, the APR written review is contained within the template of an APR document with a standardised structure as designated by your university. You should take very close note of the template and fill in every component. Do not judge that there is a closed box component that does not apply to your case. For example, if there is closed box that requires you to state 'yes/no' whether you have applied for ethical approval and, if not, to state when that will occur, make sure that you provide the necessary information. The same applies to other open-ended components. For example, if there is a request to list your pre-doctoral experience, make sure that you provide the required details. Like many documents that you will fill as a researcher following completion of your PhD, such as applications for research positions or research grants, all the various components of the written APR, not just the section that deals in depth with core research activity and supporting activities, help to build up a holistic view of you as a candidate. If you miss a component that may well rile, completely unnecessarily, one or more members of your APR panel.

In writing the section of the written APR document on your core research activity pay close attention, as in a submitted thesis, to the style of your writing. Ensure that you use appropriate academic language but also strike a balance so that you do not wallow in impenetrable terminology. An overly dense use of terminology does not help with clarity for either a specialist or generalist. The specialist may simply judge that despite your awareness of terminology you are hiding behind it as a cover. The generalist may judge that you are unable to convey a central message outside your immediate field and will quiz you especially hard on the core of your work in the verbal component of the APR. In such a case you are reliant on producing a good verbal outline and set of answers under the pressure of a viva-like situation. It is far better not to get to that scenario and so enter the verbal part of the APR safe in the knowledge that you have produced a clear core document. As an aside PGRs sometimes query the value of a generalist view in an APR, whether with regard to the written or verbal component. That is rather a narrow outlook. A generalist on an APR panel may query what is otherwise taken for granted in your field or suggest a parallel with work outside your field that is unknown to the specialist on the panel or, indeed, your supervisors.

The degree of standardisation of the APR document varies across the university sector. In the unlikely event that a template is not provided for the written review, you will need to develop a clear structure with distinct headings and sub-headings. The comments throughout this chapter on APRs will help guide you in that action.

APR verbal discussion

In most instances the APR involves verbal discussion, face-to-face or online, with one, two or more academics as outlined above. Many of the elements considered in Chapter 10 of this book on preparing for the final *viva* apply to preparation for the *viva*-like verbal discussion of the APR. One way in which your APR verbal discussion may be different is that the APR panel may not include a specialist. However, as will be discussed in Chapter 9, you always need to think of your audience when you are due to present research. In that regard the APR verbal discussion is no different from any other presentation. For some further thoughts, see the sub-section below on the APR as a trial *viva*.

APR as forward strategy

As a marker in time an APR needs to offer a forward strategy. The APR forward strategy for any one year is later subject to critical reflection in the following year. Therefore, preparation of a forward strategy has a double usage and benefit.

Planning

It is important to plan actions for any upcoming academic year not just with regard to core research activity such as reading or field work and analysis, but also through intent to attend and/or contribute towards a variety of supporting activities such as seminars and workshops or publicising work. A plan for the first year of a PhD should be articulated with supervisors within the first two to four weeks of PhD study and it should form the basis of the end of year APR critical reflection. From that point on, a similar forward strategy needs to be embedded within the APR of each subsequent year. In short, the seeds of a good APR are laid

48–52 weeks before submission of a written APR and subsequent discussion with an APR panel.

Some PGRs never attach due importance to such planning and long-term preparation and follow a comparatively *laissez-faire* approach, especially if it is not a pre-requisite set by a supervisor, faculty or university. Others just write a plan and then largely ignore it as the year progresses. From experience, the first approach is not recommended. With respect to the second approach, a plan needs to be an active document. Of course, flexibility is always important, and a plan may not be completely adhered to for very good reasons. Yet, in general it is good to have a baseline of intent that covers all likely actions that will progress the research. The *caveat* is to avoid a third approach in which the plan becomes an all-consuming activity in itself. In an APR submission and a final thesis submission what has actually been carried through has more weight than what was planned and not carried through even though in some instances, as will be outlined, the reasons for abandoning parts of a plan can give rise to informative discussion: for example, when it is decided to not use a particular technique.

Specifics: Core research activity

When planning forward it is a wise approach to think in detail and so include specifics. For example, in the first three to six months of study, your supervisory team will probably recommend that you read widely and open up aspects of work that are not immediately obvious. That emphasis on width should be specified within your plan for the first year of a PhD, leading to your first APR, rather than a vaguer statement such as to develop and engage in initial reading. Moreover, you should read with regard to theory, methodology and also style of presentation, and so truly develop a multi-sided approach to your critical reading (Wallace and Wray, 2011). That should also be specified. It is all too easy to concentrate just on theory during initial reading, especially if a particular set of journal articles or books appear to be at the core of your presumed theoretical direction. An active plan in the first year of a PhD that is referred to at regular intervals and that specifies the action of reading for theoretical content, methodology and style, will help remind you that journal articles and books can be read for various different purposes.

In subsequently developing a forward strategy for the second year of study, leading to the second APR, a continued emphasis needs to be placed on thinking in detail and including specifics. Extending the example from above, in any PhD study it is important to sustain the currency of theoretical and methodological understanding that is developed in the first year. That will involve keeping up to date with emerging journal articles, books and practitioner reports plus, depending on topic, events happening in the wider economic, social and political environment. In keeping with the agenda for thinking in detail and including specifics, the first year APR should include a listing of the specific sources that will be the focus of attention for ongoing reading. With an emphasis in your first year APR that your main forward strategy will shift towards data collection and analysis you may decide that reading will be confined to leading journals. Some fields may have a wide variety of relevant journals but from within those there will be a smaller number that are considered to be leading contributors to the field. Those will need to be specified. The example above may not be of precise relevance, but readers can decide for themselves how thinking in detail and including specifics applies to their own study in the first, second and subsequent years.

A forward strategy obviously needs specific reference to timings. It is dangerous when engaged in PhD study to be a slave to timing. For example, later in this chapter there is a section on reflection. It is argued that reflection does not necessarily materialise at a specific time and requires an ongoing approach to help it emerge. However, other timings can be included in an APR with a degree of certainty. There will deadlines to be met not least, in relation to this chapter, the deadline for submission of your APR. Forward strategy will make a note of such deadlines and work back to fix timings. For example, if the APR is due for submission on June 30 and your faculty suggests that it is discussed with your supervisors before submission, you should arrange a mutually agreed draft submission (e.g. June 1) and supervisor feedback date (e.g. June 15) so that the final submission date of June 30 is achievable.

Specifics: Supporting activities

An awareness of the need for specifics is also necessary when listing a forward strategy of supporting activities. Within every university, within any given year, it is highly likely that regular seminar and workshop series or special events are arranged for PhD researchers at university, faculty and sub-faculty level. They may cover aspects of theory, research methodology, as well as other topics such as how to gain ethical approval from the university ethics committee or writing for publication and/or grant applications. Such activities may be repeated on an annual basis or may be rather more *ad hoc*. Attendance may be voluntary or compulsory or anywhere in the continuum between the two. As a PhD researcher, you should make a deliberate attempt to know as much in advance as possible about such activities, including the timings, and make the most of them as a critical adjunct of your core research activity. Then, of course, it will be up to you to make a determined effort to plan them into the forward strategy within your APR, fitting them around your core research activity. Eventually, too, you will include them as part of your APR reflection as per the double usage and benefit mentioned above.

It is highly likely that there will also be seminars, workshops and special events geared not just towards PhD researchers but other university, faculty or sub-faculty level researchers, too. In a well-run university there will be a mechanism to publicise all such activity to PhD researchers. As a PhD researcher, you should ensure that you are included on relevant mailing lists, or pay attention to online message boards, so that you broaden the range of supporting activity that you plan into your APR.

Your faculty is probably your main research home. In general, if there is an active research culture among fellow researchers and PGRs within your faculty, you should demonstrate in the forward strategy of your APR that you will contribute to that research culture by attendance at seminars, workshops and special events. However, it is highly likely that potentially relevant activities also occur in other faculties. Whilst maintaining a balance so that supporting research activities do not start to erode time spent on your core research activity, you should also pay attention to such activities, too. In my own PhD, a change in research direction was generated because I planned, at the beginning of an academic year, to attend an out of faculty seminar series to find out what PGRs in other faculties were offered on their doctoral course. Topic-wise one of the seminars was very tangential to my own research but in retrospect became particularly useful when the presenter, who was researching UK general elections, digressed and spoke about an opportunity that she was given by an MP to browse through documents, in the UK House of Commons, that were not at that moment within the public domain. The suggestion of the presenter was simply to take up any such opportunities and more or less drop whatever else is occurring. That was very useful advice as a few months later the same thing happened in my own research. I was interviewing a CEO about the usefulness of Customer Survey Questionnaires (CSQs). He pointed to a walk-in cupboard in his office that contained several hundred completed CSQs (paper form) and he gave me until the end of the day to read them through. After a good-natured plea from me, he allowed me to return the following day, too. What I read changed the course of my research because I realised that my aim to explore antecedents of customer service satisfaction and how they develop through time within an extended customer service period could not be achieved just via use of a standard CSQ (Bowen, 2002). I was primed to take the opportunity given by the CEO because of the out-of-faculty seminar that I attended, and a reflective note I made after the seminar to take such a chance if it happened to me. When making the note, I passed off such an opportunity as an unlikely occurrence. Of course, when I reflected on core research activity in my following APR, it was useful to explain the change in direction of my research with reference to the priming process from across-faculty seminar attendance.

Across-faculty activity is becoming more important as universities develop internal networks based around designated research foci that are incubators of ideas and/or pools of collective expertise, geared towards income generation via research bids. An awareness of that trend and intent to be included in such networks and their various activities may prove beneficial to your PhD and add some extra spice to your APR.

With all supporting activities, whilst breadth of activity is a good thing you should seek to avoid using the activities as a diversion away from the sometimes more prosaic effort that is needed to sit in one place and read, or sort through data and write for prolonged periods of time without the distraction of other activities. Therefore, in your written APR the rationale for attendance in supporting activities at university, faculty or sub-faculty level should be overt and explicable to your APR panel.

There is, of course, a world beyond your university. As time moves on and you move beyond the initial stages of your PhD you should start to plan for and so include in your APR supporting activities from outside your own university. In some instances, there may be specialist courses that you will need to attend in order to cover a gap in training that is not available within your university or faculty. Examples of such training from among PGRs that I have worked with include specialist language training for a PGR prior to participant observation within an indigenous community in Cusco, Peru and specialist data analysis training for econometricians. In addition, of course, as your PhD progresses you should be planning to attend and present in conferences for other PGRs, academic researchers or practitioners (as will be elaborated on in the next chapter). As with all the other core research activity and supporting activities detailed above, the forward strategy that you specify within your APR will need to justify how your presentation contributes to your PhD progress. That will be doubly useful. The APR panel may be in a position to back your attendance and/or you can use the same argument when you make a separate application for funding to your faculty.

APR as critical reflection

The APR as a marker of time needs to include a section that looks back in the form of a critical reflection as well as a section that looks to the future in the form of a forward strategy. A retrospective listing of core research activity and supporting activities by themselves is not as useful within an APR as a listing discussed with a critical reflection. It is important that you carry out your intention as listed in the forward strategy and reflect on it within both the written and verbal component of the APR process. The reflection on any particular aspect of the forward strategy may be confined to one paragraph of the written APR and a short part of the verbal APR if there has not been any major shift in specifics. However, the reflection will be more substantial if something more significant has emerged from within the core research activity and supporting activities. Examples include the emergence of a new stream of literature, methodological approach or style of presentation.

Reflection process

In the same way that the section above on the APR as forward strategy required an overview of how to plan, so this section requires some thoughts on the process of reflection. During the recent Covid-19 pandemic it was stated by the CEO of the Anglo-Swedish drug maker AstraZeneca that the process of vaccine manufacture is different from the manufacture of orange juice and that the yield at production sites can vary (BBC, 2021). There is an analogy with the process of reflection. You may find that reflections rarely come to order and so the period that you write your APR will need to factor time into the development of your reflections and/or you will need to have a system to develop and record reflections through any given year leading up to the end of year APR. Both approaches may work and you should also think how to maximise your reflective productivity by an active awareness of contributing elements such as the time of day that best allows you to reflect, or the place and activity that best allows reflection such as lying down in a dark room, taking a long walk, or sitting in a busy café.

From talking to many PGRs I conclude that a systematic approach to reflection works best. That involves a constant reflection on the relevance of what someone writes or says in relation to one's own PhD. That becomes especially valuable if an effort is made and a routine established to make a written note of reflections during or soon after they occur: whether from core research activity (like reading or writing) or any supporting activities (like seminars, workshops and special events). Written notes are useful as an *aide memoire*. You will definitely forget specific detailed reflections, not to mention broad reflections, without a written note. Once you have a system so that you do not rest until your reflection is committed in writing, on paper or online, you will build up a fund of reflections to insert in your next written APR, albeit very succinctly, as well as the written thesis itself. The same fund can be used in the verbal part of the APR and by extension the *viva* and future presentations.

It is worth considering how the above works in practice. In an APR at the end of the first year of a PhD it is almost inevitable that you will receive questions to justify the choice of the main authors who are driving your literature review and/or a justification for the main streams of literature that you have decided to focus on. As you read one journal article after another and constantly reflect on the relevance of each article or set of articles to your work there will definitely come a point where you will be able to jot a written reflection, short or long, on whether the articles are relevant or irrelevant to your study. When taken with other reflections they can help answer any APR questioning about the key authors driving your literature review or the main streams of literature that you have chosen to focus on.

An example of a reflective approach is evident from the excerpt of an APR below. The PGR was at the end of his third year of full-time research, investigating the role of strategic practices in megachurches, hence the reference in the excerpt to prayers. Systematic reflection allowed him to make succinct and intelligent comments in his APR on transcription:

> My experience with transcription showed that it is not a transparent process but one that is interpretative (Lapadat and Lindsay, 1999), relying on the transcriber to make decisions, judgements and choices (Bird, 2005). For instance, at the start of some interviews and sometimes at the end, prayers were said by the respondents. This did not make it to the transcribed document because I decided it was not relevant to the study, which highlights the subjective nature of the transcription process. Kvale (1996) suggests that transcription should not be seen as an insignificant process but one that should be clearly and carefully described. Transcription was done manually with the aid of a transcription tool known as Otter, artificial intelligence software used to transcribe audio into text. The end product of this automated transcription was rather poor with an accuracy rate of about 20%. Particular challenges emerged where the interview involved speakers with accents other that British or American and when the recording quality was poor. As a result, I still had to listen to the recordings carefully, making corrections and basically re-transcribing each interview. Though it was a slow, tiring and mechanical process, the effort was not wasted as I became intimately familiar with the data (Braun and Clarke, 2006). I have come

to see transcription as representational and the transcribed text as an attempt to capture as best possible the interview event. Transcription, therefore, is not objective but subjective, it is practically impossible to represent every detail in text (Lapadat and Lindsay, 1999).

The same reflection process applies to any seminar, workshop or special event that you attend. Most faculties have doctoral candidates studying a diversity of topics and so you are very likely to attend seminars and workshops in which the direct, overt relevance of presentations is limited. That becomes more pronounced if you take the advice from above to attend supporting activities from across your university. However, if you adopt the mode to constantly reflect on the relevance of what someone says to one's own PhD there will never be a supporting activity that is irrelevant, even if the relevance is confined to a few minutes in any one hour. A written reflective note at the end of a seemingly irrelevant supporting activity may be very short, but it may be the link to justify the inclusion or non-inclusion of a stream of literature or a particular methodological technique, or a myriad of other elements that compose a PhD thesis. You may have noticed that in the acknowledgement section of journals and books many authors make indirect note of a reflective system. Specifically, from the range of books on how to get a PhD, Dunleavy (2003, p. xii) writes about the content of his book as a conduit for the ideas of students and staff that he '*jotted down* (my emphasis), adopted (and) tried out ... over the years'.

Direction change

The process of critical reflection will inevitably lead to some big decisions. It may be convenient if they occur at the time that you are writing your APR, but they may be made at any time during any particular year. Mention is made above about verbal APR discussion concerning the main authors who are driving your literature review and/or your chosen main streams of literature. In the early part of a PhD, PGRs are customarily encouraged to read widely, and that process can mean that multiple strands of literature are explored. It is very important to explore those strands because otherwise there is a chance that a key sub-field will be ignored. When setting out on the literature review phase of a PhD use should be made of multiple books. Some may be skim read and a smaller number read in depth, either as a whole or in part. It is standard practice, too, that in an established research area it is necessary to engage with multiple journal sources and a large number of academic journal articles. However, not all the books or journals or journal articles will be relevant. It may well be that a particular sub-field appears after some time to be less than relevant or even irrelevant to the aim and objectives of the research. In such a situation, there is a need to pull back. However, in the APR there is a need to describe what has been done. A very good APR will reflect on whether the exploration of the abandoned literature was inevitable or whether there were signals that the exploration was better called-off earlier in the process. That will also help as new strands of literature are sought further along the research process. As part of an APR it is important to document not just what you are continuing to go ahead with but also what you are not going ahead with. Here is an example of direction change as expressed in the APR of a part-time PGR at the end of her third year of study:

> This PhD research started out as a project on women and identity in private security organisations. In conversation with my two supervisors, this aim slowly morphed into something more sharply defined. This was in part because of further reading and developing better understandings of particular literatures and in part because of the practicalities and constraints of both my day job and what is possible 'in the field' (e.g. women participants are difficult to locate and recruit). This has meant the following changes to the study:
>
> - Changes to conceptualisation: the themes of female employees/women and frontline security roles made way for feminisation and everyday practice in relation to professionalism. The gendered nature of professionalization in the security industry remains of interest. Private security as a theme moved further to the background, but still provides an important context for the research.
> - Changes to empirical objectives: interview data are now accompanied by more substantial secondary data. As a result, the number of interviews is lower than anticipated and I will no longer carry out observations.
> - Addition to analysis: I will design a close reading methodology to analyse policy text in documents.

As noted from the example above, direction change is not confined to literature review. For example, with regard to methodology, an APR that covers the year during which you have determined the main methodology or techniques that you intend to employ will need to outline the rationale for your choice including what you have decided to leave out. That is especially pertinent in an APR because you may have taken several weeks or even months considering the adoption of one particular technique, for example, the use of participant observation, only to then discard it and use a combination of in-depth interviews and focus groups. Alternatively, you may have decided to modify rather than reject what you intended, for example, to use one period of participant observation in one location rather than several periods in different locations. The time spent reading about, designing and even preparing work in the field that you subsequently decide not to go ahead with may seem to you like a frustrating loss of time that you want to skim over in your APR. However, it is a good idea not to take such a view. There are several reasons why that may be the case. Letting go of an approach that is deemed by you and others around you as inappropriate, after due exploration of its possibilities, demonstrates a level of criticality that is important for PhD study. It is not something to be swept away and not referred to, whether in an APR or in a final thesis submission. At the very least, the articulation of a path in your APR that you have explored and then abandoned will act as an *aide memoire* for you when you write the relevant chapter to which it belongs (e.g. methodology chapter). It may also trigger thoughts when preparing for a *viva* and allow you to anticipate an examiner question about alternative techniques for conducting your PhD research. Studying for a PhD in business and management is not necessarily as pre-determined from a methodology point of view as in the hard sciences which are more often tied to considerable funding and predicated on laboratory access for experiments using capital intensive equipment. A discussion of a change in technique or methodology is certainly relevant in an APR. After all it may also have involved some considerable negotiation with your supervisors or even a change in supervisory team.

Research community

So far this section on the APR as a critical reflection has largely concentrated on how core research activity and supporting activities influence you and your world as gauged by your ongoing research output. However, as a member of a research community you have a wider responsibility and it is good in an APR to outline your contribution to that community. The excerpt from an APR below illustrates the contribution of a PGR beyond his immediate study:

> I was a PhD student representative over the last year and I attended all but one of the faculty academic research meetings. At the start of lockdown, I was concerned about the effects of isolation on the mental health of PhD colleagues, especially international colleagues who were either stranded away from their families or unable to return to the UK to continue their research. Consequently I started sessions which we dubbed as 'PhD Virtual Coffee' to ensure colleagues had regular on-going contact with one another. To date I have organised seven of those sessions, which all have some or other research theme or speaker and they have proved to be popular and appreciated by the 15–20 colleagues who attend.

Your APR can additionally capture and discuss reflections on supporting activities that are related specifically to your experience but may also benefit the wider community. For example, you may have gained the opportunity to attend an external training session on a particular method that is not available in your university. The APR panel will be interested in your thoughts on that for PGRs who may want to attend a repeat of the course in a following year. The same applies to conference attendance. As a member of a community, you should recognise that it is important for a faculty to build up a realistic view of whether particular conferences are worthwhile for PGRs. Your APR panel as a whole, or individual members within the panel, may be in a position to influence faculty conference support. Sometimes annual gatherings at conferences can become staid affairs and what was once reckoned to be a dynamic event loses energy. In such a circumstance, if you provide a considered opinion in an APR, monies that your faculty spends on a future cohort can be more usefully diverted elsewhere. New conferences emerge and with your input they can be pencilled in as potential alternatives. Discussion in an APR can have a wider relevance than your own APR.

Retrospective clear-up

It was stated earlier that a strong written and verbal APR will most likely emerge from forward strategy rather than a sudden burst of action as the deadline for submission of an APR becomes imminent. If you do not plan ahead and do not engage in ongoing critical reflection, the period leading up to submission of a written APR and subsequent verbal discussion will probably be hectic and anxious. In such an instance, your APR will effectively become a retrospective clear-up that relies on memory of core research activity and supporting activities with *post facto* justification. Overall, that is not satisfactory as an approach. It is far better to engage in forward looking strategy and critical reflection as outlined in this chapter.

APR as verbal articulation

Another benefit can emerge from the verbal part of the APR if it is used as a means to develop a particular articulation of your work. In Chapter 9 of this book we discuss talking about, presenting and publicising your PhD. The APR is one such event, albeit rather closeted, where that can occur. Of course, the verbal discussion of your written APR will be similar to discussions that you have led with your supervisors. However, on the assumption that your supervisor is not present, the APR at the end of the initial year may be the first discussion in which you face academics, whether specialist or generalist, who are not familiar with your work, other than what they have read in your written APR.

You need to make the most of the opportunity both by providing a good written APR and anticipating where verbal clarification and expansion are necessary. All written APRs, like a final PhD thesis, will have a word limit and so you will need to have sufficient extra details and/or conceptual understanding to expand on the written document. Some aspects of every PhD are more difficult to write about and understand than others. Your readers will inevitably have different levels of existing knowledge and understanding of what is written in different parts of your thesis. Accordingly, the provision of extra clarity and expansion are two elements that are invariably required in your APR discussion. The verbal discussion of your APR is an occasion, year on year, to check and build experience of your verbal articulation.

A further potential spin-off can occur when the extra adrenaline of the APR occasion generates a chance turn of phrase, avenue of thought, or re-visualisation (e.g. of a diagram) that is new and helpful in the longer term, after due consideration by yourself and your supervisory team, far beyond the immediate outcome of the APR. If any of the above occurs it is good practice, as per the advice on reflection, to make a quick note during the APR and then immediately record your thoughts at greater length when the APR is finished. That is standard advice for any PGR who thinks of a new addition to their work. Talking about and reflecting on your work with others is almost always a good thing (Van De Ven, 2007) and that applies to the APR discussion as much as other forms of presentation.

APR as a trial viva

In one sense, whatever the form of the verbal discussion of your APR, you might like to think of it as a trial *viva*. It is surprising how such an approach can help build up experience of doing a *viva*, often the part of the PhD process that causes the most anxiety among PGRs (see Chapter 10). In many ways, an APR is a good proxy for a *viva* as it requires preparation of written material that is submitted beforehand for subsequent discussion. It also has built in tension as one of the key moments for the year, and a formal outcome by way of written or verbal approval.

Note has already been made of the need to give due attention in your written APR to each of the elements that you are asked to prepare. It is a truism that the basis of a good PhD *viva* is a good written thesis. As with the final *viva* so, too, with the APR: The verbal discussion will have a better chance of going well if the written material that you submit beforehand is up to standard.

APR: Onward administrative use

This chapter has already made some comments about the audience for the APR: one or more academics who are specialist or generalist to your particular field. It has also mentioned that the exact composition of the APR panel may or may not include a supervisor. Whatever is the case, the APR document and discussion of its contents will most likely be referred to and commented on in a faculty report on your progress that will be signed-off by your supervisors and/or the person responsible for doctoral students. The faculty report will then be passed to the university-level administrator and so university-level research degrees committee. It may be a requirement of your university that your written APR is attached to your faculty report. The report and/or APR can be used actively at university level. As an example, each may be accessed by a university research degrees committee when considering whether to approve an application for extension of your PhD study beyond a time limit. If a PhD proceeds smoothly, year on year faculty reports/APRs may never emerge from storage for detailed consideration at university level. That highlights why you need to make an APR work to benefit you, for your purpose, whilst nevertheless ensuring that the faculty and university requirements are fully met.

Some final words of encouragement

All the recommendations with regard to the APR in this chapter help the final submission. It is useful to remember the core function and rationale of the APR rather than just working to fulfil an obligation on specified content as set by your university. By truly planning for the APR from the start of a year, recording details of core research activity and supporting activities, engaging in critical reflection and developing an ongoing forward strategy, the APR will emerge more as an active contributor to your ultimate aim of gaining a doctorate rather than as an onerous administrative exercise that absorbs unnecessary time. A full-time PGR will most probably complete two or three APRs during a period of study for PhD. A part-time PGR will complete four or five. The process of looking back in the later APRs, in which the critical reflection extends over several years, has one added benefit: it can help ensure that there is a strong thread running through your final thesis submission. Moreover, the APR can positively benefit your spirit because in taking time to review what you have done you will most likely discover that you have done more than you thought. The process of researching for a PhD consists of myriad of tasks each of which you will work your way through day after day. Once one set of tasks is completed another set emerges and iterative steps fade into background memory. The APR is an occasion to remember and highlight what has been completed. It is also a time to look forward and realise that with continued application what can seem like an everlasting project will be achieved. There are moments to celebrate as you progress through your PhD and the successful negotiation of the written and verbal components of an APR is one of those moments.

References

BBC (2021). *EU approves AstraZenica vaccine amid supply row*. Available at: <https://www.bbc.co.uk/news/world-europe-55862233>

Bowen, D. (2002). Research through participant observation in tourism: A creative solution to the measurement of consumer satisfaction and dissatisfaction among tourists. *Journal of Travel Research*, 41(1), 4–14.

Dunleavy, P. (2003). *Authoring a PhD – How to Plan, Draft, Write and Finish a Doctoral Thesis or Dissertation*. Basingstoke, UK: Palgrave Macmillan

Van De Ven, A. H. (2007). *Engaged Scholarship: A Guide for Organisational and Social Research*. Oxford, UK: Oxford University Press.

Wallace, M. and Wray, A. (2011). *Critical Reading and Writing for Postgraduates*. London, UK: Sage.

DAVID BOWEN

9 Talking about, presenting and publicising your research

Preamble

Talking about, presenting and publicising research is an ongoing project for a PGR. It starts before the PhD begins because in order to get accepted onto a PhD programme you will need to prepare a proposal and discuss it with an interview panel. It may never finish because if you enter academic life you will draw on aspects of your PhD throughout your career, like you will draw on your other academic or consultancy projects. Even if you follow another life-course you may still talk about your PhD in a work or social context. Any three- or four-year period of your life, yet alone a period as intense as one involving PhD study, will yield lessons and stories to inform and recount, sometimes as fond memory and sometimes not, for years to come. The three activities of talking about, presenting and publicising are not one and the same thing. There are also differences within each activity. However, there are some essential principles that apply to all. The **aim of this chapter** is to unpack both common principles and the peculiarities of each distinct activity. After outlining the essential principles with reference to research content (details and ideas) delivery style (written and verbal) and platforms, the chapter offers further general and practical discussion about a range of platforms (research-speed dating, lecture-type presentations, poster presentations and social media). Conferences are an important opportunity to talk about, present and publicise your PhD and the section that follows offers an exploration of what that entails. Finally, a PGR also needs to engage beyond peers and other academics. Hence, the next section offers some pointers on public engagement. The chapter ends with our customary final words of encouragement.

Essential principles

There are a number of essential principles concerned with talking about, presenting and publicising as listed below. They are introduced as discrete components although in reality they all interact.

Know your audience

This is the *sine qua non* of talking, presenting and publicising. For example, there is variability in a presentation when an audience changes from in-faculty PGR peers to across faculty PGR peers, or from PGR peers to practitioners (industry, government) or to the public. You may encounter all such audiences as a PGR, depending on your topic and stage of research. You have to modify your approach accordingly. Whilst avoidance of the overuse of academic terminology has been mentioned several times in this volume you will need to pay extra attention to that as soon as you step outside of a university. To complicate matters, practitioners may have their own practitioner terminology. If you have picked that up through prior contact with them, for example, from employee or management interviews, you may decide to use it in your presentation. If you are reading this book and you have followed such an approach, you have already demonstrated a learned or innate sense of the need to know your audience.

It is worth mentioning here that you can also learn a lot about your audience by observing them both before you start your presentation and whilst engaged in your presentation. A good presenter perceptively uses feedback from an audience from the first moment that eyes meet and for every moment from then until out of contact. You need to be that good presenter. At the very least you should pause when you think that your audience may not be following the research content of what you present or when their attention seems to flag and, depending on time available, either recap or bring the presentation to a close. In some instances, you can also learn something about your audience by prior desk research.

In an online space it is more difficult to monitor your audience because when there are many participants some of them may only be visible on a different screen or may not have their cameras switched on. However, you still need to gain what feedback you can, for example, by breaking the flow of your presentation via a pre-determined or spontaneous call for questions and comments. In an online conference presentation, you might also engage a peer or friend to monitor and alert you, as appropriate, to incoming chat.

Active listening

It is a truism of communication theory that listening is part of talking, sometimes the most important part. At the early stage of a PhD when talking about your proposal with supervisors or other academics in your field, you need to listen for streams of research, theoretical or methodological, that may be relevant in some way to your thesis. Sometimes, your supervisors may deliberately introduce and emphasise a particular aspect of theory or a methodological technique that they think you do not know about, or do not know about well enough. Listening is easy in such instances and you just need to make a mental and written note to follow through on what they emphasise. However, at other times, what is not known will be inadvertently glanced over in supervisory conversation and will only be picked up with active listening. Your supervisors may not even recognise the full relevance of their remarks. The same can apply when talking about your research throughout your PhD. For example, in the Q&A sessions of in-faculty seminars and workshops or external conferences in which you have presented your work, you need to actively listen to what people say, for example, what they think you have not included or how they think your work relates to theirs. What they say is not necessarily relevant and so later you will need a filter to help decide what to accept, modify or reject. In conference poster presentations active listening is just as relevant, as will become apparent later in this chapter.

Active questioning and commentary

Active listening overlaps with active questioning and commentary (Zenger and Folkman, 2016). As a PGR, an omnipresent question for you to exercise is the relevance of your research to that of any other researcher. That is the case whether in an informal one-to-one conversation, a poster presentation, a lecture-type presentation and Q&A, or any other communication, including social media. It does not mean that you need to place yourself front and centre without due regard for others. Such an approach will quickly alienate your PGR peers and other researchers that you regularly talk with, as well as those that you only ever meet irregularly. However, you cannot know and understand everything immediately. Accordingly, you owe it to yourself to question and comment, when appropriate, so as to sift the knowledge and understanding of what others say. That can be a mutually beneficial spark that sends you and them in a new and positive direction.

In Chapter 2 of this book (see Figure 2.1), we outline a thesis template that any research project, large or small, can follow. In Chapter 10, we outline general questions asked at a *viva voce*. It is good practice to have the template and general questions in mind at all times, not just for the direct purpose of guiding your own writing but also to engage in active questioning and commentary of PGRs and other researchers whenever they talk, present or publicise their work. To maximise active questioning and commentary you need to know what and how to question. The basis of what to question is contained within the template and general *viva voce* questions. How to question, whether as a PGR or otherwise, is another skill that can always be honed. From observation, the best questions are short. If you insert a commentary into your question, the best commentary is also short. Long questions with multiple diversions will require long answers and the person that you are questioning may, wittingly or otherwise, skirt over or around the core of your question. Long commentary also reveals you as someone putting yourself front and centre. You may have observed how the questioning of public figures such as politicians is less effective when interviewers ask long questions and add too much commentary to feed their own self-esteem as interviewers.

Questioning and commentary most often benefits from a supportive approach. For example, there is much to gain from an empathetic but non-formulaic opening remark that draws attention to a part of someone's presentation that you found useful, whether to do with research content or delivery style. Once you have done one presentation you will realise the encouragement gained from such a remark. By default, a presenter uncovers a part of themselves as they deliver a presentation and that needs to be respected in questioning and commentary. That does not mean that there is no place for critical questions and comments. Quite the reverse is the case. Well-judged critical questioning and commentary is supportive. It will help the presenter and it will help you because it forces you to reflect on the omnipresent question: the relevance of your research to what any researcher is saying.

Written and verbal fluency

It is important to set high standards with regard to written and verbal fluency. I well remember one international PGR, whose first language was not English, asking over the course of three supervisory sessions whether it was really necessary to write a final PhD thesis with perfect or near perfect written English. On each occasion there was a unanimous answer from the supervisory team: 'Yes'. That was backed up with a suggestion to attend some courses on academic writing in English as well as other informal suggestions such as making a regular effort to read good newspapers (in addition to academic journal articles) and listen to English language news broadcasts, often repeated or available in streamed form. To the credit of the PGR she took all the advice and also opted for other ways of developing written and verbal fluency, not least through social engagement with PGRs and others from beyond her own country. The result was that her written work and spoken English developed an admirable degree of nuance.

Nearly all researchers, not just PGRs, need to engage in a constant effort to improve written and verbal fluency. That includes native speakers, writing and speaking in a language learned in infancy. There will no doubt be someone reading this chapter who will think that there is some aspect of sentence structure, grammar or vocabulary that needs correction. If so, it will be good to hear from you because that is one way to improve. It may seem pedantic to some or self-evident to others, but written and verbal fluency is based on sound sentence structure, grammar and vocabulary. During a practitioner conference I recall an audience that was rather amused when a well-respected academic spelled the word 'literacy' incorrectly on a power-point slide. He was listing the advantages of recruiting university-educated employees to junior management posts. The supposed literacy of university graduates in comparison to non-graduates was high up the list. The presenter was lucky that he had industrial credibility. Your audiences, practitioner or academic, will be less than amused. Repeated mistakes in power-point slides, on a poster or even on social media will be interpreted, rightly or wrongly, in a negative way. In other words, if you cannot get the written basics of a presentation correct, you will find it more difficult to get your audience to accept any evidence or argument that you present. With regard to basics the same also applies to verbal fluency, although much empathy normally exists for a presenter genuinely trying to engage with the complexities of a second or third language.

Learning from others

There is no need to work everything out by yourself. Hopefully, this chapter provides some pointers to help you. However, there is much that can be learned from others that you are in contact with. As a PGR it is good practice, at all stages of your research, to pay attention to talking, presenting and publicising at two levels. On the one hand, obviously, pay attention to the research content. However, also pay attention to delivery style. The learning derived from dual reflection on content and style is advocated in Chapter 7 in relation to reading academic journal articles. However, it extends much wider, to all other written forms and the delivery style of others as they talk about, present and publicise research. You probably feel that some research seminars or workshops in your faculty are very good and others not-so-good. Therefore, analyse what makes them so. On the assumption that the research content is sound, it is odds-on that the very good presentation will pitch at a suitable level to its audience: for example, generalists and specialists, including you as a PGR. It will have written and verbal fluency by getting the basics correct. From active listening, the questions and comments of others in the Q&A session will highlight synergies between what is presented and their research. Interventions by a Chair will also be geared towards the audience so that so that you feel a sense of inclusion.

Seize opportunities

In the first year of running a doctoral programme it became obvious to me that PGRs needed a forum to present aspects of their work to one another. I had previously seen too many PhD presentations that were *endured* rather than *enjoyed*, partly because they were impenetrable to any PGRs other than those studying almost exactly the same topic, partly because they were too lengthy or deficient in other aspects of delivery style. Accordingly, a presentation format was devised that required PGRs to present an aspect of their research for no more than 15–20 minutes with two slides (absolute maximum), followed by 5–10 minutes of Q&A. In any one session there were two presenters, so the total session time was one hour (2 x 30 minutes). We made much of starting and finishing on time. If someone arrived even a few minutes late, they walked into a live presentation and everyone came to know that the sessions finished on time for whatever else they had to do that day. Each session was part of a series of three running over three consecutive weeks on the same day at the same time. For obvious reasons we named the sessions 'Doctoral 20-20s' which eventually morphed into the sobriquet 'Doc 20-20s'. At the end of the first session, which was very good but delivered to a sprinkling of just five or six PGRs and two or three supervisors, the lead author of this book made a vigorous call for each PGR to seize the opportunity to attend further sessions, present their work and also spread the word to other PGRs. 15+ years and 200+ presentations later the 'Doc 20-20s' still run as a series of three sessions each semester, occasionally with a 'Doc 20–20 special' such as a supervisor-PGR public conversation *in lieu* of a two-slide presentation. Since the Covid-19 pandemic the 'Doc 20–20s' have also transferred to an online format, with the modification of some additional slides (still subject to a stated maximum). The main point here, however, is that a generation of PGRs have seized the opportunity and each invariably says, privately or publicly, that the benefits far outweigh the costs. That happens despite the effort to prepare and deliver their presentation and the reality that a supportive atmosphere does not entirely diminish anxiety. Through seizing the opportunity to present, a PhD improves: the act of preparation and delivery, yet alone Q&A, sharpens a sense of what you know and do not know. That holds whether it is your first or subsequent presentation. There is mutual benefit, too, for peers and supervisors in the research community, for the reasons mentioned above.

Develop a strategy

In Chapter 7 on Annual Progress Reports, it is stressed that there is a need for a clear forward strategy. That applies to talking, presenting and publicising, too. An example can be taken from lecture-type presentations. Most universities will require that you present your work as part of research support activity. However, unless there is a legitimate, fair request made of you to create an unexpected *ad hoc* presentation (e.g. to fill in for a PGR peer who is ill), it is advisable that you follow a strategic, developmental route with regard to both the research content and delivery style of presentation. Your lecture-type presentations will improve by both learning from others and practice and so it is good to develop a forward strategy that allows that to happen. The sub-section above offers advice on learning from others. With regard to practice, it is recommended that you first try and present within your faculty (e.g. to a group of PGR peers and supervisors) comparatively early in your PhD, say, sometime within the first six months of study. If your forward strategy can also include a further lecture-type presentation of the same research content to another forum within the university at more or less the same period of time you

Talking about, presenting and publicising your research 219

will straighten up any uncertainties with research content and fast-track the development of a delivery style that you are comfortable with (e.g. high-tech or low-tech).

Once you have presented internally within your faculty or wider university, you can identify opportunities for one or more external conference (or other) presentations. In many large conferences there will be a PGR track and that may be the most appropriate stage for you to present. Further conferences can also be attended so that you move beyond the PGR conference track as your use of essential principles, range of research content, and delivery style develops. In the section after next, this chapter further explores the use of conferences to talk about, present and publicise your PhD research.

Platforms

The activity of talking about, presenting or publicising your research is helped by application of the essential principles as outlined above. There are a variety of platforms that you might seek to engage with across the course of PhD study. Some are already signalled in the discussion of essential principles. As a PGR you need to produce research content (details and ideas) to present on any platform that you use and also develop an appropriate delivery style. Delivery style can refer to written form and verbal form. Below I elaborate on some general and practical discussion points for you to consider so that you make good use of the platforms.

Research speed-dating

This platform runs across the three activities of talking, presenting and publicising your research. It is quite likely that if you join a new cohort of PGRs you will be called on within the first few weeks to offer a short pitch of your proposed work to the cohort. The time allocated is typically between two and five minutes. Research speed-dating is a challenging exercise at any stage of your PhD yet alone before your thoughts are truly crystallised, when the most you can offer may be a rather broad free-ranging talk about your intentions. However, you will have opportunities to improve your pitch because it is also a favoured icebreaker exercise at the start of events that you will attend throughout your PhD. It can also be the central exercise in events that bring PGRs and other researchers together to uncover synergies, for example, for cross-faculty or cross-university collaboration. On such occasions, normally towards the end of your PhD (or beyond) your speed-dating pitch should be more structured and honed. As such it will be a fine chance to publicise your completed research so that it enters the minds of people beyond your more confined circle. Sometimes such events are classified by other names such as research sandpits, or research hubs. They are often worth attending as they can open up connections to people and fields that are otherwise closed.

Lecture-type presentation

As a PGR it is unlikely that you will be called on to deliver a set-piece lecture, as normally understood, extending to an academic hour (fifty minutes). However, it is very likely that from six months into your PhD and thereafter, you will be required or requested to deliver a lecture-type presentation on some aspect of your PhD for something like 15–20 minutes, plus Q&A of 5–10 minutes. As you will discover, either by direct experience presenting or listening to others present, that is both ample time for a very good PhD presentation and a very long time for a not-so-good PhD presentation. The difference between a lecture-type presentation and seminar is not distinct. Your university or faculty will follow its own interpretation of any distinction. A seminar typically involves an introductory presentation by a seminar leader, for example, you as a PGR, similar to that delivered in a lecture-type presentation. However, the balance is tipped towards a Q&A session with multiple interactions between seminar attendees rather than just between you as the seminar leader and attendees. You may also be requested or required to deliver a

PGR workshop. There are similarities between a workshop and a seminar but the former normally involves more of an emphasis on an activity element, for example, a group of early stage PGRs working through the process of coding an interview transcript under the guidance of an experienced researcher.

After undergraduate study I trained to teach in high-school and eventually spent four years working in what was then the largest state secondary school in the UK. It was a defining experience in many ways. Some advice/warning from a senior-pro still jumps into my head when I walk down a corridor to give a lecture or, nowadays, get set for another Zoom presentation: 'If I ask you on the way to your class what you are teaching, just make sure you can tell me the main thing that you want to say.' That advice is central to you, too, as a PGR when you step forward to make a lecture-type presentation, lead a seminar or workshop.

There is a world of other advice on lecturing both in lengthy texts and in more pithy form online (e.g. Gosling and Noordam, 2006). Your university may also require you to do a short or long course on some lecturing basics before you engage in any teaching support as a PGR (for more detail on these opportunities, see Chapter 12). What you pick up on such courses is likely to transfer to the craft of PGR presentations. Therefore, seize the opportunity. Within the confines of space for this chapter, there is one more adage on lecture-type presentations that is worth stressing. I first heard it from a former journalist, used to spinning stories, who moved into university teaching and research. Here is his adage on presentations: tell them (briefly) what you are going to say – tell them – tell them what you have said.

Do not forget, too, what is already written above in the section on essential principles, for example, knowing your audience and working hard on verbal and written fluency. Finally, as I learned in the first week of teaching in high school, never turn your back on the audience. Rugg and Petre (2015, p. 186) reflect that each batch of speakers in a conference session (normally about four lecture-type presentations) will include one speaker who is inaudible, incomprehensible, uninteresting or using unreadable slides. Whether in a conference or other setting you should try not to be that person.

Poster presentation

There is plenty of general and practical discussion about poster presentations on the internet, some of the best of which is referenced below. Poster presentations are common platforms within faculty events and external conferences. The posters themselves are usually size A0 (841 x 1189 mm or 33.1 x 46.8 inches), A1 (594 x 841 mm) or A2 (420 x 594 mm). Finn (2018) summarises some of the uses of posters and emphasises how they can help clarify your thinking, especially in the early part of your PhD. They force you to frame something visual for others to see that contains succinct sections: introduction, overall aim or research questions, literature streams (without details), core methods, potential contributions, critical references, contact details and a photo of you. Obviously, at a later stage of PhD a poster will include other sections such as an overview of findings and acknowledgements. Finn (2018) also states that a poster is an effective dissemination tool in your own faculty. It is your research footprint at a particular point of time and can allow you to engage informally with interested people and so build up a network. Moreover, a poster can get you to a conference with all the benefits that such opportunity can create.

Many conferences have poster streams for PGRs and other researchers and the more progressive conferences make a determined effort to position the poster sessions on a par with more classic lecture-type presentations and Q&A. Finn (2018) notes that in some ways a poster is a more effective form of communication because it typically involves one-to-one rather than one-to-many communication, which helps build up your network. Rossi (2018) summarises the double intent of a poster presentation as communication and networking.

All the authors referenced so far in this sub-section are from hard science rather than social science. However, that is an advantage when it comes to a general and practical discussion around this platform because hard scientists are traditionally required to be succinct with words and place an emphasis on clear visuals. In practical terms such use of words and visuals are the two main fundamentals of a good poster. As Rossi (2018) states, a poster is an accessible, visual abstract that drives attention to your work, even from across a large display area. Purrington (2019) provides downloadable templates for you to experiment with various poster layouts and a gamut of practical advice on elements such as amount of text, connectivity between sections, use of boxes and borders, pictures and graphs, font size, colour, museum-style interactive components, paper type (matt), software, printing, storage and so on. In fact, he includes forty things to do and not to do on a poster. The full details go beyond the scope of this chapter although they are all worth your attention and may drive your interest in posters as a presentation platform. You do not need costly software: Microsoft PowerPoint can do the job.

As an articulate exponent of poster craft, Rossi (2018) argues that 90% of posters at conferences are 'terrible'. From my experience of university PGR poster fairs, that 90% figure seems like a deliberate over-estimate to stress a point. However, even if the percentage is far lower, it is clear that you can do yourself a favour as a PGR by making use of the practical advice from the likes of Rossi (2018) and Purrington (2019). Above all, more is less. There are interesting, online debates about how many words to use on a poster and it is probably less than you think (about 250–350 for size A0). Moreover, it is suggested that you include white space so that the mind can rest, unlike you'll probably see on most posters. Early cartographers used to fill gaps on their maps with ornate drawings. At least they were restful. An extra loading of dense text or visuals on your poster fills no useful purpose.

The production of your poster is only one element of a poster presentation. You are also charged with engaging those who are drawn towards it and you need to communicate your research verbally in the best way. Again, Purrington (2019) has some good advice on a verbal pitch; for example, give a two-sentence overview of why the research is interesting, do not refer to notes and, if you have to leave your site, place a post-it note with a time of return. For the truly imaginative and outgoing PGR, or the PGR worried that their poster will be allocated to a quiet or ill-lighted part of a display area, Purrington (2019) suggests creating a mobile poster so that you can go toward an audience rather than waiting for the audience to come to you. Finn (2018) also notes how a poster visual can be used to drum up footfall via Twitter, Facebook, Instagram or other social media, before or during a faculty event or external conference. In turn, a QR code on a poster can link to a blog, microblog or journal abstract. Although posters are the focus of this sub-section the various other platforms can be used in an integrated way.

Social media

Shinton (2017) recommends that the first step for any PGR interested in engaging with social media is to check out university social media regulations. Here is a summary version of a much longer social media policy from one university:

> As an official voice of **the university** you must act responsibly when posting, commenting and sharing content online. Don't post or share content that is offensive. Don't share confidential information or personal data. Be respectful and courteous at all time.

You are most probably tech savvy and experienced in social media use, but you are well advised to remember the advice above whether you are more not-online or more too-online. This section includes a general and practical discussion of social media that may help you evaluate your active or passive use of it during your PhD study. Social media is variously defined but includes different forms of electronic communication that allow users to create and contribute towards online communities that share content: information, personal messages and other material such as videos. Social media is fast moving and too close attention to any one commercial provider in this section may seem very out of date in a comparatively short period of time. Current providers include Facebook, LinkedIn, Google+ (social networking), Twitter, Tumblr (microblogging), You Tube, Facebook Live (video sharing) and Instagram, Snapchat (photo sharing). We consider below the potential that you have as a PGR to engage with social media through blogs and microblogs.

Blogs

Most of us have read blogs but fewer of us have either a solo blog or contribute to blogs in blog posts. One definition of a blog comes from the Oxford English Dictionary (2021):

> A *regularly updated* website or web page, typically run by *an individual or small group* that is written in an *informal or conversational style*.

The usefulness of blogs for talking about, presenting and publicising your work should be obvious from the definition. The italics are inserted by the author of this chapter. Their relevance will soon become clear.

Thomson (2016) explores the scholarly virtues of putting research thoughts online and points to several payoffs. She views blogs as more than an add-on to academic writing, more than light relief from what is assumed as the more serious job of constructing journal articles, chapters and books. For her, the necessary switch to a comparatively informal or conversational style challenges awareness of the writing process because it is different from what you are used to doing as a PGR: constructing proposals, literature reviews and so on. Even though we consistently argue in this book that writing needs to be accessible, every one of us can slip-up in that regard and obscure what we write. Blogs are less amenable to such slippage. There can be immediate written feedback for you in reply posts. A lack of clicks and reads may also tell you something.

To develop your own solo blog may be a step too far for many PGRs. However, you can start by submitting blog posts to an existing blog run by your faculty PGR peers, faculty researchers or other small group. Your blog post may be picked up and spread upwards through the hierarchy of blogs and bloggers so that you are read more widely and then feel able to suggest a blog post to an outlet like the LSE impact blog (LSE, 2021). To maintain a blog, whether you write as an individual or contribute posts, you and/or others will need to provide regular updates. However, as Thomson (2016) argues, that leads to another pay-off because it drives the habit of writing. Blogs also encourage brevity because the norm limits the number of words to between 500 and 1,000. Moreover, blogs are enhanced by visual appeal and that can lead to experimentation with representations (figures, graphs, pictures) that may find their way into your written thesis or help you with other platforms such as poster presentations. The use of videos and recordings in blogs can also cross platforms.

A further advantage of blogging is that if you become part of a group of bloggers, even confined to faculty PGR peers, you by default develop a community of authors. You may also feel emboldened to offer a blog post higher up the hierarchy. There are numerous listings of the top blogs for PGRs and academics in general (top 50, 25, 10 and so on). A few blogs that frequently show on ranking lists are 'Thesis Whisperer', with its associated blog 'Supervisor Whisperer' (for your supervisor), 'Patter' (from Pat Thomson) and 'PhD Life' (from University of Warwick, UK). 'PhD Life' has an objective to create an online PhD community for anyone and everyone who identifies with PhD. It has an open call for insights, comments, suggestions, questions, stories, feedback, jokes or musings (PhD Life, 2021). It is a useful exercise to develop your own ranking of top blogs, subdivided into subjects, for example, thesis writing, conference etiquette and wellbeing.

For Thomson (2016) blogging is (or should be) an endemic part of modern academic life. That perspective still requires a mindset change for many PGRs, and even more so supervisors.[55] There are negatives. You may find that your solo blog or blog posts drift toward more time and effort than is sensible and divert rather than enhance the research experience and development of your PhD. Also, of course, whilst many of the academic social media forums are filled with like-minded supportive contributors, there is a darker side to the responses that may come your way, too.

55 For example, many old school, hard-nosed economists, may still consider blogging as a second-rate form of academic dissemination at best. Yet, even the most technical coverage of econometric theory and practical application has successfully penetrated the blog world. *Econometrics Beat*, developed by David E. Giles in February 2011 (<https://davegiles.blogspot.com/>) is the most eminent and prolific example. Originally expected to reach a somewhat niche audience, by the time of Giles' final (950th) post on 31 October 2019, his blog site had recorded 7.4 million page-hits.

Talking about, presenting and publicising your research 227

Microblogs

Microblogs have various functions for you in relation to the theme of this chapter. Whilst holding to the view that too close attention to any one commercial provider can be perilous because they come and go according to vogue, it does seem that Twitter has achieved a stable prominence as a microblog. With specific reference to Twitter, Huchet (2019) describes the singular relationship between Twitter and scientists as a love story. You may have noted that if you followed the tweets from public health academics and administrators about fast emerging clinical research during the Covid-19 pandemic. However, Twitter is also the major microblogging player in business and management, and wider social science, too.

As social commentators and others point out, for example, novelists (Lockwood, 2021), there is a continuum between the not-online and the too-online extremities. For any PGR who is closer to the not-online endpoint of the continuum, a succinct summary of Twitter as a microblog may help at this point (Huchet, 2019):

> As a person (or an organization), you manage an account and post messages (under 280 characters) that can include images, links, and videos. In these 'tweets', you can tag other accounts by using @ (mentions) and keywords # (hashtags). You can connect to other user accounts and they can to yours; this action is called 'follow'. The posts from the followed users will appear on a timeline. By default, they are public and anyone can comment.

In short, through Twitter you will find academic researchers (and others) disseminating information to one another and wider communities (e.g. mainstream media, government and the public) with an immediacy that is not present through journals, conferences or indeed blogs. It takes seconds to 'tweet', 'retweet' or assign a 'favourite' and so know, share and 'like' what is going on in the field. The stated objective of much Twitter dissemination is discussion and potential collaboration, although once signed up to Twitter it does not take long to realise that there can also be a self-serving undercurrent to activity. For example, as Klar et al. (2020) note in relation to the fields of political science and communications, there seems to be some connection between tweeting about a publication and the eventual number of citations. That may seem relatively innocuous but sometimes tweeting, retweeting and liking seems overly orchestrated and so rather facile. You will have your own view.

As with blogs there are academic hierarchies in microblogging but there are suggestions that the activity has the ability or at least the potential to even out hierarchies and help build the profile of PGRs and early career researchers (ECRs). There is plenty of advice about how to build up a list of people or organisations to follow and also how to gather a following. For the former, a short-cut is to note what others in your field follow. For the latter, you will need persistence and regular well-written text (e.g. article, leaflet, webpage and blog post), visual content (picture, diagram and infographics) and video (interview, explainer video and documentary) (Huchet, 2019). 'The Leveraged PhD' (2019) blog classifies hashtags that are applied to academia (e.g. discipline specific, research writing, minorities) and includes PhD and ECR hashtags such as #PhD Life, #PhD Student and #Write that PhD. In the end you must find your own way and find your own time to work the microblogging system.

In truth, rightly or wrongly, I have never felt the compulsion to be an active micro-blogger, for example, to tweet before, during and after an event (journal publication, conference, public meeting). However, the journal article that has left the largest impression on me, by the US-based academics Eric Arnould and Linda Price, read for the first time in 1995, included a footnote that showed a very human side of the two authors that in the days before social media normally remained sealed in journal formality (Arnould and Price, 1993). Whilst those I currently follow on Twitter remain in their academic bubble for 95% of the time, they also release a part of themselves (e.g. enthusiasm for landscape or sport or a social cause) in the remaining 5%. For me that adds to my understanding of them and their work and is the benefit that I see to microblogs, above and beyond what is written above. It is the benefit that you might generate, too, if you decide to use microblogging as a way to talk about, present and publicise your research.

Conferences

As part of your development as a PGR you will need to attend and present in at least one external conference. The form of presentation that you use is most likely to be either a lecture-type presentation or poster. The conference may be geared just to PGRs or open to all researchers, either with or without a PGR track. In addition, some conferences also incorporate a pre-conference meet geared to PGRs, with seminars or workshops given by invited researchers, for example, on research methodology or other aspects related to the process of PhD study, covering a range of topics as framed within this text.

You need to discuss with your supervisors and faculty PGR tutor or similar when to attend an external conference and what conference to attend. The discussion can be ongoing or part of the Annual Progress Review (APR) process (see Chapter 7). Obviously, you will need to have something worth talking about, presenting or publicising and so your first external conference will probably not occur until the end of your first year. That will also give you the chance to practise within your faculty and smooth the rough edges of whatever presentation you intend to give. Some long-established conferences occur on an annual or bi-annual basis either in fixed or revolving locations. In such instances, the support that they give to PGRs may be well known. Other conferences may be more recently established or *ad hoc* and so rather more unknown. You can often gauge what the conference will be like and whether it will suit your situation by reading the information published in advance by the organisers on purpose, theme and conference process. It is a good idea to pay close attention to such aspects. For example, the purpose should be appropriate. One early stage PGR from my experience, who was researching social identity and consumption, was accepted to present in a small, specialist conference on the anthropology of consumption. However, after acceptance, her literature and methodology fast evolved more to psychology than anthropology and even though she was a particularly resilient character, the conference experience was difficult. The discipline of anthropology is distinct from psychology. Her revised methodological approach came under more scrutiny than she imagined, and the conference, purposed towards anthropologists, was a step too far for an early stage PGR leaning towards a contrary approach. Another PGR chose to attend a conference that purposed itself as one of the largest in the field with several thousand delegates from all over the world. There were multiple tracks. Despite the large numbers of attendees, her presentation was not well attended because delegates gravitated towards non-PGRs and speakers known through their journal and book authorship. She was unable to isolate a network of like minds among the large number of delegates. Accordingly, she felt thwarted as few people paid attention to her work and she did not build her network.

Beyond purpose, the overall theme of a conference also needs to be related in an appropriate way to what you are studying. Most conferences will be split into a number of sub-themes. You will need to identify a sub-theme for your submission, but it is wise to check that there are other sub-themes that may be related to your PhD. You will get the most from a conference that has plenty to keep you interested so that you have the pleasant dilemma of competing choices. Your lecture-type presentation or poster presentation will only occupy you for a limited time.

Regarding conference process, it is standard practice that after a call for papers you will need to submit either a short/working paper or a full-sized paper for consideration by the conference committee. The committee will also give instructions regarding submission of posters. There will be a deadline for submission of the paper and further deadlines for feedback, resubmission and upload of your presentation (or electronic version of your poster). If there is no review process, or you feel after receiving feedback that the review process is very limited, you should very carefully consider whether or not to find another suitable event. You should do the same if you are not comfortable with other aspects of process (e.g. no stated policy on use of mobile phone recording in lecture-type presentations or mobile phone cameras in poster presentations).

It is well to remember that conferences are used by some universities and other institutions to generate income for research or other activity. At the very minimum, most business and management conferences must cover costs. Your attendance and payment of fees contributes towards breaking even or surplus. Therefore, approach acceptance of your fee money with open eyes and make as sure as you can, in advance, that you will benefit from attendance. Also, on the plus side, check and double check whether there are any concessions for PGRs, not only with regard to fees but also costs of transport, accommodation, and so forth. Note, too, that you are unlikely to get such concessions if you do not pay attention to deadlines set by the organisers.

The recent Covid-19 pandemic has speeded the development of innovative ways to develop online conferences. They are likely to feature into the future as part of PGR experience, even as the pandemic subsides. In my own field, tourist behaviour and tourism development, the main academic international conference, shared by a consortium of Australian and New Zealand universities run under the acronym of CAUTHE (Council for Australasian Tourism and Hospitality Education), is staged annually with one or other university from the consortium as a rotating host. In February 2021, with Australia in international lockdown, it ran online for the first time. From the Twitter feed it was a success. The four day conference included a pre-conference PhD/ECR workshop; keynote speeches; numerous presentations and e-posters; panel discussions with journal editors; a publishers and sponsors' marketplace; a social programme including an online interactive cooking demonstration from the Sprout Cooking School in Adelaide and a live guided tour of the Sydney Opera House; opportunities for networking; the usual prizes for best paper and social media contribution, for example, online engagement and online promotion (CAUTHE, 2021). As one delegate tweeted, it was a good chance to pretend that she was in Australia. If you have not yet had the chance to see the capability of online conferences it is informative to read the website of a company such as Events Air that provided the technical event expertise for CAUTHE 2021 (Events Air, 2021). It is evident that they delivered their product beyond the now familiar capabilities of day-to-day Zoom presentations and break-out rooms. The 'Virtual Hub' offered by Events Air is described as a secure meeting space for event attendees to browse attendee profiles, request to connect with someone, start up a conversation via text, video call or messenger, or schedule a meeting. The 'Networking Group' is a virtual function area where attendees meet and exchange ideas in pre-selected or spontaneous groups according to shared interests. It is true that no amount of imagination can allow you to spend the evening on the beach or in the coffee shops and restaurants of whichever town or city an online CAUTHE conference would otherwise take place. On the other hand, as a PGR on a limited conference budget and not resident in Australia or New Zealand, the chance of attendance in CAUTHE was practically zero until 2021. However, for the online conference, PGR early-bird registration cost just AU$130. Even late registration cost only AU$175. For someone travelling from North America or Europe that is a total cost close to twenty times cheaper that a face-to-face conference.

From what is stated above, a good conference, whether face-to-face or online, offers you a very useful chance to talk about, present and publicise your work: to communicate and network.

Public engagement

For the most part the talking, presenting and publicising of your work so far discussed in this chapter has involved engagement with your peers and other academics. The sections on blogs and especially microblogs suggested the possibilities for engagement with a wider community: media, government and the public. Public engagement has always been a part of university life but there are varying degrees of commitment at institutional, faculty and individual level. In the UK, organisations such as the National Coordinating Centre for Public Engagement help to plan, fund, deliver and evaluate public engagement activities. Their online presence illustrates the scope of what is possible (e.g. NCCPE, 2021). An exploration of the relevant websites of your or other universities is also useful for general and practical discussion on public engagement activities. The University of Bath, for example, has a quick-start, how-to guide on engaging public groups with research (University of Bath, 2021a). Public engagement, as the University of Bath documentation outlines, can give you the chance to inform and inspire others, to listen to others and to collaborate with others. Those three activities form the three corners of the public engagement triangle: to transmit (e.g. through festivals, exhibitions), receive (e.g. through public meetings, online surveys) and collaborate (e.g. through open space events, steering groups). As a PGR, the above listing may seem daunting but with a mindset that seeks to engage with the public from early in the research (indeed from the start) I have seen PGRs plan and deliver all three types of engagement. There are examples of engagement, sometimes including PGRs, on university websites (e.g. University of Bath, 2021b). I finish with an endorsement of public engagement in a PhD thesis of a recent PGR who researched consumer acceptance of eating insects (Chatterjee, 2020, p. 291):

> In a naïve capacity, I have tried my best to keep the public gene alive. I have come to learn that whilst publishing and gaining academic recognition are keys to establishing credibility (we) must gain trust from our various audiences to take our research seriously. My most cherished memories and moments have arisen from interactions with the public, more than attending conferences or from developing research articles for specialised audiences. I believe that public engagement and a strong and transparent agenda with the media have created some of the impact I've wanted to see …

Some final words of encouragement

There are some occasions when you get tangled up when talking about, presenting or publicising your work. You then need to account for what has happened and have another go at another time, improving any aspect of research content or delivery style that did not work for you. In all likelihood the more you talk about, present and publicise your PhD the less you will get tangled. If so inclined, there is no reason why you should not develop your use of all the platforms above, separately or in tandem. It is all part of your PGR apprenticeship as you move towards the award of PhD. There are other things you can do. Even in a world skewing towards social media, most faculties and universities have research administrators regularly calling for copy about research for print or online magazines and newsletters. Sometimes opportunities are missed in plain sight and at appropriate moments it is good to take up their call. Also consider non-ordinary platforms. There are reasons why competitions like 'Dance your

PhD' are so popular. They are enjoyable but also have the capability to bring new insights through a different form of talking, presenting and publicising.

References

Arnould, E. J. and Price, L. (1993). River magic: Extraordinary experience and the extended service encounter. *Journal of Consumer Research*, 20(1), 24–45.

CAUTHE (2021). *CAUTHE 2021 conference online.* Available at: <https://forumgroup.eventsair.com/cauthe2021/panels-and-workshops>

Chatterjee, I. (2020). *Evaluating the Influence of Individual Traits and Information on Consumer Acceptance of Entomophagy: A Choice Modelling Experiment.* PhD Thesis. Oxford Brookes University.

Events Air (2021). *Bringing virtual and online events to life.* Available at: <https://eventsair.com/onair/.>

Finn, J. (2018). Six reasons why PhD students should make poster presentations. Available at: <https://asippathways.com/2018/04/02/six-reasons-why-phd-students-should-make-poster-presentations/>

Gosling, P. and Noordam, B. (2006). *Mastering your PhD: Giving a great presentation.* Available at: <https://www.sciencemag.org/careers/2006/10/mastering-your-phd-giving-great-presentation.>

Huchet, B. (2019). *Twitter and scientists: A love story.* Available at: <https://www.labsexplorer.com/c/twitter-and-scientists-a-love-story_185>

Klar, S., Krupnikov, Y., Ryan, J. B., Searles, K., and Shmargad, Y. (2020). Using social media to promote academic research: Identifying the benefits of twitter for sharing academic work. *PLoSONE*, 15(4), 1–15 (e022944).

Lockwood, P. (2021). *No One is Talking About This.* London, UK: Bloomsbury Publishing.

LSE (2021). *Welcome to the LSE impact blog.* Available at: <https://blogs.lse.ac.uk/impactofsocialsciences/about-the-lse-impact-blog/>

NCCPE (2021). *Do engagement.* Available at: <https://www.publicengagement.ac.uk/do-engagement.>

PhD Life (2021). *A blog about the student experience.* Available at: <https://phdlife.warwick.ac.uk/>

Purrington, C. (2019). Designing conference posters. Available at: <https://colinpurrington.com/tips/poster-design/#whyposter>

Rossi, T. (2018). *How to design an award winning conference poster*. LSE Impact Blog. Available at: <https://blogs.lse.ac.uk/impactofsocialsciences/2018/05/11/how-to-design-an-award-winning-conference-poster/>

Rugg, G. and Petre, M. (2015). *The Unwritten Rules of PhD Research*. Maidenhead, UK: Open University Press.

Shinton, S. (2017). Teaching Matters Blog: The benefits of blogging for PhD students. Available at: <https://www.teaching-matters-blog.ed.ac.uk/the-benefits-of-blogging-for-phd-students/>

The Leveraged PhD (2019). *53 hashtags for academia to expand your academic network on Twitter*. Available at: <https://theleveragedphd.com/academic-hashtags-twitter/>

Thomson, P. (2016). *Seven reasons why blogging can make you a better academic writer*. Available at: <https://www.timeshighereducation.com/blog/seven-reasons-why-blogging-can-make-you-better-academic-writer>

University of Bath (2021a). *Engaging public groups with your research*. Available at: <https://www.bath.ac.uk/guides/engaging-public-groups-with-your-research/>

University of Bath (2021b). *Public engagement at Bath: Case study – co-production*. Available at: <https://www.bath.ac.uk/publications/engagement-stories-making-public-engagement-work-for-you/attachments/public-engagement-case-study-afroditi-stathi.pdf>

Zenger, J. and Folkman, J. (14 July 2016). What great listeners actually do. *Harvard Business Review*. Available at: <https://hbr.org/2016/07/what-great-listeners-actually-do>.

GLAUCO DE VITA

10 Final checks of the thesis, preparing the *viva* and dealing with amendments

Preamble

Far too many PhD candidates still arrive on the day of the *viva* somewhat underprepared, anxious and daunted by the prospect of their oral defence of the thesis. A feeling of self-doubt, lack of confidence and last-minute panic due to the unpredictability of the line of questioning and the indeterminacy of the outcome of the examination, are not uncommon. It does not need to be this way! The **aim of this chapter** is to provide you with a greater understanding of what is involved in the *viva*, recommend when and how best to prepare for it and demystify the process by offering a clear guide of dos and don'ts, also with respect to a remotely hosted or online *viva*. Additionally, the chapter offers advice on how to deal with outcomes requiring minor or major amendments. The advice draws on many years of experience as a PhD supervisor, PhD examiner at different institutions (in the UK and abroad), Chair of doctoral examination committees and PhD Programme Director.

What is the *viva voce*? The process and the role of participants

In many countries, assessment of a PhD entails, in addition to a formal evaluation of the written thesis, a *viva voce*. The *viva voce*, which translates from Latin as 'with living voice', is an oral examination of the PhD candidate on their research. Also known as the 'oral defence', it is part of a longstanding tradition expecting the 'newly become expert' to demonstrate their knowledge, articulate publicly their *thesis* (via Latin from Greek, literally 'placing, a proposition', from the root of *tithenai* 'to place') and justify their own arguments when challenged.

The *viva* consists of a series of questions from the examiners which the candidate must answer though, as the candidate relaxes, a flowing discussion among experts should ensue. As observed by Rüger (2016, p. 31):

> Almost all vivas turn out to be discussions between experts on an equal footing; in fact, it is virtually always the case that the PhD candidate is the best expert out of the three viva participants on the specific theme of the thesis by virtue of having worked on it exclusively for 3–5 years.

In some countries, universities require a presentation to an audience of the work of the thesis before the *viva*, but not in the UK. In the UK the *viva 'is usually a private affair that takes place "behind closed doors"; there are only a few institutions that operate "public" vivas and access is still restricted to members of specific academic communities'* (Tinkler and Jackson, 2002, p. 86). The duration of the *viva* may vary, but it is usually between two and three hours. If taking longer, it is reasonable for the candidate to ask, or the chair to call for a short break since the *viva* should never become an interminable, intimidating interrogation aimed at breaking the candidate.

The main participants in a PhD *viva* are the external examiner (i.e. external to the host university), the internal examiner (a faculty member with no prior involvement with the thesis) who may also act as Chair on behalf of the university, and the candidate. In some universities a separate independent Chair is appointed. If the PhD candidate is a member of staff of the university at the time of the examination, it is a requirement that two external examiners are appointed. Some UK universities also allow or even expect the Director of Studies (DoS) or another member of the supervisory team to attend the *viva* (but no more than one) if the candidate so wishes, purely for moral support. But the supervisor is not allowed to speak throughout the oral examination, making his or her presence seemingly superfluous, harmless but of no real benefit. However, it could be argued that the mere presence of a supervisor may, in fact, act as an additional safeguard for the good conduct of the examiners. Moreover, if anything goes wrong during the *viva* and there is an appeal, the supervisor can report as a passive witness on the events and endorse (or otherwise) the candidate's claims as to what may have gone wrong. Nonetheless, the PhD candidate has the right to veto attendance by the supervisor. This could happen, for example, if the candidate feels that the presence of the supervisor would add to the pressure, or simply to avoid the risk of inadvertently looking at the supervisor for reassurance during the *viva* instead of being self-reliant. As a passive observer expected to be silent throughout the *viva voce*, a useful role for the supervisor might be that of taking notes of issues raised as the *viva* unfolds or during the feedback when the outcome is communicated, rather than the PhD candidate doing this, which may cause pauses, slow down the proceedings and irritate the examiners. In cases where amendments are required, these notes can turn out to be most helpful to offer further detail and/or provide context to the corrections requested in the examiners' final report.

The internal and external examiners are charged with the responsibility of making an assessment as per the standards of the discipline. The final decision of recommendation of award is agreed jointly, though in the case of a disagreement the judgement of the external examiner carries greater weight. Because of his or her higher standing – also by virtue of the greater independence from the host institution – the external examiner usually leads the oral examination. The role of the candidate is the oral defence, assessed against a range of criteria for awarding a PhD as determined by the expert judgement of 'senior academic peers' (the examiners). In the main, these criteria relate to:

- Having made a significant contribution to knowledge through original, independent research of a quality to satisfy peer review (or a quality in whole or in part of a standard to merit publication, whether or not subsequently published).
- Having shown an ability to position the arguments within a theoretical context by testing or developing theory and conceptualising findings.

- Having gained significant expertise with respect to research methodology for advanced academic enquiry and an ability to justify methodological choices made *vis-à-vis* available alternatives.
- Having demonstrated a systematic acquisition and an appropriate understanding of a substantial body of knowledge and relevant literature at the forefront of an academic discipline.
- Having displayed an appropriate depth and breadth of knowledge in the field of study and the capacity for critical thought.
- Having completed a written thesis of a quantity reflecting three years of full-time postgraduate study or five years part-time postgraduate study, that conforms with academic standards in terms of structure and presentation (including a full bibliography and references).

The role of the Chair is to host the meeting on behalf of the university, ensure that university rules are upheld, that the proceedings are conducted in accordance with institutional guidelines and that the required paperwork is completed and submitted accordingly. The Chair is required to attend the meeting with the examiners prior to the *viva* and oversee the oral examination and post-*viva* discussions and deliberations. The Chair is neither expected nor required to be a subject expert, to have read the thesis or to make any academic judgement of it. The Chair has authority to intervene on procedural issues, if they judge that an examiner's line of questioning is too aggressive, biased or discriminatory, if the candidate is in extreme distress or if the supervisor interferes with the oral examination. In such rare cases, the Chair has the right to call a temporary break to discuss these concerns with the examiners or the supervisor and/or allow the candidate to take a short break and regroup.

While the Chair is usually appointed independently by the university, examiners are nominated by the DoS at least two months prior to the expected date of submission of the thesis. The identification and selection of potential examiners is usually done in consultation with the candidate, possibly drawing on field experts cited in the thesis. They should have no obvious conflict of interest in examining the candidate's work (e.g. to have previously published with the candidate or have been employed at the host university within the last few years) and be knowledgeable of relevant literature, the debate, problem or phenomenon being investigated. The potential examiners are initially approached informally by the DoS, to check their willingness and availability. Once their names and CVs are passed on to the university along with the official examiners' nomination form, the composition and profile of the proposed examining team is checked to ensure that it meets the requirements of the university regulations and is academically suitable. Most UK universities require examiners to have a PhD or equivalent experience as well as some experience of at least internal PhD examination. The appointment of examiners is ultimately approved (or otherwise) by the University's Registry or Graduate School, and a formal invitation to examine the candidate's thesis is sent by the university.

Much has been written in relevant literature about how PGRs and supervisors should go about choosing the ideal examiner(s), with a multitude of pseudo criteria and recommendations being mentioned. They include, letting the PGR nominate the examiners since 'student knows best', canvassing opinions among colleagues and other PGRs as to whom has already been found to be a 'soft touch', aiming at the top of the field and 'shooting for the stars' since the older, most experienced and/or famous academics are, allegedly, more lenient, compassionate and forgiving, nominating examiners who are sympathetic to your methodological approach to avoid possible clashes during the oral examination with "*a smart Alec*" who has some sort of prejudice against your epistemological position (Kiley, 2009), and steering clear of examiners suffering from "*neuroticism*" (Dunleavy, 2003, p. 214) or the "*drawbridge*" mentality (Delamont et al., 2004, p. 145), that is, unduly harsh examiners who believe they should be the last person to enter the ivory tower of academe before the drawbridge is raised. More simply, official criteria notwithstanding (e.g. the avoidance of a conflict of interest), the choice should boil down to balancing the need for specialist academic knowledge and expertise of an examiner on one hand, and their reputation for fairness, reasoned judgement and professionalism on the other. Once honest and balanced consideration has been applied with these broad attributes in mind, the job of choosing the 'best' examiner is done and the rest is best left to the quality of the thesis and the ability of the candidate to defend it appropriately during the *viva*.

The examination process has four distinct parts. The first part, taking place before the *viva* and usually lasting up to thirty minutes over a cup of coffee, is an opportunity for the examiners to share their views of the thesis and compare notes as per their respective preliminary independent reports (see Appendix 10.1 for an authentic example of an examiner's pre-*viva*, preliminary report). During this part of the process, examiners also agree on a strategy of how to structure the line of questioning. Usually examiners have already developed a list of questions and have brought with them a copy of the thesis filled with (sticky)notes for easy retrievable reference to specific pages of the thesis. The second part is the actual oral examination of the candidate. This is typically planned to start with a series of warm up questions or a short presentation by the candidate describing the key aspects of the thesis, to kick start the examination and put the candidate at ease,[56] followed by a more in-depth probing of knowledge, understanding, choices made or suspected deficiencies of the thesis, by theme or, sequentially, chapter by chapter. The third part of the process – carried out in the absence of the candidate and the supervisor, who are required to leave the room – entails a discussion between the examiners to agree a recommendation to the university's degree-awarding committee. See Appendix 10.2 for a full menu of options of possible recommendations available to the examiners to choose from (slight variations may apply across universities and countries). It is extremely rare for any degree-awarding university not to follow the recommendation of the examiners unless there are serious, documented irregularities that have occurred during the *viva*. It is highly recommended for the Chair to get the examiners' agreement of the final recommendation of award signed at this stage by both examiners, who can then, later, finalise the exact list and wording of specific amendments required at resubmission, if any. The fourth and final part of the examination occurs when the candidate and supervisor are called back and told the outcome (recommendation of award). The *viva* Chair or internal examiner then coordinates and arranges for the examiners' final report (with

---

56   It is becoming increasingly common for business and management PhD *vivas*, to expect the candidate to have prepared a five- to ten-minute PowerPoint presentation that summarises the thesis. While it is good to be prepared for this eventuality if asked, it is important to remember that it is up to the examiners to decide whether this is the way the *viva* will start or they would rather have full control of how they wish to run the *viva*.

the complete list of amendments, if any) to be filed to the university who then officially conveys this to the PhD candidate.

Preparation for the *viva* starts when making the final checks of the thesis

The last two or three months before submission, it is of paramount importance to go through a series of critical checks of the thesis to ensure everything is in order. These final checks are crucial since they address many details and more major aspects that will be under close scrutiny when examiners receive the thesis. Some of these aspects are likely to determine the impression examiners form about the whole work and potential deficiencies, giving them prompts on areas they may wish to probe on during the oral examination. In this respect it may also be useful prior to the submission of the thesis to learn about your examiners' own research, particularly if they have published on the topic of the thesis (but do not contact them under any circumstances). Failure to cite properly in the thesis their recent, relevant contributions, would obviously be a noticeable omission (but don't conjure up a citation purely for the purpose of ingratiating yourself with the examiner!). Reading your examiners' published research could also help you form a view of aspects of the debate they place special importance on and gauge their likely reactions to your work. What kind of questions can you think reading the thesis would most likely raise in your examiners given what they have written? So, in light of these considerations, you should take this last chance to consider whether some slight changes or additions may be needed in the thesis.

Turning to the task of ensuring the thesis meets expectations of what a good thesis looks like, you should start by reviewing its content and structure. Ask yourself, does the title accurately represent the content? Does the thesis include a very concise yet comprehensive *Abstract* that clearly states the problem, highlights the significance of the study, and outlines the method(s), the key findings and the original contribution(s) of the research? Does the thesis display a logical, coherent structure? In terms of having at least:

- *Introduction chapter.*
- *Literature Review chapter(s).*
- *Methodology chapter* (explaining what you did, why and how, in terms of data collection and analysis with a clear justification for methodological choices made).
- *Presentation and Further Discussion of Results/Findings* (which also includes a discussion of the connections between the literatures reviewed earlier and the thesis' results/findings).
- *Conclusion chapter.*

The Introduction and Conclusion chapters are typically written simultaneously at the end of the PhD. Because of this, they are sometimes rushed in order to hand in the completed thesis by the deadline. Yet, these chapters are very important since they determine, respectively, the first and last impression of the thesis in the eyes of the examiners, and you only have one chance to make a good first and last impression. The last impression will come at the time the examiners have just finished reading the thesis and are about to start writing the pre-*viva* (preliminary) report. Hence, the importance of 'the feel' examiners are left with after reading the conclusion chapter is self-explanatory. With respect to the importance of the first impression, as observed by Golding et al. (2014, p. 568):

> An examiner's first impressions influence how he or she reads the rest of a thesis. If they have a good first impression, they feel they can relax and enjoy the thesis; if not, then they read more critically, looking for problems.

The 'Introduction' chapter fulfils many purposes. It needs to state the rationale of the study, the problem statement, the research question, aim and objectives. Eco (2015) also emphasises that the introduction chapter establishes *"the center and periphery"* (p. 111) of the thesis. Indeed, the introduction should clearly designate the boundaries of what constitutes what is critical, relevant, less relevant or excluded in your thesis, and it should explain why. The 'centre' is the core of the thesis; the critical part that deals with the focal object of enquiry. This is also the part that, as rightly emphasised by Dunleavy (2003, p. 50), unlike the "*Lead-in*" and "*Lead-out*" materials of the thesis, one would expect to contain the most original elements of the work, based on your novel results, findings and distinctive arguments that you can legitimately claim to have developed yourself. The 'periphery' is the domain that relates less directly to, or touches lightly on, the main object of enquiry, extending to what may be regarded as the outer or tangential parts of the territory of your study. The 'Conclusion' chapter must revisit your initial purpose, research question, aim and objectives, and economically restate the thesis' statement. It must summarise the key findings and spell out implications, provide a clear and cogent statement of the *significance* of the contribution(s) of the thesis over what has gone before (for both theory and practice), acknowledge limitations and point out profitable avenues for future research. So, do a final review of these chapters with these considerations in mind.

Still on matters of structure, ask yourself: 'Is there adequate signposting throughout the thesis?' For example, does the 'Introduction' chapter include a road map to the text in terms of outlining the structure of the thesis? Does each chapter contain an introduction or overview section and a chapter summary at the end? Do you cross-reference appropriately to different (earlier or later) sections of the thesis at strategic points throughout the text?

Moving on to aspects related to the writing itself, does the thesis properly report quotations from the literature and/or any participants? By 'properly', I mean, for example, that direct quotations from published sources report also, in addition to the year, the page number, that there aren't too many quotations packed together and that you also *interpret* quotations. Is there a *critical discussion* of the key findings, either as a separate chapter or integrated with the 'Results/Findings' chapter, that addresses the all-important 'So What' question? This is the time to also engage in at least a couple of final rounds of proofreading to ensure the thesis is as error free as possible. Avoiding such presentational errors is important because "*once examiners notice sloppy presentation and have become suspicious of the quality of the thesis, they tend to read more critically, searching for faults*" (Golding et al., 2014, p. 569).

In addition to typographical errors, recurrent presentational issues to bear in mind when doing these final checks include inaccurate mathematical notation, a wandering tense, the unnecessary and/or repetitive use of particular words, split infinitive constructions, poor spelling, errors of grammar or syntax, wrongly numbered tables, figures and section headings. I could add to the list the use of long or verbless sentences, for which – I must admit – I do not share the common antipathy. What's the hurry for a full stop? And do we always have to put a verb in a sentence, no matter how short? *Why, what a question!* (forgive the use of the exclamatory verbless clause in italics). Some of the world's most admired writers, from Virginia Woolf to David Foster Wallace, seemed to be fond of sentences which, despite or perhaps because of their lengthiness or verbless structure, stand as pieces of writing or 'fragments' one can only marvel at. But, let's face it, we are neither Woolf nor Wallace, and longer sentences can be harder to understand than short ones. Hence, when it comes to taking such 'liberties' in the thesis, especially given the widespread allergy towards sentences of this kind, better to be cautious. The same applies to using unfiltered (unnecessary) jargon or indulging in the formulation of neologisms as they too suffer from a pointless dislike in some quarters.

Consistency is also an issue that needs to be checked, including the mixed use of the active or passive voice. The former (where the subject of a sentence performs the verb's action) is generally preferred, taking the first-person singular pronoun (i.e. 'I') rather than the *pluralis majestatis* or royal 'we'. The use of the majestic plural can prompt hard-nosed examiners to ask questions about attribution, that is, whether the thesis is the fruit of the candidate's own work: 'Who is *we*?', 'Who wrote this?', 'You, and who else?', they may ask. That said, many supervisors and academic journal articles recommend that the thesis be written in the third person, for example, 'The researcher found', 'The author argues', which is also acceptable. Whether you have used the first or third person, ensure your thesis is consistent. Verifying correct punctuation throughout the text, for example, a comma splice (when two independent clauses are incorrectly joined by a comma to form one sentence) or a missing comma, is another worthy check. Proper punctuation can help the reader better understand the intended message by indicating pauses where necessary and/or laying emphasis on important ideas that are discussed in the text. Even the absence or presence of a single comma can sometimes change the entire meaning of a sentence.

For example, I once read in the 'Acknowledgements' of a thesis: "*I want to thank my parents, Sandra and God.*" The sentence bears a sacrosanct difference with "*I want to thank my parents, Sandra, and God.*", which surely is what the PGR intended to write (the missing comma makes the PGR look rather holy, don't you think?). The same holds true for apostrophes, hyphens, colons and other punctuation marks.

The above issues should all be resolved before you hand in the thesis to avoid them being picked up by examiners. You must also undertake a final check to ensure that all the sources cited in the text are properly reported in the final reference list and *vice versa*, and that the style guide for rules about formatting the final list of references – brackets, full stops, commas, capital letters, italics, volume, issue number, etc. – has been followed consistently. As a hopefully superfluous reminder, you should avoid at all costs reporting quotes from an indirect source whilst giving the impression that you have read the original. As observed by Eco (2015, p. 52): "*This is not just a matter of professional ethics. Imagine if someone asked how you were able to read a certain manuscript directly, when it is common knowledge that it was destroyed in 1944!*" The same prudence applies to citing untranslated foreign texts written in languages you are not proficient in. It is also recommendable to avoid an abundance of references to unrefereed material from non-reputable websites or the like, sources which do not carry out authoritative or rigorous peer review.

With respect to sources cited and references, it is also useful to check whether any publications originally reported (at the time of writing, which could be two years earlier, when you were working on your literature review) as working papers or articles in press, have changed their publication status. If so, you should duly update such references as per their latest publication details (advice that acts as a reminder for me to 'walk the talk' before sending the completed chapters of this book to the publisher).

Ensure you fully conform to your institution's PhD thesis submission and formatting requirements. This process entails compliance with a range of often university-specific issues regarding the allowed length (word or page limits), typescript/print, one-sided or two-sided, line spacing, consecutive page numbers, font and font size, margins, front cover, first page, submission in part fulfilment statement, academic award for which the thesis is submitted and year of submission, ethics approval certificate page, acknowledgements, list of contents, list of abbreviations, list of tables, list of figures, appendices, soft/hard binding, number of copies to be submitted, etc. These checks are *your* responsibility, not that of your supervisors.

I know! All the final checks mentioned above constitute a very tedious, time-consuming, dull, monotonous and tiresome task. Especially so when acknowledging that the process of reading, re-reading and double-checking what is by now a 200-page document needs to be undertaken with painstaking attention to detail. But don't make the common mistake of underestimating the importance of such checks. At times it can feel as if this unpleasant process, painful even, can go on *ad infinitum*. Nevertheless, I would advise to be mentally prepared and determined to carry it out *ad nauseam*, literally to the point at which it is almost more than your body can bear. These final checks are not just a cosmetic exercise. As with getting the references right, issues of style and formatting are important not only for presenting yourself as a professional academic, they inevitably affect how you and your work will be perceived.

Finally, once you have gone through all these checks, and you alongside your supervisors are fully satisfied, run the thesis through the institutional plagiarism detection software. Most UK universities also require the DoS to check the Turnitin report. Check carefully whether, even purely by mistake, there may be passages that may cause any such concerns since irrespective of whether plagiarism is complete or patchwork-based and was carried out intentionally or as a result of carelessness, it is unacceptable, unethical and constitutes a serious form of academic misconduct. If so, address any such issues by properly referencing to the original source.

Preparing for the *viva* after the thesis submission

Once the thesis is submitted, there is a time lag of about two to four months to the *viva*. You will be quite exhausted at this point and it is probably best to take a week or two off for a well-deserved break. You need to recharge your batteries also in the light of the work ahead to cross the finishing line. Indeed, during the last four or five weeks before the *viva*, it is highly recommendable to re-enter the thesis in earnest to place yourself in the best position to face the oral examination since in addition to a great thesis, what is needed to pass the *viva* is a well-prepared and confident candidate. Torres (2012, p. 9) went as far as arguing: "*The candidate's performance during the viva may be as important as the written thesis.*" Obviously, a good oral defence will not turn around fully the examiners' view of the printed thesis, but as noted by Russell (2008, p. 122):

> … a strong performance at the viva could sway them if they were unconvinced about parts of your thesis. Equally, a weak performance might make them question their inclination towards passing you.

I list below several tips that can make a significant difference:

- *Ensure you re-read the thesis a few times, cover to cover*. You should develop a mental map of where everything is in the text and know your thesis inside out. If you are already concerned about particular aspects of the thesis, aspects you are uncertain or insufficiently clear about (e.g. the advantages and disadvantages of alternative methods to the ones you used in your study, the model, specific tables of results, graphs or figures), those are precisely the areas you should spend some time brushing up your knowledge on. This is useful even simply to raise the level of confidence in your ability to deal with those difficult aspects of the thesis which may be causing some doubt or apprehension.
- *Don't worry if you notice the odd spelling error or small mistakes that you failed to spot before submission*. This is not uncommon and can easily and quickly be rectified when the final, revised version of the thesis (post-*viva*) is resubmitted. Just make sure you draw up a list of such small errors that still need to be corrected.
- *Be proactive in asking your supervisors to arrange a mock viva*, two or three weeks prior to the actual one, to be led by your supervisors if no other departmental or school expert is available (in most universities a mock *viva* is offered as a matter of routine). This trial run can help you develop the confidence to answer orally different types of questions about the thesis, defend your ideas, think on your feet and cope with the pressure. Experiential evidence suggests that a mock *viva* is found to be particularly useful to those PGRs who take it seriously and prepare well for it.

- *Register yourself in any institutional training workshops or seminars on preparing candidates for the viva.* The more you know about what a *viva* is, the process and what is meant to happen on the day, the less intimidating it will be.
- *Write a one-page summary of each chapter* and keep in mind the clear distinction between the thesis' findings, implications and recommendations.
- *Remember that what examiners will be mainly looking for is the 'contribution to knowledge'* (you need to ensure examiners understand exactly what the contribution is, and that you are able to express it clearly and concisely).

I am often queried about what questions examiners are likely to ask and whether it is worth anticipating and preparing for such questions. Inevitably every examiner will have their subjective view of the thesis, their 'take' on it, as it were. The more substantive questions will revolve around their own reading and interpretation of the work with respect to specific claims made, the wording of specific passages, your model, your results and findings, and the conclusions you draw from the evidence. Such specific questions cannot be predicted. However, this does not mean you should not aim to prepare appropriately for the oral examination since there are also more general questions that are, in one way or another, likely to be covered during the discussion with the examiners.

I list below many such questions. At the start, they will most likely ask general questions about the thesis, requiring you to offer a brief synthesis. These questions may include asking what motivated you to start a PhD or to give a three- to ten-minute introduction of your work and key findings. These are the so-called icebreaker or warm up questions, to calm you down and help you relax. Next, the examiners will delve into the details of the thesis itself, asking confirmatory, probing and, at times, redemptive questions. Such types of questions will pertain to your knowledge, comprehension, application, analysis, evaluation and synthesis. So, draw up your own list of possible specific questions, especially the ones you dread the most. Some typical 'wrap up' questions are likely to conclude the *viva*, these too are listed below. You should be prepared to answer all such questions and should practise by vocalising answers. It is not a case of needing to learn the pre-prepared answers by heart though. This would only work as a technique if you could be certain of the exact way your examiner(s) will ask a question. Moreover, reciting memorised answers may remove a healthy feel of spontaneity from the discussion. It is more about thinking about and rehearsing how you will articulate key arguments and ideas.

Typical general questions asked at a *viva voce* worth preparing for:

- Assume you are stuck in a lift with people who know nothing about your subject area. In no more than three minutes, summarise to them your thesis and what you have done, why you have done it in that way, and your key findings.
- How does the thesis fit into the big picture in the field? (i.e. within the map of the wider knowledge domain).
- What is the big idea that binds your thesis together and why is this idea important?
- What is the problem statement? Why is the problem worth addressing?
- Why did you choose this specific topic for your PhD study? What was your motivation? Why were you interested in this debate? How did your main research question emerge?
- Who are your main interlocutors in this literature and who will be most interested in your work? Who is your relevant audience?
- What is the main aim of the thesis? What is the main research question and the key, associated research objectives or sub-questions? How did you arrive at, or derive such questions and sub-questions?
- What are the boundaries of your study? Where did you draw the line on what to include in, and exclude from, your literature review?
- What previous experience, preconceived ideas and values did you bring to this research study? How important is reflexivity for your work and where does it feature?
- What is the theoretical or conceptual framework in this study? Take us through your model. How did you derive your specific hypotheses?
- What are the main findings from your review of the literature and what questions did such a critical review raise for you? What is your critical assessment of existing literature in this field? What have you learned from this literature and what was(were) the main gap(s)?
- What are the main controversies in this literature? And where do you stand in relation to these areas of dispute?

- Can you point us to evidence of 'criticality' in the treatment of existing literature in your thesis?
- Who has had the strongest influence in the development of your debate? Which are the three most important published articles that relate to your thesis? How is your study different?
- How did you go about answering your main research question and/or addressing your research aim and objectives? What methodology did you use and why did you choose that methodological approach *vis-à-vis* others? What advantages do your chosen methodological techniques/tests have over available alternatives? What are their disadvantages?
- What problems, if any, did you encounter in executing your method/techniques? How did you attempt to resolve these problems? How successful were you?
- How did you recruit your sample of interviewees? What are the weaknesses of your sample? Why did you choose this sample country or countries as your setting/context for the study? How did you select your sample frame/interviewees? Why them? What boundaries did you set for this selection?
- How did you delineate the limits around the scope of your data collection? What makes your data the most appropriate to answer your research question? Are there any other data you would have liked to have collected?
- Did themes emerge from your data (*a posteriori*) or did you bring them to the data (*a priori*)? Why did you do it in this way? Could your analysis have been done in another way?
- How do we know your results are reliable and valid? Can your results be replicated?
- What ethical issues were you confronted with in undertaking the research, data collection and analysis? How did you address such ethical issues? What protocol did you employ?
- What is your *unit of analysis*, that is, the major entity that you are analysing in your study?
- Why did you opt for follow-up, face-to-face interviews? Why did you conduct interviews before (or after) the questionnaire survey?
- How did you test the face validity of the instrument? Who did you pilot test your survey with? Why them? How representative is your sample for piloting? Did you pilot all aspects of the survey, including flow of the questions, their order, question types, clarity, etc.? Which

specific changes were made to your questionnaire as a result of the feedback from the pilot test?
- Why did you use focus groups instead of other methods? What are the benefits of focus groups?
- Why did you opt for the case study method? What are your case studies for? Are they exploratory, descriptive or explanatory in nature? What are the advantages and disadvantages of your case study approach?
- What makes your analysis 'rigorous'?
- Are your conclusions generalisable? (Do they need to be?) How can you be sure your sample is adequate to draw conclusions?
- What are the main findings of your PhD thesis? What do they add to what was known before? What surprised you about your findings and why?
- How do your results compare to those of previous studies? Are there any major differences? If so, why do your results differ? Is it due to a different sample, different data, different sample period, different methodological technique used?
- What does this figure tell us? What is the 'take away' message of this table? Take us through this diagram.
- What is the important, original contribution that the thesis makes to the body of knowledge? (N.B. this isn't just about the specific results of your work, but about spelling out the *significance* of the main findings to the existing body of knowledge and their novelty value. This is the most important criterion for award of a PhD since it is the *contribution to knowledge* what makes your work doctoral level. You should be able to distinguish between a contribution your work makes to theory, a contribution to knowledge and a policy or practice related contribution).
- What makes your thesis 'original'?
- What are the main *strengths* and *weaknesses* of your thesis? (It is useful to link your weaknesses to the limitations stated in your concluding chapter. Stick to those).
- What are the main *limitations* of your study? What would you do differently if you were able to start all over again, with the benefit of hindsight?
- What impact are your findings likely to have beyond academia? What are the main *policy implications* that stem/flow from your results/findings? What is the relevance of your work to practitioners?

- Which aspects of the work could be taken further? What are the profitable avenues for further research from your thesis? How do you see the debate developing over the next five to ten years?
- How did the project change as you progressed? How has your view of the debate changed as the study unfolded? Has your thinking changed over the course of the PhD?
- What have you learned from this PhD journey in terms of research skills or other transferable skills? (For business and management theses this question is quite common.)
- What are your plans for publication from this research?
- What do you intend to do next? A job in academia perhaps?
- Is there anything else you would wish to tell us which we have not given you an opportunity to discuss?

The day before the *viva*

Try to stay calm and relaxed about it. Despite the ominous cliché in relevant literature, the *viva* should not be thought of as something 'to survive'; you will continue to live, come what may! But it is true that many PhD candidates are gripped by a feeling of anxious uncertainty the day before the viva. Over the years some of them have come to see me in my office to be reassured, and I could read in their faces 'that feeling', which – in the absence of a better analogy – I can only describe as the apprehensive thoughts that go through one's mind in a dentist's waiting room, when one doesn't know whether what lies in store is a dreadful root canal or a clean bill of dental health. Instead, try to think of the *viva* as something to look forward to, a great occasion that affords you the opportunity to explain the good work you have done and highlight the contribution the thesis makes. What a great privilege it is to have two academic experts interested in your thesis, who are willing to have a stimulating discussion with you about it. And remember, no one, not even the examiners, knows your thesis better than you, so you are in an advantageous position to have that discussion. There is, therefore, no need to be anxious or panicky, and have a good sleep the night before. Assuming the *viva* will be done

Final checks of thesis, prepare viva, make corrections

in person, double check the time, room and itinerary, and make sure you are there a little early. Torres (2012) even suggests that, prior to the *viva*, it is worthwhile for the candidate to go and look over the room in which the *viva* is scheduled to take place *"so as to be more comfortable during the examination process [...] and to envisage a successful defence of the research"* (ibid., p. 12).

If the *viva* is to be conducted online, 'remotely hosted', find a quiet room and let anyone who lives with you know when it is scheduled to take place, both to avoid being disturbed and to prevent multiple internet users in your household to consume available bandwidth during your *viva* connection. And if you have attention-seeking pets, ensure they have no access to your space. Try out different sitting and desk arrangements to find the set up that works best for you. In addition to ensuring you have some paper and working pens, a bottle of water, etc., as per a face-to-face *viva* (more details in the next section), have your mobile (on silent of course) at hand, in case you experience technical issues and/or to give the Chair another way to contact you should there be problems with the video call connection. It is also useful to have a copy of the printed thesis with you since flicking to the relevant sections of the thesis by having to switch between computer tabs and scroll down the screen of a 200-page document can take longer and disrupt the flow.

Find out beforehand who has the responsibility to set up the video conference call, to send out the online platform invitations and to contact technical support should the need arise (these are typically the responsibility of the Chair). Whether the video call is to be done via Skype, Zoom, Microsoft Teams or Cisco Webex, try to arrange an online test with your DoS prior to the *viva*, to ensure the connection works, familiarise yourself with the videoconferencing software and check how you and your background will look on camera to increase your confidence on the day. Due to the Covid-19 social distancing measures, I recently examined a PhD remotely and the UK-based host university stipulated that three online tests had to be done by all panel members in the month preceding the *viva*. These online trials can be useful for candidates to brush up on the regulations of remotely hosted *vivas* (e.g. recording is not allowed) and test computing equipment and features. These include the use of headphones (you may find using headphones with built-in microphones useful), muting/unmuting and screen sharing features, how to avoid 'echo' sound issues and internet interference from nearby electronic devices, and the availability of good internet speed and an adequately sized computer screen. Most important of all, don't be apprehensive about doing a *viva* online or let the practicalities of remote arrangements daunt you. Yes, it's a bit unusual, but that doesn't mean that the experience cannot be a very positive one.

On the day

On the day of the *viva*, be your best self. Choose a dress code attune to the occasion, aiming to look professional, business-like, but ensuring you feel comfortable (just as you should do for an online *viva*). Don't forget to bring with you some pocket-tissues, a small bottle of water (water should be there, but better safe than sorry, a dry mouth is not uncommon when you feel your heart pounding in your chest), two pens and some paper, and a copy of your thesis. The latter must be the same version as in possession of the examiners. Specifically, the same pagination as the copy that was sent to them. It's hard to treat this piece of advice without anecdotes. After asking a candidate I was examining to go to page 18, second line, his copy of the thesis took him to an altogether different section. The rest of the *viva* lasted considerably longer as a result, with each discrepancy punctuating our intermittent dialogue over what felt like the longest three hours of my academic life. Not good!

You should also bring two copies of any published paper from your thesis to give out to the examiners in case they ask about your publication plans. And if you haven't published yet, try to use the two/three months before the *viva* also to work on such papers from the thesis. It will afford you the opportunity to have something to say in case you are asked about your publishing plans.

Place the closed thesis in front of you when you sit, at the start, and should you need to refer to it to address a specific point, be polite by asking the examiners whether you are allowed to open it on the right page.

In order to answer questions to the best of your ability the cardinal rule is to listen to them carefully. Concentrate on what you are being asked. Remember, if you do not understand a question, it is best to say, 'I don't understand the question, could you please rephrase it?' This reply could also be used to buy you time to answer, but this is a 'card' to be played only once. Alternatively, you could begin your response by rephrasing the question yourself, for example, 'if I understand your query correctly, you wish me to explain why/how ….', which again, will grant you a moment or two to collect your thoughts to help you prepare the best possible answer. If you don't know the answer to a question or don't remember something, it is best to be honest and say 'I don't know' or 'Sorry, I can't recall' rather than waffle or go off on a tangent. In your quest to show what you know, don't launch too quickly into an answer and end up misspeaking. It is far better to take your time to formulate a well-articulated answer than rush into a poor or poorly phrased reply. Short pauses and silences while you are thinking do not have to feel uncomfortable. Perception of time can be distorted when one is under pressure and what may feel like blackouts to you may in fact be perceived as natural pauses by the examiners. Short pauses can let examiners know that they should pay attention to what you are about to say, they can project thoughtfulness, confidence and control over the situation. You can, therefore, take a bit of time to reflect on difficult questions or simply ask, 'Can I write that down for a moment as I think this through?' This approach can be helpful especially in the event in which an examiner asks multiple questions at once or, even worse, a nested question (two questions, with one embedded in the other), which should be avoided but, unfortunately, is not uncommon. For difficult questions you may even wish to qualify your answer, something like 'This is a really profound question that would probably require some deep thinking to be answered fully but, off the cuff, I would say …'. Once, I was positively swayed by a *viva* candidate who, after having responded to my question with a barely acceptable answer, qualified her reply by saying: "*I hope I answered your question, but it most certainly requires further reflection to do full justice to it and I can't think of a better answer offhand*". The candidate's qualification reassured me as to her awareness of her own limitations and, at the same time, signalled her genuine interest and curiosity in expanding that line of scholarly enquiry. Most importantly, if you feel cornered by particularly awkward questions or annoyed by what you may perceive as sharpshooting, don't lose your cool.

Of course, you should expect to *defend* your thesis, but don't assume you'll be, literally, under attack. It is not a battle. Part of the examiners' job is precisely to question aspects of your work and satisfy themselves as to whether such aspects require intervention or not. Don't be adversarial and don't ever antagonise the examiners. Avoid at all costs coming across as arrogant by interrupting or speaking over them. Be always very respectful also when you wish to stand your ground. Consider carefully what you'll defend strenuously and what you would be prepared to concede. Remember, it is crucial to defend claims of significance, originality of the thesis and its contribution to knowledge. However, no research is perfect and acknowledging that some parts of the work could have been done differently or better, shows intellectual maturity. After all, to err is human and, as the aphorism goes, it is a sign of weakness to avoid showing signs of weakness. On this account, good judgement is paramount since defending obvious shortcomings of the work, especially about relatively minor issues, will not serve you well and is likely to irritate examiners. As per the sensible advice offered by Rüger (2016, p. 34), "*one should not fight when it is about trivial things: for one, it will not cost one much work to concede small points, for another fighting these has the danger as coming across as unnecessary bellicose.*"

Good judgement should also be exercised in avoiding grandiose claims or comments that undersell the value of the research (Rüger, 2016). Be confident but not over-confident. As recommended by Eco (2015, p. 183), you need to balance academic pride with humility:

> When you speak, you are the expert. [...] you have no right to hesitate if you have done good work. [...] Be humble and prudent before opening your mouth, but once you open it, be dignified and proud.

Don't be long-winded but, equally, avoid giving monosyllabic answers; getting a candidate to talk about the thesis should not feel like pulling teeth. In their engaging, tongue in cheek coverage of "*How to fail a viva*", Rugg and Petre (2004, p. 175) also list, among other items, answering questions about 'why you did what you did' with the infamous "*my supervisor made me do it*", and displaying "*a lack of interest*", "*intransigence*", "*rampant cynicism*" and "*flippancy*". I couldn't agree more. These behaviours assail in distinct ways, but all have the power to ravage a *viva*.

After the viva: Dealing with minor or major amendments

Appendix 10.2 provides an example of the menu of PhD award recommendations available to examiners (but please note that this may vary slightly across universities and countries). The vast majority of PhD *vivas* in the UK result in an examiners' recommendation to award the PhD subject to very minor corrections, minor amendments or major amendments (outcomes 4.2 to 4.4 in Appendix 10.2). Other outcomes in the list such as the recommendation of downgrading the award to a MPhil are less common and the probability of an outright 'Fail' below 5% in the UK. Of course, as noted by Phillips and Pugh (1994), an outright fail should not occur at all, but if it does, it is as much a failure of the supervisors as it is of the candidate. Usually, a natural selection occurs, meaning that those PGRs most likely to fail will already have been lost along the way of the PhD programme as a result of the PGR decision to withdraw before completion or by the university's decision following the official annual progress reviews of the candidate's work. In cases where supervisors have serious concerns about the quality of the thesis (despite their repeated attempts to help the PGR get the PhD back on track, one would hope), they should advise the PGR of this. Yet, in such cases, most universities will still allow PGRs the option of carrying on and submitting the thesis for examination regardless.

Each recommendation of award carries a given timeframe allowed (see, as an example, Appendix 10.2). Of course, you are not obliged to resubmit the revised version at deadline. You can submit earlier, but you must ensure that you and your supervisors are happy with the revisions carried out. You must also attach a letter that details clearly how you have addressed *each and every* point that had been raised in the examiners' report listing the required amendments. The letter should also indicate where such changes are in the revised thesis.

When addressing the final report of amendments, it must be appreciated that this is not a time to argue with examiners over the relevance or otherwise of their qualms about your thesis, let alone dispute their requests or recommendations. The ultimate verdict on your PhD award now lies firmly on how satisfied they will be with your revisions. If you believe that what the examiners are requiring you to do is inappropriate or the final verdict of the examination unfair, check your university's official appeal regulations. But bear in mind that in nearly twenty-five years of academic practice, I have yet to come across a successful appeal of the outcome of a PhD examination, let alone of the examiners' required amendments. Simply disagreeing with the examiners' expert academic judgement will not suffice. Academic judgement is a guiding principle at most universities. Serious, demonstrable procedural irregularities or behavioural breaches (such as negligence or misconduct by an examiner) must occur to constitute reasonable grounds of appeal that are permissible in light of the university's stated rules, policies, codes and guidance, and the rules of external bodies such as the Office of the Independent Adjudicator (OIA) and the Quality Assurance Agency (QAA) for higher education. Hence, above caveats notwithstanding, my advice is to comply fully and amend accordingly. In this sense, the approach is not quite the same as attending to the issues, reasonable or otherwise, raised by anonymous reviewers after submitting articles to journals for the purpose of publication. In the case of responding to journals' reviewers, authors are allowed much greater leeway in making their case. Moreover, there is less at stake, thus granting you the freedom to decide whether and how suggested amendments about a journal article should be dealt with. I have quite a few anecdotes about my personal clashes with journals' anonymous reviewers over objections that I considered to be unjustified or questionable. Oh, wait a minute, that's next chapter. Here I am discussing post-*viva* revisions.

Completing a PhD is immensely rewarding but the journey itself can be taxing. In relevant literature, the mental challenge of completing a PhD has been compared to running the London marathon or swimming the English Channel (Russell, 2008). It has also been suggested that, after the *viva*, a sense of grief can be experienced, since the thesis had become the central focus of the candidate's life (Murray, 2009). The *viva* itself may be a disappointing experience for some candidates. Expectations, too, can play a part in making people miserable. I once even heard a newly conferred 'Doctor' who had just passed her *viva* with 'no corrections' express her sorrow for how "*easy*" and "*uneventful*" the oral examination had turned out to be: she referred to it as "*an anti-climax*". More commonly, candidates are up for celebration, but even a pretty successful outcome of 'minor corrections' often leaves candidates with an unwanted further 'last hurdle' at a time when they are exhausted and do not want to see the thesis ever again (Rudestam and Newton, 2001). Some may have already secured employment thus even minor corrections would impose additional sacrifices to find the time to undertake the revisions and finish the PhD. Nevertheless, it is recommendable not to lose momentum. Hence, try to complete the required amendments as soon as is practicably possible.

Once you receive the examiners' final report of the required amendments (which should provide specific instructions as to what is to be addressed), typically sent from the university's Graduate School or the Chair within one month of the *viva*, you must ensure you are clear as to what the process is to ratify the changes. Who will ratify the corrections and accept the revised version of the thesis? Who can communicate with whom to ask for clarification on aspects of the report(s)? Irrespective of all of this, the candidate is encouraged to continue to work with supervisors who should oversee the successful completion of the revisions.

The above-mentioned procedures can vary slightly across universities and countries and they also depend on the recommendation of award. For very minor changes (up to one- or three-month timeframe), it is usually the internal examiner only who is charged with ratifying your revised version of the thesis. For major amendments, it could be the external or both the internal and external examiners. Also ensure that you (and your supervisors) are clear as to whether you (or your supervisor) may be allowed to communicate with the examiner in charge, or to see if they would be prepared to look at a draft version of your revisions (which is most unlikely) before you officially submit the revised version of the thesis. The latter must be accompanied by a letter reporting the changes made as per the examiners' written list of corrections in their final report. This accompanying 'Letter of Amendments' usually contains a table with the examiners' comments on the left hand-side column and, on the right hand-side column, details of the changes made as a result of the comment and where they are located in the revised thesis. Whatever you do, do not procrastinate and do not miss the last and final deadline.

Some final words of encouragement

Don't be anxious or scared of the *viva*. Build a positive mindset to enjoy the moment. Think of this moment as the pinnacle of your scholarly efforts and achievements to date. Not just 'the last hurdle' but a splendid opportunity to show and elaborate on the quality of your research, how much you have done and what a significant contribution your PhD thesis makes. You are unlikely in your future academic life to have the opportunity again to have two interested subject experts listening to you talking for a couple of hours about the research you have done. Look forward to and relish this opportunity. You are yourself an expert now. It won't be long before people will have to start calling you Doctor.

Appendix 10.1. An authentic example of an examiner's pre-viva report (see note)

---

3 Examiner's pre-viva report

This is a well-structured thesis investigating the determinants of inward service FDI in **XXXX**. Overall, it demonstrates an adequate level of originality and significance, particularly in terms of its service sector focus and primary data collection and analysis. However, the writing leaves much to be desired. It needs polishing and proofreading and there are a few other issues that still require consideration. Subject to a very good viva, I would be inclined to recommend a 'Pass, with minor amendments' but 'major amendments' remains a possibility. At the *viva* I wish to probe on the candidate's wider understanding of the subject and aspects of the thesis that need further clarification, elaboration or amendment as indicated by the non-exhaustive list of concerns below:

- Chapter X lacks a clear graphical representation and an adequate discussion of the trend in inward FDI across sectors and over time. A graph and related discussion must be added to clearly cover the issue of the evolution of inward FDI in services in **XXXX** *vis-à-vis* industry and agriculture.
- Still in Chapter X, it would also be useful (possibly delving into the data on inward service FDI in **XXXX** to be added as per the point above) to elaborate further on what the candidate means by 'services' – because there is a need to highlight the distinction between consumer and producer services (the latter referring to firms providing services to other firms as intermediate inputs), a distinction that is largely ignored in this work.
- In Chapter X (literature review), the discussion of the exchange rate as an FDI determinant (sub-section **X.X.X** on pp. **XX-XX**) is pedestrian and insufficiently up to date.
- The literature review also neglects the role of intellectual property rights as a determinant of FDI, an important omission since they too are expected to affect service FDI inflows.
- In Chapter X, on p. **XXX**, it is written: "*HX Market size has a positive and significant impact on Inward Services FDI irrespective of the type of service.*" But later in that same page it is stated: "*The results [...] show that a moderate negative relationship can be found [...] Therefore, hypothesis X is supported.*" Why? Surely **HX** is not supported. **HX** predicts a positive relationship and the result unveils a negative association. This needs to be squared/amended.

3 Examiner's pre-viva report

- Table **X.XX** on p. **XXX** summarises the results. The second column reports the sign of the hypothesised relationship for each variable. In the case of market size, it reports a negative sign. Why? I don't understand that. The larger the market size, the larger expected FDI inflows in services (as well as manufacturing). Hence, the sign should be positive, not negative. And why the last column (outcome) of this table states that this hypothesis is supported? This needs to be squared/amended.
- In the same Table **X.XX**, on p. **XXX**, I am also puzzled by the 'cost reduction' hypothesised sign.
- I spotted several sources cited in the text that are not reported in the final list of references. This needs to be resolved, see, for example, '**AUTHOR, YEAR**', first line of p. **XXX**.
- A thorough final round of proofreading is needed since the thesis contains many typographical and grammatical errors.

Note: To ensure anonymity, any text referring to chapter numbers, page numbers, dates, geographical locations, etc., has been obscured to avoid traceability to its origin.

Appendix 10.2. An example of the menu of PhD award recommendations available to examiners (but please note that this may vary slightly across universities)

Examiners' final recommendation of award
Based on the thesis submitted and following the *viva voce* examination, the examiners' final recommendation is: (choose an item among 4.1 to 4.7):   4.1   The candidate be awarded the degree unconditionally.   4.2   The candidate be awarded the degree, subject to the completion of very minor corrections (one month).   4.3   The candidate be awarded the degree, subject to the completion of minor amendments (three months).   4.4   The candidate be awarded the degree, subject to the completion of major amendments (one year).   4.5   The candidate be required to make substantial amendments to the thesis for re-examination (one year).   4.6   The candidate be invited to resubmit for examination for the award of another research degree, e.g. MPhil (one year).   4.7   The candidate be failed, without the opportunity to revise or resubmit the thesis.

References

Delamont, S., Atkinson, P., and Parry, O. (2004). *Supervising the Doctorate – A Guide to Success*. Berkshire, UK: Open University Press and McGraw-Hill Education.

Dunleavy, P. (2003). *Authoring a PhD – How to Plan, Draft, Write and Finish a Doctoral Thesis or Dissertation*. London, UK: Macmillan International Higher Education.

Eco, U. (2015). *How to Write a Thesis*. London, UK: MIT Press.

Golding, C., Sharmini, S., and Lazarovitch, A. (2014). What examiners do: What thesis students should know. *Assessment & Evaluation in Higher Education*, 39(5), 563–576.

Kiley, M. (2009). 'You don't want a smart Alec': Selecting examiners to assess doctoral dissertations. *Studies in Higher Education*, 34(8), 889–903.

Murray, R. (2009). *How to Survive Your Viva*. 2nd Edition. Berkshire, UK: Open University Press.

Phillips, E. M. and Pugh, D. (1994) *How to Get a PhD*. 2nd Edition. Maidenhead, UK: Open University Press.

Rudestam, K. E. and Newton, R. R. (2001). *Surviving your Dissertation: A Comprehensive Guide to Content and Process*. 2nd Edition. London, UK: Sage.

Rüger, S. (2016). How to write a good PhD thesis and survive the viva. Knowledge Media Institute, The Open University, mimeo (available at: <http://people.kmi.open.ac.uk/stefan/thesis-writing.pdf>).

Rugg, G. and Petre, M. (2004). *The Unwritten Rules of PhD Research*. Maidenhead, UK: Open University Press.

Russell, L. (2008). *Dr Dr, I Feel Like … Doing a PhD*. London, UK: Continuum International Publishing Group.

Tinkler, P. and Jackson, C. (2002). In the dark? Preparing for the PhD viva. *Quality Assurance in Education*, 10(2), 86–97.

Torres, A. M. (2012). *PhD Viva Guide: A springboard for your PhD viva preparation*. NUI Galway. Available online at: <https://www.nuigalway.ie/media/graduatestudies/files/phdvivaguide/phd_viva_guide.pdf>.

GLAUCO DE VITA

11 All you wanted to know about publishing from your PhD but never dared ask!

Preamble

Publishing is an integral part of science and a cornerstone of the research process. This explains why the reputation and prestige of individual academics and universities alike rely on publications. Peer-reviewed journal articles are possibly the most important indicator of how academic knowledge is validated and demonstrated, and research quality assessed, with an individual's publication track record usually used as a key criterion for academic appointment or promotion. Yet, there are few subjects more prone to confusion and anxiety for postgraduate researchers (PGRs) than that of how to get one's research published in peer-reviewed journals. Let me reveal from the outset that getting published in top-notch journals often causes pressure also for senior academics, even professors. We have all had some papers rejected at one time or another and we all carry the scars of sporadic unhappy experiences with the editorial and refereeing process. But, although there is no magic formula on how to publish consistently in highly ranked journals, there is certainly value in sharing views and experiences on 'something that works' when crafting, submitting and revising a research manuscript for publication, especially to help PGRs avoid the common mistakes that even more experienced researchers often make throughout this process. The **aim of this chapter** is to help PGRs and supervisors alike gain valuable knowledge on various aspects related to writing for publication and how to increase the probability of success in getting published.

Whether, with whom and when PGRs should publish from their PhD research

The typical question that frequently comes up from PGRs during seminars I run about publishing is that of whether, with whom and when they should publish from their doctoral research. These are issues some PGRs feel too intimidated to raise directly with their Director of Studies (DoS), often due to the inherently asymmetric power relationship.

Whether to publish from the thesis

Starting with the question of whether PGRs undertaking a doctorate should feel compelled to publish from the doctoral thesis prior to their *viva* (if at all), the answer is that it depends. With the exception of a PhD by published work, publishing from the thesis is not yet part of doctoral degree requirements.[57] It follows that PGRs should prioritise the research and the writing of their thesis. If they are making good, early progress on their research, have adequate support from supervisors and have the time and mental clarity needed to publish journal articles, this can be a secondary focus. How 'secondary' the focus should be, of course, depends on the type of employment the PGR is seeking upon graduation. For example, a sponsored part-time PGR who is keen to resume his or her full-time work in industry may legitimately rule out the decision to add to the pressures by seeking publication in academic outlets of high repute. On the other hand, PGRs who intend to embark on a career in academia should be aware that publishing from their PhD research is increasingly seen as a requirement in the HE sector. Competition for that 'first job' in

---

57 That said, there are early signs that this may change. For example, at the University of the West of England, the PhD regulations have been altered recently to allow arts, humanities and social science doctorates to model the STEM format of a series of published (or submitted, or in preparation) manuscripts to be topped and tailed with an introduction and conclusion, much like a PhD by publication.

a university is becoming fierce, whether as a lecturer or as a research assistant (as amply discussed in the next chapter). Hence, despite the large amount of work required to publish, PGRs able to meet the challenges and who succeed in getting published as they graduate, will position themselves favourably in the academic job market. The more journal articles published from the PhD research, the better.

Those PGRs wishing to work in universities, especially highly ranked Russell Group or Ivy League academic institutions with the highest levels of research productivity, and who have no publications at graduation, may want to consider postdoctoral positions. The postdoc will give them the time and space to work on increasing their publication record after attainment of the PhD as a way to gain additional training and expertise in research and quickly build a strong track record of publications once the onus of completing the thesis is over.

On co-authoring with supervisors

PGRs who stand in good stead to publish while still undertaking their doctorate often also wonder whether they should 'go it alone' or whether there is an expectation to share 'named authorship' of any publications with their supervisors. To answer this question it is important to understand first that during 'model', 'best-practice' supervisory relationships, the generation of ideas is often an iterative process that is heavily informed by, and builds on, the duality of the interactions (discussions) between the PGR and the supervisors. This means that, to different extents, in any completed PhD thesis, the direction of the research, the chosen methods and even the resulting findings and implications, will most likely be very different from 'the final product' that would have been obtained with a different supervisory team. This is thanks to many different steering inputs and supervisory contributions throughout the process. It follows that, although it may not be apparent, in reality, PhD research outcomes can never be completely deemed the product of exclusive and independent single authorship. This is so by virtue of the extensive feedback and advice regularly provided by supervisors to the PGR throughout all the stages of the work, from the refinement of the main research question and objectives through to the Socratic questioning underpinning the choice of method and the resulting analysis of findings. That said, this supervisory input alone cannot suffice in justifying a supervisor's inclusion as a named co-author in a PhD thesis-based paper written exclusively by the PGR. Especially in light of the PGR-supervisor asymmetric power relationship, and the potential for free-riding and intellectual exploitation of the PGR, professional ethics dictates that named co-authorship of articles stemming from doctoral research should only be warranted in cases where such named co-authors have actually contributed directly by investing time and effort in the ensuing paper. It is critical, therefore, that PGRs and supervisors have a clear and open discussion at an early stage of the PhD about any publishing plans and associated joint authorship of articles from the thesis, and about each other's expectations in terms of relative contributions and working arrangements.

Concerns and caveats above aside, joint publication between PGR and supervisor, ought to be seen as a very beneficial strategy. PGRs should proactively seek to work and publish jointly with their supervisors as the PhD work unfolds. Under no circumstances should PGRs still undertaking their doctorate establish separate working relationships to publish from the PhD thesis with parties external to the supervisory relationship unbeknown to, and without the explicit agreement of, their supervisors. Kamler (2008) emphasised that co-authorship with supervisors is a significant pedagogic practice. In commenting on a real account from interview with a female graduate, Kamler (2008, p. 287) eloquently elaborates on the tremendous benefits of writing for publication early in the research and co-authorship with supervisors – seen as an important tactic in preparing for postdoctoral work – as follows:

> In this account, the graduate emphasizes the value of mentoring for establishing a publication record and a professional identity. The process is described as a difficult apprenticeship ('very hard work', 'a hard process') initiated by the supervisor, where the inadequate writing ('pretty crap') needs to be shaped and disciplined ('training ground'). What stands out is the recognition of the importance of learning to speak in discipline-specific ways and a framing of this work as collaborative. There is a marked shift to the plural pronoun *we* to describe the difficult work of getting published

as a joint effort. The candidate knows the prestigious journals of her field and can survive rejection, because she has the support of her more experienced supervisor to guide her through the process. It is we rather than I who deals with the potentially devastating experience of being 'knocked back', as well as strategic decisions about resubmission. Taking joint responsibility appears to minimize the stress of rejection and enhance knowledge about the publication process.

From her analysis of the data, Kamler (2008, p. 292) concludes: "*It was co-authorship that produced international refereed publications – without it, it did not occur.*" It goes without saying that, past that first joint article, should the PGR feel ready and keen to attempt to put into use the skills learned by trying to publish a single-authored article, they should then make that clear to the supervisory team and give it a try, with their supervisors' blessing and support. It is also useful to think of research pieces in short-article journals, such as research letters and notes, Blogs and book reviews as excellent ways of beginning to single-author at the start of an academic career.[58]

It is worth noting at this point that a good PhD thesis can, in principle, allow several papers to be generated. Key findings and results can be split for the purpose of multiple, focused contributions for different journal articles. But these are not the only chapters of the thesis you should be trying to convert into publishable papers. The literature review chapter(s) too could be used to craft a strong critical or systematic, up-to-date review article of the state of the field. But beware, the best review articles do not

---

58 A PGR who kindly offered feedback on an early draft of this chapter, asked for more detail on the actual benefits of writing book reviews, pieces of writing often constrained by a tight word limit and which do not count for REF purposes. With this aim in mind, I appropriate Brian Dillon's (2020) anecdotal wisdom from his book, *Suppose a Sentence*, a spellbinding collection of literary essays. He writes: "*The very first thing I wrote professionally were 300-word book reviews for Time Out magazine in London. I thought then, twenty years ago, and sometimes think fondly now, that I could happily do that job till the end of my days, and never tire of its rigours or wish for a longer word count. The constraint of the task taught me how to write, which I thought to mean, for better and worse, how to maximize style, thought and range of reference in a piece of writing that would end up, on the printed page, about the size of a bus ticket.*" (ibid, p. 93) Brian Dillon won the Irish Book Award for Non-Fiction 2005 and was shortlisted for the Wellcome Trust Book Prize 2009.

just summarise the current thinking on a topic. They offer a conceptual contribution, outline profitable directions for further research and not only help other researchers keep abreast of key developments in a specific debate, they shape the future directions of that debate. Several high-quality journals exist with such scope, for example, *The International Journal of Management Reviews* in the area of organisation and management studies or, in economics, the *Journal of Economic Surveys*.[59]

The extent of supervisors' contribution should be particularly evident in the steering, re-writing, editing and polishing that typically goes into the crafting and revisions of that first joint article stemming from the PhD work. Indeed, to some, it would seem strange, atypical and potentially illegitimate, to exclude supervisors from authorship of the first article deriving from the work of the PhD thesis. Working even more closely with supervisors and attempting to publish from the work-in-progress of the PhD research whilst still undertaking the doctorate, could also be a very effective way to strengthen the collaborative relationship between the PGR and the supervisors. This collaboration would concomitantly ensure that mentoring extends to aspects of publishing so as to meet all the stated requirements of what constitutes an original and significant contribution to knowledge, as to be evidenced by the published article. An additional benefit of publishing while still undertaking the doctorate is to obtain valuable feedback from the peer-review process of the manuscript. Such feedback can then also be used to inform further refinements of the thesis itself.

When to publish from the thesis

With respect to the question of *when* should work on any publication from the research start, this too depends. It depends on the progress of

---

[59] For a couple of examples of papers published with two of my past PGRs (and second supervisors) in these journals, see De Vita, Tekaya and Wang (2011) and Noon, De Vita and Appleyard (2019).

the research, whether the PGR and supervisory team have sufficient time to devote to it without detracting from the writing and supervision of the PhD thesis itself (e.g. the potential need to undertake additional primary data collection if needed), the requirements associated with having to meet other deadlines connected with milestones dictated by the institutional PhD progress framework (e.g. annual progress reviews), and the quality of the work itself, which may affect how laborious and time consuming the conversion of the still raw PhD material to the standard required to publish an article in a good journal is likely to be. Hence, there is no set, pre-established timing for when such publishing endeavour should start. It is a matter of open and honest discussion between the PGR and the DoS to regularly review the feasibility and timing of writing for publication and reach a joint decision while taking all such factors into account.

Motivations for writing academic papers and common barriers

Motivations

As noted above, there are powerful reasons for wanting to get published even before completing a PhD. In this section I discuss several other motivations aside from the obvious expectation of publication for those PGRs intending to embark on an academic career that entails research as well as teaching.

First and foremost, akin to one of the most laudable motivations for doing a PhD, the desire to publish should stem from one's intention to contribute to the body of existing knowledge and/or increase understanding of a subject or phenomenon being studied. After all, just like a PhD thesis, to 'make the cut' for publication in a top journal, the article must make a significant, original contribution to knowledge. Early Career Researchers (ECRs) who have secured work as lecturers, assistant professors or research assistants, may be driven to publish in more and increasingly better-quality academic outlets to increase their probability of promotion. For academic staff who already lecture in universities but do not have a doctorate the pressure to obtain such a qualification may itself lead to the decision to publish around the topic of their expertise to then pursue the option of obtaining a 'PhD by publication'. In many countries, right up to the early 1990s, it was not uncommon to embark on an academic career without a doctoral degree, which is now increasingly seen as a *conditio sine qua non* for academic appointment in universities.[60] Building a track record of strong publications can also be motivated by the desire to increase one's chances of obtaining research funding. Indeed, few would disagree with the view that the probability of securing funding from research councils and/or blue-chip funding bodies, is greatly enhanced by having a strong publication record, especially for a principal investigator. Such a track record attests to the suitability and proven ability of the researcher to carry out a research project from the idea stage through to successful completion.

The various motivations outlined above do not constitute an exhaustive list. In fact, perhaps the most powerful motivation of all relates to the fact that research and writing, just like teaching, is not just a job, but a vocation. We write and publish because it is a great pleasure, because we have a natural affinity with ideas and scholarly enquiry, and because we have something significant to say and contribute. This is a very powerful intrinsic motivation that can help researchers deal with the inevitable challenges and, at times, lows, inherent in the process of trying to publish. Although it can be hard to do research, if you genuinely love it, it won't feel like work. As the precept often attributed to Confucius goes: "*Choose a job you love and you will never have to work a day in your life.*"

---

60   But don't automatically doubt the expertise and disciplinary competence of an academic just because they don't have a doctorate. Several non-PhD holders have been awarded the Nobel Prize over the years, across many academic disciplines.

Barriers

In the pursuit of publication, there are just as many barriers as there are reasons for wanting to publish. A typical barrier to even getting started may be a perception by the PGR (or even ECR) of being insufficiently equipped. If so, the PGR (ECR) should discuss this openly with the supervisors (or research mentor). Perhaps it is just a question of timing, which would call for postponing the task of writing a paper. Alternatively, it might be an issue of having to brush up or getting *au fait* with specific methodological techniques, also to increase self-confidence as one approaches the task of data collection and/or analysis.

Another common barrier prevalent among PGRs is fear of failure, which should never stop an individual from attempting something new or taking on a new challenge. There is nothing nobler than miserably failing at something in life provided we give it our best. As colourfully epitomised by Jack Nicholson's character in the movie 'One flew over the cuckoo's nest' – we can then say, "*I tried, god dammit. At least I did that.*"[61] Failures are an inevitable part of any successful journey, so give yourself permission to fail. Borrowing the words of Samuel Beckett from his (1983) novella 'Worstward Ho', no matter how many times you fail, just "*Try again. Fail again. Fail better.*"

Of course, if one lacks a genuine commitment to do research and publish, then my best and most honest advice is, *don't do it*. Go and find something else to do. Something you can get really excited about. Good research is difficult and costly, requiring considerable time and many sacrifices. It follows that without a genuine passion for, and commitment to the arduous task of doing research, one is unlikely to produce good outcomes or derive any enjoyment from it.

---

61 In the movie, the rebellious Randle Patrick McMurphy (played by Jack Nicholson) who pretends to be insane in order to serve his sentence for gambling in a mental hospital rather than in prison, stands up to the abusive stance of Nurse Ratched, who terrorises the ward. After claiming to be able, and subsequently failing, to lift a heavy control panel in the tub room in an attempt to escape, his response to the derisory looks of the other inmates in the asylum, 'But at least I tried', is a call for the others to chase their dream of freedom.

In this respect, PGRs as well as ECRs should be particularly mindful of another barrier that I term here 'negative motivations', such as the infamous axiom 'publish or perish'. Beware of such negative motivations. They are misleading in my view. Great achievements and the ability to excel at something, whatever that something is, while enjoying it, are hardly ever driven by a sense of obligation or fear of the consequences of non-compliance.[62] There are fuelled by genuine love and passion for the activity itself.

Doing your 'homework' before you start

Like any new activity one undertakes, my first bit of advice is to think ahead and do your homework before embarking on the task itself. The first question you should ask when aiming to publish a research article is 'within which debate is my contribution to be located?' Is it, say, the resource-based view, IT outsourcing, the international expansion process, digital marketing, cybersecurity, foreign direct investment, whistleblowing, sustainability? You should view these debates as social learning networks, 'communities of practice' that need to be understood before you enter them and join the debate (De Vita, 2016). You should try to become very familiar with the content of the debate by asking, 'What has gone before?', 'What are they debating as I arrive?', 'What do they already know and agree on?', 'What do they disagree on? Why?' and, most importantly, 'How can I add to that?' You should become acquainted with your interlocutors in that debate. Ask yourself, 'Who am I conversant with in this community?', 'Who are the respected elders or authorities in this field?', 'Who works with whom?' (You can find out via conferences and by checking Web of Knowledge/Science; Google Scholar; ResearchGate, etc.). You should be able to develop a mental map of your field, top world authors in your chosen debate, from those

---

62 Research has also shown that the 'publish or perish' culture can contribute to stress among faculty members (see, e.g., Miller et al., 2011).

academic pioneers who initiated the debate through to the recent rising stars who are now shaping and advancing it (De Vita, 2016).

It is also of paramount importance to develop an understanding of what are the underlying theories of reference of the debate you wish to enter. Is there an established epistemological paradigm driving the debate (positivism, constructivism, etc.)? In essence, the question is, what are the assumptions about the nature of 'reality', 'truth', 'knowledge' and 'being in the world' that underpin the debate, a question, therefore, about the epistemological and ontological stance you are about to engage with. Much about epistemology and ontology has to do with the academic discipline of provenance of the community populating the debate. Are they historians, economists, psychologists, anthropologists, geographers, lawyers, language teachers? This is important since especially within the broad church of business and management, we all bring from our respective disciplines of provenance a set of cultural (field-specific) assumptions and methodological traditions which, in turn, influence our expectations of what constitutes good research. Critically, one should also ask questions about the history and geography of these ideas. Why would a specific debate develop in a certain geographical area, and at a certain time? How policy driven is the debate? To solve what problem in society? To benefit whom?

Of significance is also what should be a conscious decision of how one intends to introduce and establish oneself in this community. As a *Novice*? As an *Experienced researcher*? As an *Outsider*? This choice is important since it should influence and be reflected in your style of writing. A replication study intended to take someone else's work apart (see, e.g., De Vita and Trachanas, 2016, *Energy Economics*) authored by researchers with decades of publishing experience, will be written greater authority and confidence than, say, a paper led by a junior researcher fresh from obtaining her PhD (see, e.g., Luo, Tanna and De Vita, 2016, *Journal of Financial Stability*), which inevitably requires greater caution, particularly in the treatment of 'what has gone before' in that debate. Finally, it is useful to develop an understanding of where 'the experts' or 'respected elders' are having this debate. Which conferences do they go to, to talk to each other? Which journals do they publish in? Which journals are hosting such debates?

Choosing the right journal, not just a suitable journal

There are thousands of journals worldwide across the economics, finance, accounting, law, and business and management fields. Your target journal could be the journal cited the most in your manuscript or the journal most frequently giving space to that debate. However, also consider the perceived quality as determined by journal rankings (De Vita, 2016). Academic journal ranking lists such as the Academic Journal Guide (AJG) produced by the Chartered Association of Business Schools (ABS), guide to the range and quality of journals in which business and management academics publish their research.[63] Although the quality ranking of journals is a controversial issue (particularly for those who find it harder than others to get published in highly ranked journals), by and large, there is broad agreement on the leading, most prestigious (3 and 4 star-rated) journals across journal quality ranking lists. More importantly, whether we like it or not, such lists are widely used by individual academics and universities alike to form a *prima facie* view of the quality of track records of publications when looking, for example, at CVs for academic appointment or promotion purposes.

Having established that the ranking of a journal is important, in choosing a target journal one should also consider the relevance of the manuscript to that specific target journal. You should read the 'aims and scope' and recent issues of the journal identified to get a feel for what the

63 The AJG, more commonly known as 'the ABS list', is based upon peer review, editorial and expert judgements, and citation rates. The list ranks journals according to four main ratings. All journals rated '4' (or the 4* distinction category), are judged to be top journals in their field, publishing the most original and best-executed research. '3' rated journals are described as publishing original and well executed research articles, and they are also highly regarded. They are very selective in what they publish, and papers are heavily refereed. Journals in the '2' category publish original research of an acceptable standard. Papers are fully refereed, but these journals' citation impact factors are often somewhat lower than the more prestigious ones. '1' rated journals are regarded as publishing research of a more modest standard and as undertaking a considerably less stringent review process. Few journals in this category carry a citation impact factor.

journal is about and what type of contributions would be welcome. You should also ensure that there is alignment between the quality level of the paper and that of the journal you target. There is no point in sending a manuscript that the authors themselves deem to be of 'average quality' to a top-notch journal just to see what happens or in the hope of getting some feedback. In fact, such a strategy is likely to backfire since, over time, after numerous consecutive desk rejections, it might stain your reputation with those journals. Similarly, you would ultimately be left short-changed in sending your very best manuscript to a low-ranked journal. Even if published, it would be a wasted effort.

One should also consider the trustworthiness of the journal. Unfortunately, not all publishers follow the standards required to produce quality publications or follow ethical, best practice.[64] On these matters, PGRs should be guided by the experience of their co-authoring supervisors. They should also seek to obtain as much feedback as possible on the manuscript from respected researchers within their reach before deciding, in agreement with their supervisors, which journal to submit the manuscript to. Other considerations when deciding where to submit an article include:

- The likely *duration of the review process*, since in very good journals the review process can, over several rounds, take well over a year. I once had a paper 'under review' for eighteen months, which after further revisions finally came out in print after three years from initial submission.
- The *size of readership* and *geographical reach* of the journal. The journal's website usually indicates if it is intended for a regional, national or international readership and the target region, country or area. You may be able to gauge these features also by looking at the size and composition of the editorial board and their affiliations, information that is usually readily available.

---

64 There is a useful resource. 'Think. Check. Submit.' (see <https://thinkchecksubmit.org/>) that helps researchers identify trusted journals and publishers. This international, cross-sector initiative aims to promote integrity and build trust in credible research and publications.

- The *opportunity to make your publication available Open Access*, the benefits of which include raising the visibility, use and impact of your research and enabling a wider audience to have access to it.
- *Other tactical reasons*, such as journals associated with professional bodies. Publishing there can make you part of these communities and increase the probability of funding.

However, the considerations above should not be at the expense of the perceived quality of the journal. Again, look at the journal quality lists (SJR; ABS 2015, Harzing's 2016 'list of lists', or their future updated versions), especially if used in your field and institution. A 'quick and dirty' metric to gauge the quality of a journal is its impact factor, based on the number of citations that articles published in that journal receive. The higher a journal's impact factor, the more frequently articles in that journal are cited by other articles. The impact factor can, therefore, give a rough indication of how prestigious a journal is in its field.

Once you have selected the journal, research it as an anthropologist would. After all, if you think about it, a 'debate' can be viewed as a 'territory' (an academic territory) and the scholars populating that debate as a 'tribe', with its own cultural norms, assumptions and ways of doing things.[65] Ask yourself, 'How do they do things here?' (e.g. quantitative *versus* qualitative), 'Do these papers follow a standard structure?', 'What norms and conventions do the authors follow?', 'How do they talk to each other?', 'What style and register do they use?' You should speed read the last few issues of the target journal and read carefully articles that may relate to your topic, debate, data and methodology – cite such articles if deemed appropriate and make sure that there are no notable citing omissions (De Vita, 2016). I would also encourage you to identify potential reviewers from authors cited in the manuscript, especially if published in your target journal since nowadays many editors build their pool of reviewers from authors who previously published in their journal.

---

65   A classic book entitled 'Academic Tribes and Territories', published in 2001 by Becher and Trowler, illuminates the distinctive cultures of disciplines. A book I would encourage every researcher to read irrespective of their disciplinary field.

Writing the paper

By no means does this section intend to cover all aspects related to how to write a paper. Ten books on the subject would not be enough. First, because like a work of art, every paper is different, unique. Second, because even within the business and management discipline, the variants across different academic related fields (accounting, economics, business law, marketing, tourism management, critical management studies, organisational behaviour, etc.) as to what is expected of a good article, are simply too many to contemplate. More modestly, the aim of this section is to provide suggestions on some aspects of paper writing and highlight critical areas that require special attention, areas that even experienced researchers often neglect.[66]

The title

The first such area, is the *title* of the manuscript. Indeed, it is surprising how, despite having spent several months writing a paper, many academic authors spend so little time thinking about or revisiting the title. Even the few 'how to' PhD guides that do cover the topic of publishing articles from the PhD material, appear to say next to nothing on the subject. Gosling and Noordam (2006, p. 92) write, *"A good title is an art in itself. Give your article a strong title for maximum impact."*, but do not offer any further details on either the *"art"* of title writing or how to achieve such

---

66   The suggestions relate to paper writing in general, since aside from the obvious differences between writing for the thesis and writing for a journal article, aiming to write a journal article from a PhD thesis poses no additional challenges. The differences include structuring the article into sections rather than chapters, having to deal with much tighter word limits *vis-à-vis* the lengthiness allowed of a thesis, adhering to varying formatting requirements depending on the journal one is submitting the manuscript to, and adopting a narrower focus by presenting only the selected key findings rather than all the findings produced as part of the PhD study.

"*maximum impact*", which I take to mean getting the editor and readers' attention. So, let me elaborate.

To get the editor and readers' attention, the title should not only reflect the actual content of the study but also indicate that the article will tell them something useful. Phrasing the title as a question can be helpful in this respect, this also applies to the title of your thesis, but for journal articles it is certainly worth thinking more creatively about how to phrase a title in a way that could appeal to the reviewers and readers' sense of wonder by being intriguing, fascinating or even provocative. These are the titles that stick in people's minds and capture attention.

Let me explain by example. I must have read hundreds of articles published over the years in *The Economist*, the international weekly magazine that focuses on international affairs. Yet, if I were asked to name papers I remember to have read in *The Economist* in my lifetime, the first that comes to mind is because of its title. 'Room without a view' it was called,[67] ironically paraphrasing the famous 1908 book by Edward M. Forster. The article was about the boom in 2012 of the cheap 'no frills accommodation' in London's hotel market, akin to the 'capsule hotels' pioneered in Japan in the 1980s. A great title I thought at the time, which captured my imagination and got me interested in reading the article in the first place.

I too, from time to time, indulge, for better or worse, in seeking titles that, by drawing on famous movie titles – renowned to be formulated to simultaneously attract attention and concisely nail the essence of the story – could be of wide appeal and get readers interested. Examples include 'Hotel outsourcing under asset specificity: "The good, the bad and the ugly"' (De Vita and Tekaya, 2015) and 'The "Apollo 13" of macroeconomic policy: The "successful failure" of the UK quantitative easing anti-crisis monetary mission' (De Vita and Abbott, 2011).

The latter was a critical evaluation of the unprecedented Bank of England's 2009 mission aimed at rescuing the UK economy from the real prospect of economic depression by an unconventional monetary experiment known as Quantitative Easing (QE). My conclusion was that the QE 'mission' did not meet its aims. Measured strictly against what QE set out

---

67 See <https://www.economist.com/britain/2012/01/14/room-without-a-view>.

to achieve, QE had clearly failed to boost spending and lead to a speedy recovery. However, the absence of a counterfactual meant that I could not exclude that QE was, at least to some extent, effective in affecting these variables. All in all, at the time of writing the article (2011), the economic climate appeared to be more stable than what most scenarios had envisaged at the start of the crisis, when the collapse of the entire financial system and a full-scale economic depression were distinct possibilities.

What I needed was a bold, catchy and snappy title that could capture my dichotomous conclusion, and I could not think of one. Until, that is, I heard the voice-over at the end of the Hollywood blockbuster movie *Apollo 13*. The Apollo 13 was the third mission expected to land on the Moon. Two days after launch on 11 April 1970, an electrical fault caused loss of power. The crew was forced to use the lunar module as a 'lifeboat' for the return trip to Earth. The voice-over noted that the mission was termed '*a successful failure*' because despite the failure of the mission to land on the Moon, the astronauts were brought home (back to Earth) safely. I had found my title! The 'Apollo 13' analogy perfectly captured my conclusions from the analysis of the anti-crisis 'rescue mission' via QE. It provided me with an accurate albeit allegorical depiction of the Bank of England's QE mission as 'a successful failure' in that although 'the monetary mission failed' to accomplish its aims, it could have been deemed to have been 'successful' in, at least, preventing the economy getting worse.

Clarity

Another critical aspect of paper writing is *clarity*. Writing with clarity is a concept that seems yawningly obvious, until you actually try to explain it. We attempted this in Chapter 4, but it is worth extending the discussion here. Part of the challenge is that clarity is a conceptual Swiss Army knife. It's what you need to nail a central idea and avoid getting lost in the weeds of a debate; it's also what enables you to be coherent and intelligible. Obviously, there is no substitute for a good idea but how coherent, logical and well-constructed is the main argument? Good writing is essential. By 'good writing' I don't just mean an error-free manuscript with no typographical and grammatical mistakes or errors of syntax. What I mean is 'beautiful writing', a craft to be appreciated for its ability to communicate thought and to delight.

Beautiful writing

Beauty is not the main goal of academic writing of course, but scholarly work is the perfect canvas for the expression of intellectual beauty. The relation is akin to that of valour to war. No matter in which specific (battle) field your work is located or how technical the contribution is, words matter. You should think of your words (what you say) and style (how you say it) not just as your basic tools but as your most powerful weapons. However, don't forget that beautiful writing should be reader-centred; meant to serve the reader, not the writer. It should make it easy for the reader to understand what's going on, make the reader feel richer and want to read more. Beautiful writing is a bit like music, it has tempo and rhythm. It also shares properties with maths: it is accurate, precise, logical and structured. But it is, fundamentally, an art, aimed at crafting a text capable of *capturing* the reader's interest and imagination and at provoking reflection. Interestingly, etymology tells us that the word 'text' derives from the Latin *textum*: the woven texture of a web. As vividly described by Theodor Adorno in his *Minima Moralia*:

> Properly written texts are like spiders' webs: tight, concentric, transparent, well-spun and firm. They draw into themselves all the creatures of the air. Metaphors flitting hastily through them become their nourishing prey. Subject matter comes winging towards them. (Adorno, 1951, *Minima Moralia - Reflections on a Damaged Life*, p. 87 of 2005 translated edition).

In contrast, when all these attributes are lacking, language can exert its power as a stranglehold, a cage all too apparent in poorly written PhD theses or articles in which the limits of language not only heavily hinder the ability to express thought but also *constrain* thought.[68]

---

68   As Friedrich Nietzsche wrote: *"We cease to think when we refuse to do so under the constraint of language; we barely reach the doubt that sees this limitation as a*

Obviously, it takes time to develop full command of a language and master the art of writing. Some writers seem like they are born with natural writing talent but most of us have to work hard at it. Especially for non-native speakers of English the challenges can be considerable, as I know all too well. Unfortunately, there are no shortcuts or quick fixes available to master the art of writing. As pointedly noted by Umberto Eco (2015, p. 147), one of the most revered Italian scholars of the study of sign processes (semiotics) and the production of meaning, *"If there were exhaustive rules, we would all be great writers"*. Here, therefore, the best advice I can give is to try harder, push and challenge yourself to edit, re-edit and re-edit once again. Ask yourself, 'Why this word and not another?', 'Does this sentence offer a meticulously calibrated arrangement of a few joined words of English?' Don't look for just the right words, find the best ones, with each sentence perfectly weighted. Seek to tease out the best out of the text and make it flow. A good article, like fictional narrative, should draw you in and feel like a descent. You are telling a 'story' after all. As powerfully expressed by Charles David Wendig, the popular American author, comic book writer, screenwriter and blogger, readers should feel that there is a sort of gravity to the narrative that draws them down, down, deeper and down.

The best writers strive to continue learning all they can about honing their craft. Generally, the more one reads, the better at writing one becomes. Hence, try to learn from the best, also outside your field of study, across disciplines and genres, from philosophy through to fiction. Reading widely exposes you to other styles, other voices and other forms of writing. Especially if authored by great writers, such texts will reveal writing that is better than your own and help you improve. But, to gain direction in your own writing, read with an eye on the mechanics of composition, paying special attention to form (description, narration, exposition or argumentation), style (word choice, fluency, and 'voice' or personality), the way the sentences are constructed and connected, and the way in which a logical arrangement of sentences shapes a harmonious paragraph.

---

limitation. // Rational thought is interpretation according to a scheme that we cannot throw off." (Nietzsche, 1886–1887, *The Will to Power*, p. 283 of 1968 translated edition).

In addition to George Orwell, John Steinbeck, Italo Calvino and David Foster Wallace, I usually recommend the works of Peter Singer, the contemporary Australian moral philosopher, for his superb ability to convey complex, profound and often controversial concepts via a simple, direct, yet powerfully cogent prose. I also find Steven Pinker, the Canadian American cognitive psychologist and linguist, a brilliant writer, and his thought-provoking books, startling. Pinker seems to have written about just about everything, how the mind creates language, nature *versus* nurture, the history of violence, the improvement of the human condition over recent history, and even a writing style manual (*The Sense of Style*, 2014) that won Plain English Campaign's International Award for 2014, so take your pick. And, of course, you cannot go wrong with Nobel Prize novelists such as Ernest Hemingway, renowned for his economical and understated style, and Gabriel García Márquez, the master of magical realism in storytelling. Their texts are sublime examples of mesmerising writing and how to capture the reader's interest and imagination. A typical example I offer, is the very first sentence of García Márquez' (1981) book *Chronicle of a Death Foretold*, a real page-turner of a novel, which goes, "*On the day they were going to kill him, Santiago Nazar got up at five-thirty in the morning to wait for the boat the bishop was coming on*" (p. 1). After reading this first sentence, one cannot but feel compelled to want to continue to read to find out more.

Main purpose

Of equal importance is the need to convey the main *purpose* of the paper, which should be made unambiguously clear from the outset. How clearly specified is it? What is the motivation for this paper? Why is it important to fill this gap? (and don't try to fill in a much-needed gap). Indeed, while originality is important for the thesis as well as publishing from it, as suggested by Dunleavy (2015, p. 244), "*Research students are often perplexed to find that meeting the requirements for originality in the doctorate does not in itself guarantee the publishability of their material*". This can be due to a lack of clarity as to the main purpose, the *importance* of filling a specific gap in the literature, or an inadequately cogent discussion of the *significance* of the overall *contribution* the study makes, critical attributes for 'publishability' that often override in importance the criterion of originality. You should clearly state the specific hypotheses or questions that are to be addressed by the study. Highlight its *rationale, relevance, significance* and *topicality*. As already amply discussed in Chapter 4, you should state clearly what the paper contributes to the debate. How does it add to what has gone before? Most importantly, spell out the *theoretical contribution*.

Theoretical contribution

But what constitutes a legitimate theoretical contribution? Let's be honest, as noted in Chapter 4, we seldom generate a new theory from scratch. Instead, in most cases, all we can aim at, is to improve existing theories. So, what constitutes enough of a theoretical improvement to qualify as a sufficiently significant contribution to warrant publication in a top journal? This is the million-dollar question about publishing in top journals. David A. Whetten precisely tackled this question in an article published in the *Academy of Management Review* (Whetten, 1989). Although the article was written over three decades ago, I believe it still commands benchmarking significance. Hence, in what follows, I draw heavily from it to concisely summarise the salient features at play.

Whetten (1989) starts by clarifying that there are three core elements of a theory: the '*What*' and '*How*' describe *What* factors affect other factors and *How* they do so (the mechanism or theoretical channel). The '*Why*' explains the underlying logic or reason for the relationship or phenomenon examined. As Whetten (1989, p. 491) states: "*Together, these three elements provide the key ingredients of a simple theory: description* and *explanation.*" Although, in principle, it is possible to make a theoretical contribution by simply adding or subtracting factors (the '*Whats*') from an existing model, or by identifying new channels (the '*Hows*'), Whetten warns that these extensions rarely satisfy reviewers of top journals as to the *significance* of the contribution. Whetten further argues that the most fruitful albeit most difficult avenue of theory development entails adding to the

Why: the explanation of the phenomenon, the underlying logic. Adding to the *Why* commonly involves borrowing a perspective from other fields, which alters our ways of seeing in ways that challenge the underlying rationales or assumptions supporting accepted theories. On this account, it should be noted that pointing out limitations in current conceptions of a theory's range of application – which Whetten (1989) terms the *Who, When, Where* conditions – does not in itself constitute a theoretical contribution, unless applying a theory in new settings leads to a *"feedback loop"* through which we learn something new about the theory itself as a result of working with it under different conditions. That is, new applications of an existing theory should not merely reaffirm the applicability of the theory, but improve it (Whetten, 1989).

Let me give you one concrete example from my own research of how we can fruitfully borrow from other theoretical perspectives in other fields to make a significant theoretical contribution in our debate. The example relates to a co-authored paper of mine (still under review), entitled 'Is the Fisher effect asymmetric? Cointegration analysis and expectations measurement' (see Cushman, De Vita and Trachanas, 2021). For those of you who are not familiar with economics, let me clarify that the relationship known as the Fisher effect (Fisher, 1930), that a change in expected inflation will change the interest rate in the same direction by the same amount, has been a cornerstone of monetary and macroeconomic theories and has caused much debate and controversy for over ninety years.

In this paper, we investigated whether the interest rate response to inflation could be asymmetric. The asymmetry postulated is that the long-run change in the interest rate is larger when inflation rises than when it falls. So, this is the 'new *description*' of the theory. But why? Where is our new '*explanation*'? As we write in the paper:

> The possibility follows from behavioural and economic psychology hypotheses that *we borrow* to construct an asymmetric model about the relation between inflation expectations and actual inflation. (emphasis in italics added)

So, as suggested earlier, we borrow from other fields – namely, behavioural and economic psychology – to add to the '*Why*'. We alter a theory borrowing from other theories to develop a model of an asymmetric relationship between the interest rate and inflation. Using quarterly U.S. post-war data (from 1953q1 to 2019q1), in the paper we also test whether such asymmetry has existed in the Fisher effect using a recently developed asymmetric cointegration procedure. This means that in the paper we also test the asymmetric model we develop, and we summarise our *contribution* as follows:

> As in many past papers, the interest rate response to inflation is found to be less than one-to-one, but our novel finding is that it is asymmetric: the interest rate response to inflation rate increases is about 15% larger than to decreases. The asymmetry result has implications not only for the Fisher effect, but also for uncovered interest [rate] parity.

Rigour, significance and final caveats

In writing the paper, of considerable importance is to include a 'Data and Methodology' section that adds rigour. Even for 'action research', at least a methodological note is in order. Rigour was discussed at length in Chapter 4, but it is worth adding that any good paper should include at least a rationale for choices and selections made with respect to methodological techniques, setting and context, data sample, cases, organisations, etc. For example, why does the paper focus on a specific industry, group of firms or countries? Why a sample size of 3, 33 or 333? Why was that sample period selected? Why was that start date and end date chosen? The answers to these questions cannot be left to the imagination of your readers. You should also spell out the *significance* of the findings as well as the implications and recommendations (for policymakers, businesses, etc.) flowing from them. Final caveats, in the form of an explicit acknowledgement of limitations and profitable avenues for future research, are also useful when ending the paper.

Once the article is completed, one should ask oneself the proverbial 'how long is a piece of string' question, that is, the question of whether the article has reached the quality level worthy of journal consideration. Experienced co-authors should be able to advise you on this but you should still aim to get comments from other academics in your circle and present at relevant conferences to get feedback to improve the paper as much as you can before submission.

Submission and review process

Good journals have a very low acceptance rate, some as low as 2%. They employ two, sometimes three or even four (anonymous) expert reviewers. It follows that the probability that even a good quality paper receives favourable reviews from all of the reviewers is inevitably low (most journals use a *double-blind review* system, where the identities of both authors and reviewers are hidden). Yet, favourable reviews should not be seen as a matter of luck (though the quality of reviewers and reviewers' reports can seem like a lottery sometimes), but of painstaking work coupled with dogged determination to constantly improve the standard of the work one can produce.

Once you and your co-authors are confident about the quality of the paper, ensure you undertake yet another solid round of final proofreading and polishing. Yes, polishing, to give the paper the shine it deserves. Of course, 'all that glisters is not gold',[69] but there is nothing worse for a reviewer than receiving a manuscript poorly written, with typographical errors and/or writing inconsistencies still present throughout. What does it say about the paper and the authors? It suggests that the paper is untidy and the authors careless. Read the 'guidelines for contributors' published on the journal's website and comply fully with the journal's house style in terms of format, word or page limit, referencing style, formulae and equations, tables, figures, footnotes or endnotes, etc. 'Sell' the paper in the cover letter. Not just *here it is*. Sell the rationale, relevance, topicality and spell

---

69   A reader of a draft of this chapter queried the form of this figure of speech. Here I adopt a sixteenth-century version of the popular expression that employs the term 'glisters' rather than 'glitters', as used in Shakespeare's play *The Merchant of Venice*. The aphorism is generally used to convey the point that not everything that is shiny and *prima facie* attractive is valuable.

out the reason for choosing that journal *vis-à-vis* others (De Vita, 2016). And if you are contributing to a debate that has already been hosted in the pages of that journal, tell the editor so.

After months of waiting, when the manuscript comes back ... three, six or nine months later, read the reviews carefully. The outcome may be:

- *'Accept'*. Very, very rare *at first submission*. And, if so, don't be jubilant, this is no triumph. It only indicates that the journal you submitted to is a very poor one, one which does not undertake rigorous peer-review. In fact, it may even be a scam journal that conveniently neglects to mention 'author publication charges' until late in the process.[70] If you are eager to hear the phrase "*Practically perfect in every way*", watch *Mary Poppins*, don't submit articles to serious academic journals.
- *'Accept with revisions'*. 'Minor' changes required? This is rare. Moreover, amendments should never be regarded as 'minor' anyway. These revisions should be taken very seriously because the journal could still reject the paper at a later stage of the review process. Indeed, I heard many tales from colleagues over the years whereby the reviewers selected by the journal in the second or third round differed from those who had provided comments in the first review round, with altogether different objections about the manuscript, which can be most annoying.
- *'Revise and resubmit'*. Treat these revisions as major even if not explicitly described as such. The journal is interested in your manuscript but there are no guarantees. You must put all your efforts to address the issues raised by the editor and in the reviewers' reports.
- *'Reject and resubmit'*. You are still allowed to resubmit. Evidently a considerable re-think and re-write is expected, along with a substantial reworking of core elements of the study. But don't give up because

---

70   These are ethical breaches and predatory practices by scam journals that regularly engage in phishing by sending cold emails to academics, and which accept almost all submissions. They are not to be confused with the legitimate 'submission fees' (£50-£150) charged by some highly rated, reputable journals (e.g. *Journal of Money, Credit and Banking*) to help to fund editorial and peer review administration costs, or the 'post-acceptance fees' charged by almost all subscription-based journals should the authors have opted for colour printing and/or open access publishing (e.g. via OnlineOpen).

they may still be interested in considering a significantly revised and improved version of the paper.
- *'Outright desk reject'*. You need to rework the paper and consider an alternative target outlet. Note, also, that a desk rejection does not necessarily mean that the manuscript is of low quality, they may be just suggesting that it is not of interest to, or suitable for that journal.

How to deal with the outcomes of submissions and reviewers' reports

If the manuscript is rejected, don't let it crush you. I know, it's difficult not to take a rejection to heart, but don't lose sight of the fact that they are rejecting a version of the manuscript you have written, not *you*. One gets rejections from top journals more often than not. I still remember a lecture from a tutor of mine at the University of Cambridge in celebration of his Nobel Prize award, where he shared anecdotally – and with a modicum of sarcasm – that he too had experienced journal rejections for some of his work. Who are we to expect any different? Getting articles rejected from time to time is inevitable. It is part of 'the game' we are in. Despite the disappointment, you should find the strength to regroup and rework the paper by considering the reviewers' comments and doing the extra work needed before you send the manuscript to another journal. If the outcome is minor or major revisions, don't procrastinate. Do the revisions. Attend to them promptly. Don't rush them, of course. Revise carefully. But don't wait until you have time, *make time*.

Deal with each point raised. Take note of all the changes made to the manuscript and where they are located in the revised version of the manuscript. This process will aid the development of the 'Response Letter', which should spell out how and where you have dealt with every point raised by reviewers. The crucial aspect of undertaking revisions is to appreciate that especially harsh or even unfair criticism can often profitably be used to rework and improve the paper by arguing your case and by providing counter-arguments in the paper itself, not just in the Response Letter (De Vita, 2016).

Let me give you an example from my own research, with reference to a co-authored paper of mine, De Vita and Kyaw (2017). The manuscript postulated and tested a new relationship, between tourism specialisation, absorptive capacity and economic growth. One point raised by one of the three anonymous Reviewers, read as follows:

> Reviewer 1.6: The study only considers tourism specialization as a nonlinear variable, by including its squared version. However, this is a restricted assumption, and leaves open the question whether other independent variables could also be nonlinear. The author(s) should consider a model, which also includes the squared versions of the other independent variables.

Upon reading this comment, my co-author and I were in shock. We both deemed the objection unhelpful, unjustified and unreasonable. Why would we wish to re-estimate a myriad of regressions while also including the squared value of all the variables in our model? There was no theoretical justification for doing so. In principle, we were inclined to accommodate reviewers' requests for changes as much as possible. However, we were not prepared to do something meaningless purely for the sake of pleasing the Reviewer and 'sell our soul to the devil' so to speak. As we explained in the Response Letter:

> R1.6 Response: The key objective of our study is the estimation of the inflection point at which the growth-enhancing effect of tourism specialization begins to experience diminishing returns. There is, therefore, a clear theoretical rationale for including the squared specialization term in our regression to measure the posited diminishing returns. Estimation of a fully nonlinear model is beyond the scope of this paper and lacks theoretical justification, at least as far the purpose of this study is concerned.

The response above is cogent and theoretically justified. But it does not suffice. First, because it merely shows to the Reviewer that he or she was blatantly wrong. While this may well have been the case, the perverse satisfaction to explicitly show how wrong or silly a Reviewer's point is, should have no place in the attempt to extract value from the feedback, irrespective of how misplaced you consider that feedback to be. Second, because, in itself, our response above does not translate into any improvement in the paper. It is, solely, a response to the Reviewer. These are the reasons why we did not merely leave our response at that. We went a step further, adding the following text to our response (and the paper):

> Nevertheless, as suggested by Reviewer 1, postulating, modelling and estimating a fully nonlinear model could provide a profitable direction for future research and we now explicitly acknowledge this suggestion in our final paragraph of the paper, on p. 26, as follows:

> '*Second, although we introduced nonlinearities in our regression through the inclusion of the squared tourism specialization term in order to test whether its growth-boosting effect is susceptible to diminishing returns, future studies may consider the possibility of nonlinear dependencies of the other independent variables and/ or the non-linear causal properties in the relationships characterizing the growth model in question.*'

The above additions highlight how, even in cases where requests for amendments are mistargeted, one should always try to find a way to respond accordingly, avoid antagonising the reviewer and, most importantly, use the reviewers' prompts to further enhance the paper itself.

But, of course, there are limits that should not be crossed by Reviewers since veracity and integrity impose clear moral and ethical limits to what can be legitimately claimed when anonymously assessing a paper on behalf of a journal. If there is a proven lack of conformity to truth and fact in a Reviewer's report, with totally unfounded comments denoting a lack of proper reading of what is in the paper already, these must be exposed and resolutely contested.[71] For example, for a different paper I co-authored, Reviewer 1, point 4, read as follows:

---

71   In fact, in principle, where such misgivings occur, they should be picked up by (and pointed out to) the journal's Associate Editor, whose primary role is the management of the peer review process. The responsibility of the Associate Editor extends to helping authors navigate multiple and sometimes conflicting reports by reviewers. It should not be forgotten that manuscripts are accepted for publication on the basis of merit and appropriateness, based primarily on the Associate Editor's decision.

Reviewer 1.4: Many regression equations were estimated without full justification or proper explanation.

On this point, our lengthy reply in the Response Letter was uncompromising, see below, and we still had the paper accepted by that journal in the end[72] (see De Vita, Li and Luo, 2021).

> R1.4 Response: With respect, we must point out that this is a totally unfounded and unfair comment. For example, on p. 15, we clearly motivate and explain why we report the number of 'after matching' observations as additional diagnostics estimated for each algorithm, as follows: 'King and Nielsen (2016) recommend that when using PSM, the researcher should closely follow the advice in the literature and provide full information and diagnostics to readers so that they can understand what was done. They also argue that PSM is more efficient in cases where relatively large sample sizes are available after matching so as to both avoid going past the point of complete randomization and evidence that the difference after matching between PSM and a completely randomized experiment is small and inconsequential. We follow their advice by also reporting as a diagnostic measure in Table 1 to 5 the number of observations (or units) "after matching", for each algorithm.'
>
> We also convincingly justify and clearly explain our robustness regressions reported in Table 8 that use pooled OLS and cross-section OLS based on data averages of the outcome variable and covariates, also citing relevant literature to validate our choice, on p. 18, as follows: 'Finally, to determine the sensitivity of our results to the methodology employed (PSM), we also re-estimate the model using pooled Ordinary Least Square (OLS) (columns 1 and 2 of Table 8), a regression method commonly employed in empirical studies linking legal origin to financial, economic or social outcomes (see, e.g., D'Amico & Williamson, 2017; Rambaccussing & Power, 2018), and cross-section OLS (columns 3 and 4 of Table 8). At the cost of losing many country-year observations for the covariates, the latter cross-section OLS empirical exercise may be justified by the fact that our treatment variable (legal origin) is constant over time, hence we take averages (over the full sample period) of the outcome variable and covariates and use a cross-section of countries rather than a panel, as done, for example, by Beck et al. (2003).'

---

72   The narrative here is not a subtle attempt to brag about our success in dealing with the reviewer's criticism - though, I must confess, for days afterwards I shared that story as a tale of triumph - but rather to convey the message that standing one's ground, when justified to do so, does not necessarily lead to a rejection.

> Given the examples above, we are genuinely at a loss as to how the Reviewer could suggest that our regression equations were estimated without full justification or proper explanation. This is clearly not the case and we kindly ask the Reviewer to reconsider.

Despite the latest example reported above, no matter how disheartening or even soul-destroying peer reviews can be, by and large, they tend to be fair and constructive. Peer reviewers – just as well as Editors and Associate Editors – aren't out to get you. They are colleagues, experts, giving their own time – most often for no remuneration – to read your work and offer feedback. Most importantly, despite concerns about shortcomings of the review process relating to bias and inconsistency, ineffective filtering of error or fraud and the suppression of innovation due to echo-chamber effects, the peer-review process genuinely helps to make published papers much better than the versions originally submitted.

After all, formal peer review has been part of the academic/scientific publishing process for hundreds of years,[73] for good reasons. Reasons that go well beyond the unavoidable necessity to select – out of a myriad of submissions aiming to appear in the limited (and costly) number of pages of the most prominent journals – the best articles. These reasons include the lack of better alternatives to scrutinise the accuracy and validity of the work, its ethical appropriateness and the reliability of research submitted for publication.

Publication strategy: Some general pointers

The intention of publishing as many articles as possible in stellar, reputation-enhancing journals, is a laudably ambitious aim. However, it

[73] ELSEVIER's website notes: "*The Philosophical Transactions of the Royal Society is thought to be the first journal to formalize the peer review process under the editorship of Henry Oldenburg (1618–1677).*" (see <https://www.elsevier.com/reviewers/what-is-peer-review>).

is not a strategy as such since it does not entail a plan designed to achieve the overall aim. At the other extreme, being 'unfussy' about academic outlets, merely opportunistic or purely reactive to publishing opportunities as they present themselves in terms of what, with whom or where to publish, is not ideal to cater for a well-planned career progression. What is needed is a reasoned, well-thought-out publication strategy. One that can help maximise academic impact, choose and prioritise among available alternatives for publication and aid the long-term development of an optimal portfolio of research outputs.

A carefully planned publication strategy can also help prevent potential conflicts in the direction of scholarly research, by guiding alignment between individual research interests with both institutional research strategies and external funding drivers. For ECRs, a well-considered publication strategy is particularly important to ensure that early publishing endeavours actually benefit a young scholar's career.

One of the most important considerations in terms of publication strategy is that of the competing tensions between specialisation *versus* diversification. Whilst specialising on a single debate by writing papers exclusively in a narrow area can bring fast recognition (if successful) and allow relatively junior researchers to quickly make a name for themselves in the field, it is a highly risky, 'all eggs in one basket' strategy. Diversifying the research portfolio, at least to some extent, working on two or three debates for possible publication, is, therefore, a sensible approach for ECRs. You should pursue those topics until you produce a couple of very good publications. If you have a strong hit in one debate, then redouble your effort to establish your name in that debate before you move on to another. Without clear evidence of success over, say, three to four years, consider moving on to a different debate in your field.

And, of course, work on your research and publications also with an eye to achieving and demonstrating broader impact, with effects beyond academia, be it societal, attitudinal, cultural, environmental, economic or related to policy influence and change. Pathways to impact include public engagement, stakeholder co-creation and targeted strategies for knowledge exchange and dissemination.

Other general pointers worth considering are:

- Don't put two or more good ideas from your PhD thesis in one paper. An issue of focus, plus what will you work on next? Better to separate them into two or more papers.
- Aim to produce a couple of high-quality papers per year whilst ensuring you secure at least four or five top publications every five years, a time span that aligns to the REF cycle here in the UK.
- Having three papers in different journals is better than having three papers in the same one, if the relative quality of the journals is perceived to be the same.
- Be careful with having *most* of your papers with more than four co-authors (a matter of degree, not kind). In our field, it raises issues (or even suspicions) of relative contribution and attribution. Of course, this does not mean that you shouldn't aim to publish collaboratively.
- Working with others, including in cross-disciplinary research collaborations and, where possible, as part of international teams, is important. Multi-authored articles based on international research collaborations, especially if transdisciplinary in nature, have also been shown to result in higher citations rates.
- When you are ready, consider also a 'single authorship'. It signals that you can do it all, from the conception of the idea through to publication, single-handedly.
- Focus on quality rather than quantity. A couple of very high-quality publications in stellar journals in the first three or four years of an academic career are worth immensely more than dozens of average quality articles published in low-ranked journals of little or no repute.
- Beware of displaying negative patterns or trends in your publication track record. Reaching high peaks shortly after completion of the PhD, aided by supervisors as co-authors, to then drop to an abysmally low-quality level or with several 'dry spells' over the following years, does not look good.

Some final words of encouragement

Getting published, especially while still undertaking a doctorate, takes great tenacity, determination, huge focus, skill and a thick skin. Those who obsessively work on honing their craft and sharpening their competencies, collaborate with supervisors, present at conferences and persevere by not taking 'no' for an answer, however, will most likely succeed.

References

Adorno, T. (2005). *Minima Moralia – Reflections on a Damaged Life* (originally published as *Minima Moralia* by Suhrkamp Verlag, 1951). Translated from the German by E. F. N. Jephcott. London, UK: Verso.

Becher, T. and Trowler, P. R. (2001). *Academic Tribes and Territories*. Buckingham, UK: Society for Research in Higher Education and Open University Press.

Cushman D. O., De Vita, G., and Trachanas, E. (2021). Is the Fisher effect asymmetric? Cointegration analysis and expectations measurement. [currently under review]

De Vita, G. (2016). Coventry University Research Blog: 'Five Top Tips on Getting Your Research Article Published'. Available at: <http://blogs.coventry.ac.uk/researchblog/five-top-tips-on-getting-your-research-article-published/>

De Vita, G. and Abbott, A. (2011). The 'Apollo 13' of macroeconomic policy: The 'successful failure' of the UK quantitative easing anti-crisis monetary mission. *Public Money and Management*, 31(6), 387–394.

De Vita, G. and Kyaw, K. S. (2017). Tourism specialisation, absorptive capacity and economic growth. *Journal of Travel Research*, 56(4), 423–435.

De Vita, G., Li, C., and Luo, Y. (2021). Legal origin and financial development: A propensity score matching approach. *International Journal of Finance and Economics*. In press, doi: 10.1002/ijfe.2167

De Vita, G. and Tekaya, A. (2015). Hotel outsourcing under asset specificity: 'The good, the bad and the ugly'. *Tourism Management*, 47, 97–106.

De Vita, G., Tekaya, A., and Wang, C. (2011). The many faces of asset specificity: A critical review of key theoretical perspectives. *International Journal of Management Reviews*, 13(4), 329–348.

De Vita, G. and Trachanas, E. (2016). 'Nonlinear causality between crude oil price and exchange rate: A comparative study of China and India' – A failed replication (negative Type 1 and Type 2). *Energy Economics*, 56, 150–160.

Dillon, B. (2020). *Suppose a Sentence*. London, UK: Fitzcarraldo Editions.

Dunleavy, P. (2015). *Authoring a PhD: How to Plan, Draft, Write and Finish a Doctoral Thesis or Dissertation*. London, UK: Macmillan International Higher Education, Red Globe Press.

Eco, U. (2015). *How to Write a Thesis*. London, UK: MIT Press.
Fisher, I. (1930). *The Theory of Interest, as Determined by Impatience to Spend Income and Opportunity to Invest It*. New York: Macmillan.
García Márquez, G. (1981) *Crónica de una Muerte Anunciada*. Bogotá: Oveja Negra. The translation quoted is from 'Chronicle of a death foretold' (1982) by Gregory Rabassa. New York: Ballantine.
Gosling, P. and Noordam, B. (2006). *Mastering Your PhD. Survival and Success in the Doctoral Years and Beyond*. Berlin, Germany: Springer-Verlag Berlin Heidelberg.
Kamler, B. (2008). Rethinking doctoral publication practices: Writing from and beyond the thesis. *Studies in Higher Education*, 33(3), 283–294.
Luo, Y., Tanna, S., and De Vita, G. (2016). Financial openness, risk and bank efficiency: Cross-country evidence. *Journal of Financial Stability*, 24, 132–148.
Miller, A. N., Taylor, S. G., and Bedeian, A. G. (2011). Publish or perish: Academic life as management faculty live it. *Career Development International*, 16(5), 422–445.
Nietzsche, F. (1886–1887). *The Will to Power*. 1968 Edition Translated by Kaufmann, W. and Hollingdale, R. J. New York: Vintage Books. Available at: <https://archive.org/details/FriedrichNietzscheTheWillToPower/page/n1/mode/2up>
Noon, P., De Vita, G., and Appleyard, L. (2019). What do we know about the impact of intellectual property rights on the foreign direct investment location (country) choice? A review and research agenda. *Journal of Economic Surveys*, 33(2), 655–688.
Pinker, S. (2014). *The Sense of Style: The Thinking Person's Guide to Writing in the 21st Century*. New York: Penguin.
Whetten, D. A. (1989). What constitutes a theoretical contribution? *Academy of Management Review*, 14(4), 490–495.

GLAUCO DE VITA

12 Preparing for life after the PhD and career options

Preamble

As noted in the opening chapter of this book, many PhD guides tend to neglect information relating to life after graduation and career options post doctorate. The few texts that provide some coverage of these issues, being written for a wider audience of PGRs across all disciplines, are too general in scope, thus lacking the specificity required to offer targeted advice. The **aim of this chapter** is to fill this gap, with a focus on doctoral graduates within business management related fields and the social sciences. The chapter places emphasis on how PGRs can best prepare for life after graduation as their doctoral studies unfold rather than after the *viva voce*. Additionally, it discusses employment opportunities available to PhD graduates not only within but also outside academia, and how PGRs could think more creatively about their future working life and career paths given the changing nature of labour markets and constantly evolving career prospects. Useful online resources, global recruitment boards and networking platforms, are also considered at strategic points throughout the chapter along with the practicalities of applying for jobs.

Preparation for life after graduation should start *during* your doctoral journey

Few comparable texts deal with issues related to life after graduation, career options within and outside academia, and the practicalities of applying for jobs. In some that do, the subject is confined to a brief postscript (e.g. Russell, 2008). The gap is acute especially with respect to the coverage of challenges and opportunities for UK PGRs from business and management and the social sciences. This is a serious omission given the importance of 'employability' as one of the measures of the worth of a PhD qualification. After all, a doctorate doesn't just attest to a scholarly achievement, it also confers a sort of expert's licence to practice. Yet, many PGRs are often simply too embarrassed to ask questions pertaining to their job search despite the importance of those questions for their futures. Significantly, most of the few texts that do deal with such themes tend to advise PGRs to start applying for jobs as soon as they get their *viva* date or even after the celebrations post *viva*. My advice is different. In a nutshell, there is no point in waiting until the thesis submission or the completion of the *viva* before considering career options and how to go about applying for jobs.

Of course, for some PGRs the very decision to embark on a PhD may have been driven from the outset by the desire to go into a different career, in academia or elsewhere, or to enhance their professional development as part of their existing career (possibly returning to their existing employer in higher level positions once they have completed their doctorate). Especially doctoral candidates who completed their PhD part-time while holding a job, may have already planned for their career to evolve along a pre-determined path rather than take a significant shift in trajectory. If so, the 'what next?' question has already been contemplated at an early stage. But this group's experience and process of career choice constitutes an exception. For far too many PGRs, consideration of career options and what to do with their lives after the PhD comes too late in the process (Rugg and Petre, 2004).

Although planning your future career may be the last thing on your mind during the testing times of your doctoral journey, giving at least some thought to what to do after the PhD, especially in terms of the question of whether you wish to target a job within or outside academia, is important. Early consideration affords the soon-to-be job seeker the opportunity to alleviate the arduous task of securing the right employment rather than just any employment when the time comes. This strategy doesn't just have the advantage of allowing you to spread the burden of the many micro-tasks involved in applying for jobs over a longer period of time. For example, by scanning the relevant job market sooner rather than later and learning more about the sector of interest in advance. It also affords you the opportunity to develop demonstrable evidence of relevant experience and competencies that can be put on your Curriculum Vitae (CV) before realising too late what it is you may still be lacking. The latter approach is critical to give yourself the best chance of competing for the job you dream of.

Although some job-seeker's tasks such as keeping your CV up-to-date apply irrespective of the sector of employment you wish to enter after graduation, in offering advice on how best to prepare for life after the PhD during the course of your doctorate, it seems opportune in the coverage that follows to distinguish between a career in academia and one outside the Higher Education (HE) sector. After that, I will discuss how PGRs may think more creatively about their future working life and how to shape their career path.

Preparing for a career in academia

Competition for jobs in academia is becoming increasingly fierce. Although the UK HE sector has expanded considerably over the past three decades, doctoral graduates have grown disproportionately over the same period. At the same time, full-time permanent academic roles have suffered a decline, also due to the latest rounds of job cuts and redundancies arising from many UK universities' response to the fall in international student enrolments stemming from Brexit and the Covid-19 crisis. This means that unless you develop your academic profile and CV in order to meet HE institutions' own professional needs as the PhD unfolds, you may find that even a doctoral qualification, by itself, no longer suffices in granting an interview for a permanent job as a lecturer or assistant professor in universities in the UK (especially the good ones) or abroad. Unfortunately, there are still many PGRs who fail to plan and prepare for a career in academia early enough. They seek a job in the HE sector after the *viva* only to discover that to be appointable for that first academic post they eagerly long for, they need at least some teaching experience and a good 'REFable' publication.

As already emphasised in the previous chapter, PGRs who intend to embark on a career in academia should be aware that publishing from their thesis is increasingly seen as a requirement by universities wishing to recruit fresh PhD graduates as lecturers or assistant professors. The more journal articles you have and the more prestigious the journals in which such articles are published, the better. Kamler (2008) notes that co-authorship with supervisors early in the doctoral journey is a significant pedagogic practice that can evidence the robustness and know-how of emergent scholars and enhance their publication output. Kamler (2008) describes this mentoring for establishing a publication record and a professional identity as part of a wider process of 'apprenticeship'. PGRs should try to capitalise on this opportunity early in the process.

Those 'fresh' PhD graduates who, for whatever reason, want to work in universities but have yet to publish, could consider applying for post-doctoral positions via 'postdoc fellowship' schemes that are regularly advertised as part of the recruitment strategy of HEIs. This would grant them the time and space to work on increasing their publication record. Such schemes, which used to be considered as the traditional first stage of the postdoctoral pathway to a tenure track academic career, offer the opportunity to start this journey whilst undertaking a period of guided research.

Usually such fellowships provide a training period or further research mentoring during which successful candidates can develop skills, knowledge and experience while participating fully in the research environment of the faculty or department. Specific roles often entail being involved in funded research projects led by more senior academics, to then move on to lead their own independent research in industry or academia at the end of their tenure. Obviously, appointment to such postdoctoral positions (usually open to applicants who have already submitted their thesis or have recently completed their PhD) is also highly competitive in nature. These schemes are designed for first-class postdoctoral researchers who have demonstrable evidence of having consistently delivered high-quality research usually proxied by prizes attained during their doctorate, a 'no

Preparing for life after the PhD and career options

corrections' *viva* outcome or having been awarded a PhD ahead of the expected completion date, and/or are able to evidence a robust research proposal as an independent researcher. PGRs who are still enrolled in the doctoral programme or have just completed their PhD can also try to contact the career advisor of their own university for assistance with their postdoctoral application, especially if it is the university advertising such postdoc positions.

In terms of specific postdoctoral fellowship schemes worth highlighting, British citizens and any nationals from the European Economic Area, regardless of where their doctorate was obtained, or anyone of any nationality who has a doctorate from a UK university, is eligible to apply for the annual British Academy Postdoctoral Fellowships.[74] This is a three-year award made available to an annual cohort of outstanding early career researchers (ECRs) in the humanities and social sciences. The scheme provides funding to cover the costs of a 36-month fellowship at a host institution of your choice. In line with the general nature of these schemes as described above, the purpose of this specific award is to enable the award holder to pursue an independent research project, towards the completion of a significant piece of publishable research.

Postdoctoral fellowships are also regularly advertised by the Economic and Social Research Council (ESRC). Such fellowships, aimed at those in the immediate postdoctoral stage of their career,[75] are administered by the ESRC Doctoral Training Partnerships (DTPs) to provide the opportunity to consolidate PGRs' PhD through developing publications, their networks and their research and professional skills. Other postdoc opportunities can be searched on specialised websites such as 'FindAPostDoc',[76] 'jobs.ac.uk'[77] or, if you are considering moving within Europe for a research post, the European Commission 'Euraxess' recruitment tool.[78] The latter

---

74 See <https://www.thebritishacademy.ac.uk/funding/postdoctoral-fellowships/>.
75 See <https://esrc.ukri.org/funding/funding-opportunities/postdoctoral-fellowships/>.
76 See <https://www.findapostdoc.com/>.
77 See <https://www.jobs.ac.uk/>.
78 See <https://euraxess.ec.europa.eu/>.

promotes and supports researchers moving within Europe and allows you to post your CV for recruiters to see, free of charge.

Kamler's apprenticeship model discussed earlier in relation to establishing a publication record and a professional identity, should also be extended to encompass teaching experience. This is because appointment in UK HEIs would, in most cases, require the new academic to undertake a non-trivial amount of teaching and supervision, if appointed. Some lecturing and/or tutoring experience in HE, therefore, even if gained only in the capacity of teaching assistant and, better still, evidence of teaching/ tutoring quality (demonstrated by positive student feedback), could go a long way in offering reassurances to the university applied for that the candidate has already developed at least some understanding of students' learning needs, strategies to solicit interest and participation in large as well as smaller classes and, ideally, aspects related to assessment. Experience of marking and feedback is particularly useful, especially if gained by using the now increasingly common learning management platforms used in universities such as Blackboard, Moodle and Aula. In most UK universities, PGRs also have the opportunity to undertake various teaching and learning modules, some of which carry credits leading to a Certificate in Teaching in HE (commonly known as CEertHEd) or Postgraduate Certificate in Teaching in Higher Education (PGCTHE).

Such courses can be very useful for PGRs to improve their professional practice and evidence knowledge and competencies complementing any hands-on classroom experience. For example, at Coventry University PGRs can, as part of the taught modules available to them to gain the annual development credits required during their PhD, undertake the 20-credit module 'Introduction to Teaching and Learning in HE'. This is a professionally accredited 'AdvanceHE' module aimed at those new to teaching and supporting learners within HE, on completion of which successful participants can register for Associate Fellowship with the Higher Education Academy (HEA). The latter recognition is another feather in one's cap when applying for an academic position in UK universities. However, in some UK universities, such courses are selective thereby only serving a subset of the doctoral researchers wishing to become academics. For PGRs who proactively seek to make use of and end up benefiting from such a wide array of development opportunities to complement their doctoral research pathway and teaching experience, the doctoral journey can truly provide a sound, authentic apprenticeship for preparing them for an academic career.

As boldly stated by Harland (2010, p. 298): "*The concept of the apprentice-academic has a clear logic for the contemporary university lecturer.*" Yet, the development of PGRs also as teachers is still insufficiently prioritised by universities. *De facto*, a large part of the responsibility to develop the all-round employability of doctoral students is too often still left to their own initiative and the goodwill of keen supervisors who are prepared to offer advice and general guidance beyond the PhD thesis itself. I have regular conversations with many PhD supervisors at my institution about the importance of also discussing with their PGRs the theme of career options. Whilst some are easily persuaded, others agree to do so reluctantly going by their nonverbal cues. And even those keen supervisors who recognise the importance of developing the future generation of academics and are happy to extend their mentoring to matters other than the writing of the thesis – often lack information on aspects of employment and career options, especially information pertaining to jobs outside academia.

Clearly, it is HEIs themselves that should embed all-round career advice processes as part of the wider framework of PGR development. Whilst much progress has been made by UK universities in this respect over the last ten years, UK HEIs should take full responsibility and deploy further resources to develop the employability of their doctoral students at 360 degrees. This is needed especially in light of the fact that current employment prospects are different when compared to those faced by previous generations of PhD graduates, with an increasing proportion of PhD holders now finding employment in non-academic roles. This greater emphasis on what I term here '360-degree employability development', therefore, would make the experience of doctoral study more relevant for those wishing to work within HE as well as those intending to work outside the walls of academia.

Let's now turn to the scanning of the academic job market and some of the practicalities of applying for positions in UK universities or abroad. Most, if not all, universities and research institutes around the world list the vacancies they have at any one time on their website. Evidently, this search is particularly encouraged when a likely applicant wishes to target a specific university, perhaps because of its geographic location or because of prior knowledge of a relevant job opening being advertised by that specific institution. Such a targeted search offers the benefit of obtaining all the details made available about the position being advertised, including the online link to complete the job application. The pages of the 'Times Higher Education' (THE) – the weekly magazine reporting specifically on news and issues related to HE (formerly known as 'The Times Higher Education Supplement' or THES) – also hosts adverts for academic jobs. Now there is also an associated website, 'THEunijobs',[79] that offers quick online access to a rich global job board for both jobseekers and HE employers. Launched in January 1998 by the University of Warwick, 'jobs.ac.uk' is another incredibly useful website that has grown to become the top recruitment site in the HE sector, advertising and helping with the recruitment of academics within the UK, Europe and across the world. For those PGRs with a specific interest in exploring job offers in the US academic market, The Chronicle of Higher Education[80] is another useful website to check out and, like 'jobs.ac.uk', it allows you to sign up for weekly alerts.

With respect to the practicalities of job hunting, your CV and choice of referees, are of paramount importance. A great CV does not by itself guarantee a job interview but if you get it wrong, it will certainly mean you won't be shortlisted. Obviously, every CV (and cover letter) is different as you want to highlight why you want *that job*, with *that employer* (university) and why *your set of skills makes you suitable for the position* you are applying for. However, there is an expected structure of how a CV should look, so here are a few tips.

The first part of your CV, at the top of the first page, should contain your name and contact details. Do not title your CV 'Curriculum Vitae', a waste of valuable space. Use your name as the title instead. When it comes to contact details, your postal and email addresses and telephone/mobile number(s) are essential, of course. But here you can also add links to your Google Scholar,[81] ResearchGate,[82] and Academia.edu

---

79   See <https://www.timeshighereducation.com/unijobs/>.
80   See <https://jobs.chronicle.com/>.
81   See <https://scholar.google.com/>.
82   See <https://www.researchgate.net/>.

accounts[83] and/or LinkedIn[84] profile, but only if they add value and are up to date. Number the pages and try to stay within a reasonable length, no more than four pages for those new to academia (and better if shorter if you are applying outside the HE sector). Brevity is important because recruitment panels charged with shortlisting responsibilities often have to sift through 30+ applications/CVs for an academic position, so they simply don't have the time to read anything too lengthy. Your CV, therefore, needs to be short and sharp to get your message across quickly. Focus on experience and achievements that show how you meet the essential and desirable criteria of the job specification and filter out irrelevant details, including hobbies and interests not pertinent to the position you are applying for. Don't forget to proofread your CV carefully and use a professional font, reasonably sized (e.g. Calibri or Arial, minimum 11 point), with consistent formatting throughout, avoiding narrow margins and densely populated lines. These aesthetic details may be seen merely as the icing on the cake of your CV, but sometimes that thin layer of frosting makes all the difference.

More substantively, you should think of your CV as a sort of marketing document to sell yourself to the prospective employer. It should tell them about you, your educational qualifications, your professional history, skills and achievements (each listed in reverse chronological order, using bullet points). But remember, the purpose of a CV and accompanying cover letter is not just to list what you have done in the past and/or for other organisations, is also to highlight why you are the best person for the job and to let the potential employer know *what you will be able to do for them*.

Although there may be other applicants who are more qualified, with more teaching experience and publications, you should never lose sight of the fact that in assessing your experience and achievements, one significant benchmark will be the judgement as to whether they are commensurate with what you could have reasonably done or achieved in the time you had. Academics in recruitment panels know all too well that an applicant who has just completed a PhD cannot be expected to have already accumulated years of teaching experience and a dozen publications. So, don't think you

---

83   See <https://www.academia.edu/>.
84   See <https://uk.linkedin.com/>.

are fighting a losing battle from the start and don't assume that other likely applicants are necessarily better placed to compete for the lectureship or assistant professor position you are going for just because this is your first academic job application.

You should also choose your referees with care. This is one of the things that applicants often get wrong. References help reassure likely employers as to your suitability for the post to be filled. This is the reason why referees' comments are so important. Whilst it is rare to come across an overtly hostile reference, a 'bad' reference is not that uncommon and usually entails a lack of sufficient detail to offer any reassurances as to the suitability of the candidate. Think about what employers in the HE sector look for in a reference. References need to validate information the candidate has put on their CV and provide a detailed appraisal of both the merit of the applicant's profile and their suitability to undertake the work to a high standard. It is essential, therefore, that references offer detail and context. Less helpful are character references that just give a general support statement. They don't tell recruiters much. Academic references need to comment on you as well as your scholarly achievements. It follows that your nominated referees need to know you, and your work, to be able to comment on your track record and to make a reasoned judgement as to whether you have the requisite skills and experience to fulfil the essential and desirable attributes listed in the job description/specification.

Think tactically about who to name as your referees. It would look strange not to include your Director of Studies (DoS) or a member of your supervisory team as your main academic referee for an application to work in academia. The more authoritative your referees are, the better. A reference from a well-known academic in your chosen field would certainly carry more weight than one from someone whose research interests are less closely connected to your own or the post applied for. During the process of nominating referees, some important 'must-dos' and 'no-nos' include:

- Asking your desired referees for their permission before nominating them; annoyingly, many applicants don't.
- Choosing referees who you are confident will have the time to do a proper job since a rushed or very short reference is rarely a strong one.
- Trying to avoid nominating all your referees exclusively from overseas.

- Checking that your referees will be available during the time they are likely to be contacted for a reference (some UK universities require references in advance of the interview while others after it, before the formal offer is made to the candidate selected).
- Ensuring that your chosen referees know what is required of them.
- Sending your chosen referees your CV, cover letter, application that you submitted and job specification/description of the post applied for, so as to give them enough detail about you, the context and how you meet the relevant criteria for appointment.

If you are shortlisted for interview, you are likely to be nervous. Tell yourself not to be. As advised in relation to facing the *viva*, try to stay calm and relaxed. Interviews for university positions are not a dark ritual to be fearful of. They are fairly predictable and you can prepare for them, especially for posts at lower levels of the academic hierarchy (lectureship, assistant professorship or the like). Talking to your supervisors and/or other senior scholars in your personal network about the interview process is a good starting point. They are likely to have been part of interview panels in the past and their knowledge will help you to form reasonable expectations and anticipate potentially tricky questions.

Also, do as much research as you can beforehand. About the university, the school or department, and even the interview panel members if they are known to you in advance. What is their mission? What are their values and strategic objectives? What do they want to be known for? Are they teaching- or research-driven? Who do they see as their main rival institution(s)? What kind of students does that university have? Who works in that school or department and what do they work on? What do you bring to them and how do you fit into, or complement, their existing teaching and research specialisms? Then, draw on this knowledge of the institution to tune in your pitch and to answer questions at interview, particularly if they ask the proverbial 'Why do you want to come here?'. Showing you have done your homework about them will give interviewers the right impression, that you really care about this position at their university, and that it is not just one more in a string of interviews for you.

The interview process will probably entail two parts. The first part will most likely involve giving a twenty-minute or so (Power Point) presentation on your academic achievements and past, present and future research. Alternatively, you may be asked to do a mini lecture of a similar duration simulating delivery to a specified student group. This is a very important part of the selection process. Hence, make sure you give your best possible presentation. Do dummy runs beforehand and, on the day, stick rigidly to time since overruns are likely to carry a penalty.

The second part of the process is the interview. The interview panel typically comprises of a panel Chair, likely to be the most senior panel member (a Dean, Pro-Vice Chancellor or the like), your would-be Head of Department or Head of School, and at least one subject expert. In some cases, an academic external to the faculty and/or a representative of the Human Resources department are also in attendance. Panel members will usually operate in turn, based on an agreed sequence, and ask the same predetermined questions as they ask other candidates. They will also probe further on your CV and statements made in your online application or cover letter, with a specific interest in establishing how well you meet the essential and desirable criteria for the position. The higher they score you against these criteria, the higher the likelihood you'll be offered the position. So, ensure you don't fail to expand on them.

Crucially, it is *how* you come across that makes the difference. Don't put on airs! You need to strike an effective balance in displaying confidence while maintaining humility (this is just as important at interviews for jobs outside academia). After all, they will also be looking for someone who would be a pleasure to work with. Competent, diligent, reliable and, most importantly, sufficiently flexible in terms of courses to teach as well as research plans, which need to align to their thematic priority areas. They'll be mostly concerned about whether you would 'fit' into their culture, personally and professionally, how well you would be perceived by students and colleagues, and how willing you are to:

- do *more* than your fair share of teaching and administration.
- develop new courses/programmes.
- collaborate on research projects.
- initiate and lead grant applications.
- contribute to their next REF submission through 3 and 4 star-rated publications.

- engage with external networks and other public stakeholders that can bring kudos to the university, provide additional sources of income and help enhance the impact of your work outside academia.
- be a 'good citizen' in terms of service to the university, such as tutoring and offering pastoral care, mentoring/supervising, representing your peers, organising events, contributing to student recruitment open days, serving on committees, taking on co-ordination and/or leadership roles, and publicising/marketing your activities.

The list above offers invaluable prompts. However, just like the actual content to put in the thesis, it is *your* task to think constructively about what you could say at interview to show awareness, impress and demonstrate you are ready for a job in academia.

Preparing for a career outside academia

As emphasised by Hancock (2019) and Young et al.'s (2020) recent contributions to the doctoral education 'employability debate' that was originally initiated by Craswell (2007), the traditional postdoctoral academic pathway is no longer the norm. Twenty-first-century PGRs are challenged by a constantly evolving employment landscape and their current prospects are different when compared to those of previous generations of PhDs (issues I will expand on in the next section of this chapter). This leaves many doctoral graduates even more uncertain as to how to prepare for their future. Moreover, it is not always obvious to them how the specific skillsets they have developed throughout the PhD can directly translate to career skills outside the walls of academia.

Obviously, no qualification (or HE institution) can guarantee a job, let alone a great one, at the end of your studies. However, obtaining a PhD guarantees that you will have more choices open to you than you had before you embarked on the doctoral journey. As discussed in Chapter 1, rest assured that the value of a PhD in terms of transferable skills, disciplinary knowledge, professional acumen, single-minded determination and intellectual ability, is recognised far beyond academia. Academia and business may seem worlds apart, but you may be surprised at how transportable your skills are from one to the other.

Many of the tips and homespun philosophy offered in the previous section about putting together a good CV and presenting yourself at interview apply also for job hunting in non-academic sectors. However, some important caveats are worth highlighting.

The biggest problem is that few doctoral graduates are career savvy and many frequently undersell themselves to non-academic employers. Within academia, the value of the doctorate is generally well understood. However, outside academia you may come across a wide variety of perceptions. You should try, therefore, to get an understanding of how the organisation you are targeting may view a doctorate. There may still be some recruiters who hold the erroneous impression that a PhD merely confers theoretical knowledge. Others still, may feel a little intimidated or even 'threatened' by such highly qualified candidates who may be expected to display an annoying air of superiority. Irrespective of the validity of these perceptions, where present, you must be prepared to unpretentiously pre-empt such misconceptions.

Crucially, you must also spell out the myriad of skills you possess in a way that speaks to them. If you don't know where to start, one way of getting a feel for the skills you must have already mastered as part of your PhD is to have a look at Vitae's 'Researcher Development Framework'.[85] The framework explicates attributes of researchers in a way that may help you better articulate your skills to potential employers, in a way they understand. This process should entail presenting yourself as a fellow professional and translating the experience and skills you acquired in academia by using the occupation-specific competency terminology they are familiar with. For example, if you have taken part in organising conferences during your time as a PGR, you could rightfully claim to have developed 'event planning skills'. This is what 'skills translation' is about. The point here is that the market needs highly skilled, competent PhD graduates and your task

---

85 See <https://www.vitae.ac.uk/researchers-professional-development/about-the-vitae-researcher-development-framework>.

is to convince employers that you possess the knowledge and skills they are looking for.

As noted in the previous section, several recruitment websites exist that specialise on academic jobs. For non-academic jobs, it is first worth thinking about which type of job and which sector you want to consider. In this process, it is critical to remember not to underestimate the many skills developed while undertaking a PhD that are transferable to a range of different jobs across industries. The good news is that business and management as well as social sciences doctoral graduates are in demand in many industries. For example, the central (national) government, particularly in its policy making function, is obviously always in need of highly qualified civil servants with proven research skills. Although salaries are generally below those offered by the private sector, working with government offers several perks such as generous annual leave allowances and better (public sector) pension schemes. Research Councils are another obvious employment domain to explore in seeking relevant job openings. They employ thousands of people and offer many positions whose job requirements align with the attributes and skills of doctoral graduates passing through the doors of business schools and social sciences departments.

In Chapter 5 we discussed the value of *networking* also as a means to develop the assertive communication skills that you need to seek 'helpful conversations' with relevant others in professional circles. Indeed, in addition to academic conferences and professional bodies, private or public sector organisations you had the opportunity to interact with during your PhD, should also be seen as 'relevant others' who may be able to offer additional help, including further networking opportunities that could be of value in your job search.

Whatever the source of your job-leads, you should not make the mistake of considering the boundaries of your disciplinary expertise as the demarcation line of industries to be regarded as being beyond your target range or reach. Regardless of the topic of your PhD, whether it is in, say, digital marketing, economic geography or human resources, your research skills constitute valuable assets, irrespective of the industry. Hence, jobs related to industrial research, think tanks and policy institutes or management consultancy,[86] constitute other potentially appealing prospects for life after graduation. The same applies to working in industries such as pharmaceuticals or engineering (or emerging industries such as automation & robotics or cybersecurity), which do not employ solely chemists or engineers, and can offer lucrative careers with many opportunities for progression. Furthermore, managerial roles, whether as business development or product manager, are available across all industries. Likewise, analyst positions, as a market research or intelligence analyst, tend to require the very data collection and analysis skills that doctoral graduates possess. Hence, irrespective of the sector, they can offer ideal work environments to apply and sharpen your competencies.

Although the above mentioned occupations are just some examples and by no means provide an exhaustive list of job prospects, it is worth adding that there are other alternative 'ethical' careers that may be laudably pursued by PhD graduates keen on making a more direct, positive difference in the world. With over 180,000 registered charities in the UK alone,[87] creating thousands of job opportunities in specialised areas of research, the Charity or Not-For-Profit sector is also a tempting prospect, particularly for those looking for a distinctive way of 'doing good' through their work. The nascent field of 'Meta-charities', which don't seek to help people directly but promote and evaluate the work of other donors and Charities,[88] and 'Cause Prioritisation Research', aimed at assessing and prioritising within and across charitable areas and worthy causes (e.g. migration, global warming, global health, education), are also growing fast.

---

[86] Top consulting firms that recruit many people every year include not only the big four, EY, PwC, Deloitte and KPMG, but also McKinsey, BCG, Bain and many others.

[87] The largest and more popular Charities in the UK include, Macmillan Cancer Support, British Heart Foundation, Samaritans, WWF, Marie Curie, National Trust, The Fairtrade Foundation, UNICEF and Oxfam.

[88] Examples of Meta-charities include 80,000 Hours (<https://80000hours.org/>), Giving What We Can (<https://www.givingwhatwecan.org/>), GiveWell (<https://www.givewell.org/>) and The Life You Can Save (<https://www.thelifeyoucansave.org/>).

Preparing for life after the PhD and career options

They offer great opportunities to put PhD graduates' knowledge and skills into use to make the world a better place.[89]

If you are still wondering what a career outside academia could look like, it would be a good idea to find out more by browsing the myriad of post-PhD interviews, profiles and autobiographies available on specialised, reputable websites. For example, 'Vitae'[90] has a whole section devoted to careers outside academia and you can browse dozens of profiles of PhD holders working in industry, the third sector or who set up their own business and are now fully fledged entrepreneurs. Another useful website is 'PhD Career Guide'.[91] This online resource endeavours to bring to light the many career options available to PhDs as well as useful tips to decide which career path would be most rewarding given your professional interests and career goals. Recognising that expanding your professional network can offer an additional source of information, advice and inspiration for the transition from academia to industry, 'PhDs at Work'[92] provides another useful online space. It offers yet another opportunity for making new connections and gaining knowledge from many doctoral graduates who have already managed this transition and who now work across all sectors and industries. The 'Think Ahead Blog'[93] developed by the interdisciplinary Researcher Development team at the University of Sheffield, is also a useful online tool to read the 100+ profiles and posts written by researchers who have secured careers outside of academia. Just go to the 'Categories' menu and use the 'careers beyond academia' hashtag, #sheffvista, to access the full list of personal profiles and read about the many career paths open to

---

89 I am not suggesting that a highly lucrative job in say, banking or finance, is, in any way or necessarily, an unethical career choice. As observed by Peter Singer in his compelling exploration of effective altruism in *The Most Good You Can Do* (London: Yale University Press, 2015), "*For those with the abilities required for successfully earning to give, including the ability to find the work sufficiently interestingly to do it well and the character to maintain a strong commitment to giving much of what one earns to effective charities, earning to give can be an ethical career choice.*" (p. 55)

90 See <https://www.vitae.ac.uk/>.

91 See <https://phdcareerguide.com/>.

92 See <https://phdsatwork.com/>.

93 See <https://thinkaheadsheffield.wordpress.com/>.

PhDs. As part of their 'Flagship Skills Project', the British Academy too has published case studies aimed at providing further evidence for the diversity of career pathways taken by doctoral graduates. Their focus is on PhD graduates in the arts, humanities and social sciences, with specific reference to those who pursue careers outside academia or roles which traverse the normal distinctions between academia and other sectors.[94]

Staying in touch with your own university by being part of the Alumni association can also provide another networking opportunity with, and source of relevant information from, past students and PGRs who are now active in the world of work. Of course, finding the 'perfect job' straight away might be a challenge, especially at times when the state of the economy is not good. In such circumstances, although early jobs may not represent the ideal position, they will offer the opportunity to improve prospects over time and the job market value of a PhD will continue to hold when the right opportunity comes along.

Additionally, many UK universities now regularly organise *ad hoc* events for PGRs to connect with the university's 'employer partners', as they refer to them, to hear directly from these organisations' representatives about what they are looking for and the range of live roles available. At Coventry University, for example, the Talent Team (a specialised university unit for professional careers support, development advice and employer engagement) organises the annual *Talent Connect Careers Fest* that includes employer presentations, advertises graduate opportunities, offers workshops and panels, and discusses hints and tips for job applications.

Earlier in this chapter, I discussed how aspiring academics can improve the visibility of their work by, for example, uploading their profile and list of publications on online academic databases such as Google Scholar, ResearchGate, Academia.edu and IDEAS/RePEc.[95] However, nowadays, jobseekers should also be mindful of one's reputation online based on social

---

94 See <https://www.thebritishacademy.ac.uk/programmes/employment-and-skills/career-pathways-postgraduate-research-students/case-studies/>.
95 IDEAS is one of the largest bibliographic databases dedicated to Economics and available freely on the Internet. Based on RePEc data, it indexes over three million research outputs that can be downloaded in full text. Authors can register at no cost and create an online profile (see <https://ideas.repec.org/>).

media activity and posts, which can make the difference between securing an interview and missing out altogether.

Indeed, many organisations now tend to do background checks on applicants before shortlisting by browsing through details available online. You need to be mindful of your reputation online because, as they say, the internet never forgets, meaning that a negative online history or a bad online reputation can be hard to erase. Indeed, many recruiters use social media as one of the ways to gather information about a candidate and, even poor grammar and syntax on the posts you make on social media can turn out to be a major turnoff for them. Thoughtless remarks or unpleasant arguments visible online, especially on controversial or sensitive subjects are, therefore, best avoided. The same applies to compromising photographs or statements (including in your personal website if you have one or blogs) that can come across as offensive, especially those affecting other people's beliefs, religion or sexuality.

The bottom line is that social media should be profitably exploited to help you build your reputation online not ruin it. So, take time to go through your Facebook and Twitter accounts to check if there are any 'less than desirable' entries you might have posted in the past and remove them if necessary. The same applies to Instagram. The 'take-away message' here is to use social media responsibly while trying to take advantage of it. LinkedIn, for example, a platform which is enjoying a growing popularity within the academic community, could cleverly be used to market your skills, enhance the visibility of your work, boost your reputation and expand your network (also for the purpose of collecting data).

Preparing for a longer, boundaryless and protean career

In the previous sections I have discussed how, as a fresh PhD graduate, you can kick start a career and life path that defines you and your values, within or outside academia. However, it must be said, the two paths are not necessarily mutually exclusive. Indeed, the coverage in this chapter has, so far, implicitly worked under the assumption of the traditional model of a three-stage approach to our working lives, namely, education, securing a job for life and retirement. Yet, things are radically changing, with developments that, on one hand, challenge the traditional model of our working lives and, on the other, present us with new opportunities.

Significant changes in today's work environment such as, *inter alia*, technological advancements, flattened hierarchies and decreased job stability due to, for example, global financial crises and pandemics, have undoubtedly decreased individuals' opportunities to pursue a career within one single organisation during their lifetime. In the book *The 100-Year Life – Living and Working in an Age of Longevity*, Gratton and Scott (2016) also alert us of a remarkable transition that will see new generations living and working for much longer than previous ones. As they put it:

> We are in the midst of an extraordinary transition that few of us are prepared for. If we get it right it will be a real gift; to ignore and fail to prepare will be a curse. Just as globalization and technology changed how people lived and worked, so over the coming years increasing longevity will do the same.

Indeed, life expectancies have been rising by up to a quarter of a year per annum since the mid-nineteenth century, and there is no indication that the trend is slowing down. Gratton and Scott (2016) draw on a 2009 scientific study on ageing populations (see Christensen et al., 2009, published in *Lancet*) to show that if the trend doesn't flatten, more than 50% of individuals born in wealthier countries since 2000 may live to be 100!

Social, economic and technological changes increasingly lead to a discontinuous and more fragmented career context in which transitions occur more frequently than ever. Rising longevity, in turn, means that such more frequent transitions will occur over longer and constantly rising timespans of people's life. Doubtless, state pension ages will continue to rise across the world, and new generations will not be able to benefit from final-salary pension schemes that are already on the verge of extinction. It follows that new generations will have to work for much longer (probably into their 70s or even 80s) and in the context of a more unstable and uncertain labour market. Turbulence and transitions are likely to become the norm in the future, with many traditional jobs disappearing and new ones emerging.

Although it is fair to point out that the traditional career is not dead, not yet anyway, such instability and unpredictability will undoubtedly force many individuals to juggle multiple careers and transition between jobs several times during their lifetime. This means that they will need to educate themselves continuously. Not just a question of brushing up on knowledge and upskilling, but about making significant investments at different stages of their life in new learning and re-skilling (Gratton and Scott, 2016). But having to do things differently from previous generations also warrants the opportunity to learn to structure one's working life and shape one's career in new and possibly more exciting and fulfilling ways.

The academic literature has already concerned itself with some of the challenges and opportunities inherent to such shifts within this career perspective. Two concepts appear particularly relevant here given the purpose of this chapter: the *protean career* (Hall, 1976; 2004) and the *boundaryless career* (Arthur, 1994; Arthur and Rousseau, 1996).

Let's start by unpacking the former. Etymologically, the term *protean* comes from the Ancient Greek *Prōteús*, a prophetic sea god in Greek mythology who possessed the power to change into different shapes or forms at will. The adjective 'protean', therefore, denotes versatility, plasticity and adaptability. As such, the notion of the 'protean career' is very much about an individual's value-driven, self-directed personal career management, one that leverages on the ability of being open to change, flexible and adaptive in terms of both performance and learning demands (Briscoe and Hall, 2006).

The 'boundaryless career' concept was originally developed by DeFillippi and Arthur (1994) in response to labour market changes resulting from increasingly more pervious organisational boundaries. The concept was further developed to encompass an individual's ability to navigate "*the changing work landscape by enacting a career characterized by different levels of physical and psychological movement*" (Sullivan and Arthur, 2006, p. 9). The physical mobility dimension reflects individuals' preference to move across different jobs, occupations, organisations, industries and geographies. Individuals' psychological mobility refers specifically to a 'boundaryless mindset' characterised by "*the perception of the capacity to make transitions*" (ibid., p. 21) and a desire to initiate and pursue different working relationships and projects across different organisations.

The above two concepts are not uncontroversial, of course. They have sparked a healthy debate in related literature at both the theoretical and empirical level. But academic debate notwithstanding, the concepts are useful to highlight three important implications for PGRs who are preparing for their future working life and planning their career.

The first implication is that PhD graduates do not simply face a dichotomous, academic *versus* non-academic, career choice (in fact, the two paths can profitably complement each other). Drawing from the concepts explored above, the choice includes employing a deliberately polyhedric approach to shaping their future work life and choosing a multifaceted career path that incorporates both boundaryless and protean orientations.

Second, particularly when having to navigate your way through a challenging job market, *resilience* is likely to be a key resource to draw on as you write new chapters in your life. Resilience does not necessarily mean just continuing in the same way, that is, putting more and more effort into doing the same thing. It can mean occasionally stopping, taking stock and reflecting on where you are heading and your approach; helping you gain or refine a true sense of purpose. This, in turn, may help sharpen the ability to better align your decisions with your own core values and find a broader and more meaningful understanding of your sense of direction.

The final important consideration to be drawn from the above discussion relates to the fact that as the changing nature of labour markets and careers evolve, PhD graduates are likely to be more and better equipped than most individuals to adapt to this changing environment. Indeed, particularly doctoral graduates in business and management related fields, have already acquired much knowledge, expertise and many competencies to effectively deal with the challenges and the lifelong learning and skills demands of the boundaryless and protean careers that are becoming increasingly prevalent in a globalised, technologically advanced, knowledge-based economy. For example, during periods marked by economic downturns, including those stemming from global financial crises or pandemics, there will always be some organisations who are 'winners' (expanding and investing) within thriving sectors and some who are 'losers' (contracting) in sectors most negatively affected by the downturn. As a doctoral graduate you have the advantage of an excellent set of expert research skills to help you identify where the new opportunities will be.

PhD graduates have a proven willingness, agility and flexibility to mobilise in the pursuit of learning, learning how to learn and improving the self, to overcome obstacles and achieve ambitious goals. To return to our introductory chapter on the nature of doctoral research and becoming a PGR, these skills attest to the demonstrable capacity to be continuous, self-directed learners and expert innovators, well versed in dealing with uncertainty.

Some final words of encouragement

Securing the right job, especially if you are not used to looking for one, can be a real challenge. But while no aspect of finding employment is easy and there are many things you cannot control, try to stay positive and find comfort in the thought that most PGRs are successful in starting a career within the first year from completion of their doctorate. Start thinking about career choice early in your PhD and gain a clear and informed understanding of what it is you are looking for. Be proactive in seeking to develop relevant experience, skills and connections during your doctorate and, when the time comes for applying for jobs, fuelled by grit, dogged determination, willpower and the support of those around you, take failure as part of the process and don't let it stop you from keeping up momentum in pursuing your dream job. As the famous saying goes, the future belongs to those who believe in the beauty of their dreams.

References

Arthur, M. B. (1994). The boundaryless career: A new perspective for organizational inquiry. *Journal of Organizational Behavior*, 15(Special Issue), 295–306.
Arthur, M. B. and Rousseau, D. M. (1996). *The Boundaryless Career: A New Employment Principle for a New Organizational Era*. New York: Oxford University Press.

Briscoe, J. P. and Hall, D. T. (2006). The interplay of boundaryless and protean careers: Combinations and implications. *Journal of Vocational Behavior*, 69(1), 4–18.

Briscoe, J. P., Hall, D. T., and DeMuth, R. L. F. (2006). Protean and boundaryless careers: An empirical exploration. *Journal of Vocational Behavior*, 69(1), 30–47.

Christensen, K., Doblhammer, G., Rau, R., and Vaupel, J. W. (2009). Ageing populations: The challenges ahead. *Lancet*, 374(9696), 1106–1208.

Craswell, G. (2007). Deconstructing the skills training debate in doctoral education. *Higher Education Research & Development*, 26(4), 377–391.

DeFillippi, R. J. and Arthur, M. B. (1994). The boundaryless career: A competency-based perspective. *Journal of Organizational Behavior*, 15(4), 307–324.

Gratton, L. and Scott, A. J. (2016). *The 100-Year Life – Living and Working in an Age of Longevity*. London, UK: Bloomsbury Publishing.

Hall, D. T. (1976). *Careers in Organizations*. Glenview IL: Scott Foresman.

Hall, D. T. (2004). The protean career: A quarter-century journey. *Journal of Vocational Behavior*, 65(1), 1–13.

Hancock, S. (2019). A future in the knowledge economy? Analysing the career strategies of doctoral scientists through the principles of game theory. *Higher Education*, 78(1), 33–49.

Harland, T. (2010). Educating the doctoral student: Don't forget the teaching. (Chapter 24, pp. 292–299). In: Walker, M. and Thomson, P. (Eds.). *The Routledge Doctoral Supervisor's Companion: Supporting Effective Research in Education and the Social Sciences*. London, UK: Routledge.

Kamler, B. (2008). Rethinking doctoral publication practices: Writing from and beyond the thesis. *Studies in Higher Education*, 33(3), 283–294.

Rugg, G. and Petre, M. (2004). *The Unwritten Rules of PhD Research*. Maidenhead, UK: Open University Press.

Russell, L. (2008). *Dr Dr, I Feel Like … Doing a PhD*. London, UK: Continuum International Publishing Group.

Singer, P. (2015). *The Most Good You Can Do*. New Haven and London: Yale University Press.

Sullivan, S. and Arthur, M. (2006). The evolution of the boundaryless career concept: Examining physical and psychological mobility. *Journal of Vocational Behavior*, 69(1), 19–29.

Young, S., Kelder, J.-A., and Crawford, J. (2020). Doctoral employability: A systematic literature review and research agenda. *Journal of Applied Learning & Teaching*, 3(Special Issue 1), 97–107.

About the authors

GLAUCO DE VITA BA (Hons), MPhil, PhD, FHEA, is Professor of International Business Economics and Strategic Director of the PhD Programme in the Centre for Business in Society (CBiS) at Coventry University. A Cambridge University alumnus and a former senior analyst for an American multinational, Glauco joined Coventry University in 2015 from Oxford Brookes University Business School where he held a Chair and also worked as Associate Dean for Research and Knowledge Exchange. Glauco has over seventy publications based on leading-edge contributions in various areas of economics, international finance, and business and management. Some journal highlights include: *Economics Letters*; *Journal of International Money and Finance*; *International Journal of Finance and Economics*; *Energy Economics*; *Journal of Financial Stability*; *Urban Studies*; *International Journal of Management Reviews*; *Journal of Business Research*; *Journal of Small Business Management*; *Annals of Tourism Research*; *Tourism Management;* and *Journal of Travel Research*. He has published extensively also in management education (e.g. *Studies in Higher Education*), where he has also earned an international reputation. He has a track record of successful bid writing, including as ESRC principal investigator, and considerable experience of successful supervision of master and doctoral students as well as PhD examining (Bath; Cardiff Metropolitan; Edinburgh Napier; Reading; Warwick; York; University of Cape Town, RSA; etc.). He is a member of various editorial boards and a Fellow of The Higher Education Academy (UK). He also served as a member of the Advisory Panel to the UK Government Department for Business, Innovation and Skills.

JASON BEGLEY BA (Hons), PhD, is Associate Professor at Coventry University, currently located in the Research Centre for Business in Society (CBiS). He has been Academic Director for Postgraduate Researchers within the Centre since 2015, as well as being Faculty Lead in Postgraduate Research, supporting Coventry University's PhD programme since 2016. He has supervised numerous doctoral researchers to successful completion, primarily in the field of economic development. He has also published in the areas of economic history, business history and economic development. His most recent research has been published in the *Cambridge Journal of Economics* examining convergence trends and occupational change in Ireland. In 2019 he co-authored a book focusing on economic development, globalisation and sectoral change in Coventry City, published by Routledge. He is a member of the Irish Quantitative History Group based in Trinity College Dublin, as well as the Cambridge Population Group in the University of Cambridge.

DAVID BOWEN MA (Oxon), MSc, PhD, PGCE, FRGS, is Reader and Head of Doctoral Programmes in the Oxford Brookes Business School, Oxford Brookes University. In that role he has overall responsibility for the recruitment and progression of 80+ PhD students and 30+ students on the professional Doctorate in Coaching and Mentoring (DCM). He has a range of publications with a focus on tourist behaviour and tourism destination management, especially in relation to the environment and politics, and research methodology. Some journal highlights include: *Journal of Travel Research, Annals of Tourism Research; Tourism Management; Tourism Recreation Research; International Journal of Tourism Research; Tourism Geographies;* and *The Service Industries Journal*. David has supervised fifteen students to completion at PhD or DBA level and has examined numerous PhD theses in various systems including UK, Italy and New Zealand.

Index

ABS (Association of Business Schools) 25, 278, 280
Abstract 76, 243–244
academic
    fraud 123–124, 296
    misconduct 124, 248, 260
active listening 213–214
amendments 237, 239, 242–243, 259–262
annexes 106, 184
annual progress reviews (APRs) 53, 128, 191–210, 259, 273
appeals 239, 260
appendices 78, 106, 248
apprenticeship 146, 233, 270, 304, 306–307
approach
    abductive 86, 89
    deductive 77, 86, 87, 89
    inductive 77, 86, 89, 96
attribution 64, 246, 298
audience 183, 192, 194, 208, 212–213, 216–217, 221, 223, 233, 238, 251, 280
awards xi, 3, 21, 23–24, 26, 71, 80, 143, 156, 233, 239, 242, 247, 253, 259, 260–261, 265, 305

Begley, J. ix, xiv, 325
biases 54, 90, 92–93, 98–99, 101, 240, 296
bibliography *see* references
blogs 70–71, 224–229, 231, 271
book reviews 70–71, 271
Bowen, D. ix, xiv, 57, 64, 68, 70, 198, 326
brainstorming 30, 56

calendars 129
Calvino, Italo 286
careers
    academic 5, 142–143, 169, 271, 273–274, 298, 303–313, 322
    boundaryless 319–323
    ethical 316–317
    options 301–323
    outside academia 313–323
    protean 319–323
case studies 88, 97, 152, 183, 253
categorisation of literature 67
citations 25, 34, 35–36, 57, 228, 243, 278, 280, 298
clarity 18, 27, 29, 30, 68, 104–107, 207, 283–286
co-authorship (with supervisors) 270–271, 304
code of practice 169
coding 52, 97–98, 221
comments (from supervisor) 42, 91, 115, 116, 120, 180
conceptual frameworks 28, 33, 38–39, 107, 174–175
conceptualisation 33, 38–39, 89
conclusions (chapter) 68–70, 76, 175, 244–245, 253
confirmability 98
Coventry University ix, xiv, 79, 104, 128, 133, 136, 152, 153, 154, 306, 318
Covid-19 132, 133, 181, 184–187, 200, 218, 227, 231, 255, 303, 320, 322
crises (how to deal with) 159–188
criteria (for award) 10, 239–240

critical thinking 5, 90–93
criticality 71, 90–93
culture shock 131, 160
Curriculum Vitae (CV) 26, 303, 307–309

data
    'big data' 102
    collection 8, 22, 40–41, 58, 77, 88, 96–97, 100–104, 151, 154, 160, 181–187
    management 8, 56, 100–104, 151, 181–184
    management plan 181–184
    research 8, 100–104
databases 34, 55, 57, 101, 103, 318
De Vita, G. 93, 130, 131, 133, 162, 163, 272, 276, 277, 278, 280, 282, 288, 291, 293, 294, 295, 325
deadlines 44, 113, 117, 120, 125–126, 129, 130, 131, 159, 165, 174, 176, 187, 196, 206, 230, 231, 244, 259, 262, 273
defence (oral) *see viva*
Dillon, Brian 271
Director of Studies (DoS) 21, 113–124, 127, 146, 180, 238, 240, 248, 268, 310
disability 22, 142, 166–168, 186
disagreements (with supervisors) 124
discrimination 169–171
distractions 129
double blind (reviews) 290
Dunleavy, P. 21, 29, 80, 202, 241, 245, 286

Eco, Umberto xi–xii, 13, 20, 247, 258, 285
Eisenhower, D. D. (Eisenhower principle) 127
English (use of) 25, 44–45, 162, 215–216, 285–286
epistemology 26, 86–87, 88, 90, 241, 277

ESRC 86, 141, 145, 146, 148, 305
ethical approval *see* ethics
ethics 8, 93, 104, 121, 163, 192, 197, 248, 270
examiners
    aims 105, 107, 238–242
    appointment 238, 239–241
    choice of 240–241
expectations 80, 91, 114–118, 161–162, 243, 261, 270, 277

first-generation researchers 159, 178–179
focus groups 96, 97, 102, 204, 253
footnotes 106, 290

Gantt chart 127–128, 135
gap (knowledge) 18, 30, 36, 52, 53, 67, 68, 69, 81, 82, 87, 95, 140, 174, 175, 251, 286
Giles, D. E. 226

Hemingway, Ernest 286
HESA
    degree recipients 142
    employment (doctoral candidates) 142–143
    job satisfaction 143
Hutchinson, Alex 129

impact 148, 253, 280, 297
impostor syndrome 160, 176–177
induction 152
information literacy 49, 55–58, 64
institutional
    barriers 161–173
    culture x, 161, 163, 197, 276, 312
integrity 94, 123, 183, 279, 294
international candidate 42–45
interviews 182, 184, 186, 201–203, 2014, 221, 252, 303, 308, 311–314, 317, 319

introduction (chapter) 13, 68, 76, 78, 222, 244–245, 268
isolation 133, 162, 164, 165, 168, 177, 186, 187, 205
'ivory tower' (of academe) 241

jargon 246
job
    interview 303, 308, 311–314, 319
    market 268–269, 303, 307–310
    search 302–303, 304, 307–311
journal
    rankings 25, 35, 278, 279
    submission 278–280

Kamler, B. 270–271, 304, 306
Keynes, John Maynard 83
Kolb, D. A. 87

Language 162, 193, 199, 215–216, 284–286
Learning
    continuous 321, 322–323
    experiential 87, 140, 160–161
    from others 216–217
    lifelong 322
    self-directed 10, 27, 44, 153, 323
    self-regulated 9–10
'less is more' 92
Literature
    review 28, 32–38, 49–71, 76–78, 84, 87–88, 91, 94, 174–175, 201, 244, 271
    search 55–58, 94–95

Managing
    'managing up' x, 113–124
    time 124–130, 164
Márquez, Gabriel Garcia 286
mature candidate x, 164, 177

mental health 166, 167, 173–175, 131–134
mentoring 270, 272, 304, 307
method *see* methodology
methodology 12, 38, 39–41, 94, 95, 97, 99, 100, 122, 152, 174, 175, 186, 197, 204, 240, 241, 244, 252, 253, 275, 289
microblogs 224, 227–228
'more is less' 223
motivation 9–10, 76, 273–276

neologisms 246
networking 154–156, 222, 224, 231–232, 315, 318
Nietzsche, Friedrich 284, 285

Office of the Independent Adjudicator (OIA) 260
online portals xii, 34–35
ontology 88, 277
open access 34–35, 56, 280, 291
originality 10, 66, 75, 78–82, 117, 258, 263, 286–287
Orwell, George 286

perfection 75, 179–180
Petre, M. 221, 258–259
PhD
    by publication 24–25, 268, 274
    'three papers' 77–78
Phillips, E. M. xi, 9, 79, 80, 164, 259
Pinker, Steven 67, 286
plagiarism 117, 124, 248
planning 8, 45, 125, 194–195, 302, 322
post-doctoral fellowships 304–305
Postgraduate Research Experience Survey (PRES) 2, 142, 166, 173
presentation
    lecture-type 229–232
    poster 222–224

prioritisation 126–127
problematising 92
procrastination 129, 175–176, 180, 187, 262, 292
proofreading 116, 117, 180, 245, 263, 264, 290, 309
public engagement 232–233
publication
    strategy 296–298
    submitting for 290–292
Pugh, D. S. xi, 9, 79, 164, 259
punctuation 37, 246–247

questionnaire 38–39, 96, 102, 152, 174, 198

regression diagnostics 96
repositories 34–35
referees 41–42, 267, 310–311
references
    job 41–42, 310–311
    thesis 41, 56, 63, 76, 78, 91, 117, 240, 247, 248, 264
referencing 37, 68, 247, 248, 290
reflection 90, 92, 118, 196, 199–202, 205–207, 209
reflexivity 90, 93, 98, 251
reliability 93–98, 99, 101
research
    'action research' 93, 289
    objectives 30–32, 52, 89, 175, 251
    proposal 17, 20, 25–45, 305
    qualitative 96–100, 102, 103, 152
    quantitative 40, 95–96, 101, 102
    question 11, 26, 27, 28, 29–30, 31, 32, 33, 38, 53, 76–77, 79, 81, 84, 89, 95, 99, 100, 251
    speed-dating 219–220
Researcher Development Framework (RDF) 7, 146–149, 314

Research Evaluation Framework (REF) 79, 94, 271, 298, 304, 312
role of supervisory teams 114–124, 146–147, 155, 160, 162, 171, 176, 180, 238, 239
resilience 322
reviewers xiv, 260, 280, 282, 287, 290–296
revisions
    article 279, 292–296
    thesis 121, 239, 242–243, 259–262, 265
rigour 75, 94–100, 289–290
rite of passage 6–7
role
    of DoS 113–124, 146
    of PGR 113–124
routines 128, 134
Rugg, G. xii, 221, 258, 302
Rüger, S. 80, 238, 258

schedule 120–121, 127–129, 130, 133, 134, 135–136
scientific method 90, 95
self-awareness 128, 134
self-contract 128
self-efficacy 7, 10
sentences
    long 107, 246
    verbless 246
Shakespeare, William 290
signposting 68, 105, 245, 268
Singer, Peter 286, 317
skills 134, 140–156, 162, 164, 254, 304, 313–319, 322–323
social media xiv, 129, 211, 214, 216, 224–228, 231, 233, 319
Socrates 90
software training 150
Steinbeck, John 286

Index

supervision 21, 113–124, 139, 146–147, 273
survey 96, 100, 102, 183, 186, 252
survivor syndrome 37–38
tacit knowledge xiv, 140, 155, 160–161
teaching 2, 155–156, 170, 172, 221, 274, 304, 306–307, 309, 311
theory
    grounded 96
    theoretical contribution 82–89, 287–289
    theoretical framework 76, 87–88, 89
Thesis
    structure 75–78
    template 27–28, 175, 214
Thomson, Pat 51, 53, 54, 61, 64, 226
Time
    calendar 129
    longevity 320
    'time management' 164, 124–130
    'to do' lists 128, 130
title 243, 281–283
training and development 139–157
transferable skills 142, 254, 313–315, 316
Twitter 224, 227–228, 231, 319

uncertainty 6, 11–12, 179, 254, 323
university rankings 20, 25, 43

validity 60, 94–99, 101
viva
    mock 183, 249
    preparing for 194, 207–208, 243–259
    questions 250–254
    remotely hosted 187, 255–256

Wallace, David Foster 246, 286
wellbeing 114, 120, 131–134, 166, 173–175, 187
Whetten, D. A. 85, 287–288
Wiles, Andrew Sir 11
Woolf, Virginia 246
word limit 206, 271, 281
work avoidance 175–176
writer's block 130
writing
    academic 215–216, 225
    'beautiful writing' 284–286
    style xiii, 105, 277, 286

Lightning Source UK Ltd.
Milton Keynes UK
UKHW021452170122
397285UK00009B/1997